The Heroic and Creative Meaning of Socialism

Revolutionary Studies Series

The Heroic and Creative Meaning Of Socialism: Selected Essays of José Carlos Mariátegui

Edited and Translated by
MICHAEL PEARLMAN

HB

Humanity Books

an imprint of Prometheus Books

Published by Humanity Books, an imprint of Prometheus Books

Inquiries should be addressed to
Humanity Books
4501 Forbes Boulevard, Suite 200,
Lanham, Maryland 20706
www.rowman.com
Distributed by NATIONAL BOOK NETWORK
800-462-6420

Library of Congress Cataloging-in-Publication Data

Mariátegui, José Carlos, 1894–1930
    The heroic and creative meaning of socialism : selected essays of José Carlos Mariátegui / edited and translated by Michael Pearlman.
        p. cm. - (Revolutionary studies)
    Originally published: Atlantic Highlands, NJ : Humanities Press International, Inc. 1996.
    Includes index.
    Originally published in hardcover.
    ISBN 978-1-57392-381-8 (cloth) 978-1-57392-451-2 (pbk.)
    1. Socialism. 2. Socialism—Latin America. 3. Peru—Politics and government—1919–1968. I. Pearlman, Michael. II. Title. III. Series.

HX72 .M3646 1995
335'.0098—dc20   95-30978

Dedicated to the children of the Amauta
For Lori

Contents

PART III. PERUVIAN REALITY

PART IV. LATIN AMERICA

PART V. MARXISM AND PHILOSOPHY

Preface

The work of José Carlos Mariátegui, with its international scope, exemplifies the vision of this Peruvian thinker and theoretician, which has maintained its contemporary relevance because of the originality and freshness of his writings and the exemplary nature of his life, inspired as it was by the most thoroughgoing socialist ethic. Passing away in 1930, before his thirty-sixth birthday and with barely twenty years of theoretical preparation and intellectual and journalistic production tied to his work as political guide and theoretician, he has left an indelible mark in Peru and Latin America. The commemoration of the centennial of his birth, on June 14, 1994, assembled a diverse group of scholars from both inside and outside Peru who discussed his literary, esthetic, and political work throughout the year of remembrance. The relevance of the Amauta's[1] thought is due to the originality of his propositions and the great intellectual autonomy that distinguishes his writings. The Marxist method used by Mariátegui is an instrument for the interpretation of reality from a broad perspective that includes both the main developments of Marxism and the most important currents of modern thought that enrich and complement the original Marxist postulates. This deliberate heterodoxy was criticized during the era of sectarian dogmatism that reigned in the former Soviet Union and the countries of Eastern Europe and disappeared into the rubbish along with "really existing socialism." José Carlos Mariátegui is the only radical thinker in America who has attained an autonomy and intellectual and political presence comparable to that of the great European figure, Antonio Gramsci.

The intellectual climate was prepared for this commemoration of the centennial despite the reversal of the Eurasian socialist states. The principal work of José Carlos Mariátegui, *Seven Interpretive Essays on Peruvian Reality*, has been translated into the major European and Asian languages. Other of Mariátegui's contributions are found in anthologies published in Italian, German, and Russian, and selections from his writings are being prepared in French and Japanese. What was missing, then, was an English-language anthology; this book comes to fill the vacuum.

Michael Pearlman, in this collection which bears the apt title *The Heroic and Creative Meaning of Socialism*—emphasizing the bold and germinal sense of Mariátegui's socialism—has succeeded in presenting a general vision of the thought of José Carlos Mariátegui and the major facets of his political, philosophical, literary, and artistic conceptions.

Part I, "Europe and North America," presents his principal essays on international topics, the "contemporary scene" viewed from Mariátegui's keen perspective with a method that he calls "a bit journalistic and a bit cinematic." Part II, "The Anti-Imperialist Struggle," assembles the substantial contributions that characterize the authentic anti-imperialist position of the Amauta, by way of the polemic that this theme inspired at the end of the twenties.

Part III, "Peruvian Reality," contains his principal essays analyzing our national reality, with special attention to the indigenous question and the concrete aspects of the struggle on the political, party, and union fronts. The study of the Peruvian problematic constituted the central preoccupation of the Amauta. Part IV, "Latin America," contains a well-assembled collection of works about the subcontinent from his broad perspective and with his previously indicated theoretical autonomy that elucidates the often imprecise and ambiguous concepts of Indo-Iberian America and "Pan-Americanism." The Mexican revolution is examined here in its true significance.

Part V, "Marxism and Philosophy," contains memorable pages of criticism of the positivist, reformist, and electoralist views of the Second International, as well as contributions to an authentic, creative development of Marxism that is also distant from the distorted vision of the Third International. Part VI, "Literature, Art, and Culture," assembles the major offerings of the Peruvian thinker on world literature, vanguard art, and the relationship between reality and fantasy, a subject of particular fascination for Mariátegui.

The introduction, which is complemented by a chronological outline, is a general vision of the interwoven eminence that was the life and work of José Carlos Mariátegui, and the superior ethic that inspired his ideals and sentiments. It is a well-done work of synthesis by Michael Pearlman, who was responsible for the selection and division of the material into six sections.

It is fitting for Humanities Press to publish this anthology, which will occupy a privileged place among the recent works by and about José Carlos Mariátegui produced in Peru, in other countries of America, and in Europe and Asia.

—Dr. Javier Mariátegui
Lima, Peru

Note

1. For this and other untranslated Spanish and Quechua terms, see the glossary.

Acknowledgments

The editor would like to thank Luis Castro, for introducing him to Mariátegui's ideas from the perspective of a Puerto Rican revolutionist; Marc Becker, Paul Le Blanc, and Jim Henle for their useful comments on the introduction; Djata Bumpus, for his usual scathing criticism; José Carlos Mariátegui III and the staff at Empresa Editora Amauta in Lima for their encouragement, collaboration and gracious provision of materials, without which this collection would have been much poorer both textually and spiritually; and Lori Salem, without whose advice, support, and love, the editor would be, also.

Introduction

The life and work of José Carlos Mariátegui, widely considered one of Latin America's greatest Marxist theoreticians and activists, remain relatively unknown in the English-speaking world. At home, nearly the whole of the Peruvian left acknowledges him as a mentor—in fact, two political movements honor him in their very names (the United Mariáteguista Party [PUM] and the Sendero Luminoso, whose name is derived from their slogan, "Follow the shining path of José Carlos Mariátegui"). Across the political spectrum and around the continent, Mariátegui is recognized as being among Latin America's greatest essayists, literary critics, and social thinkers. Yet, Eurocentric intellectuals who pay obeisance to the Gramscian tradition are still largely ignorant of the work of America's own Gramsci. One reason is that the only work of Mariátegui which has been translated into English is his *Seven Interpretive Essays on Peruvian Reality*, which, while one of the finest Marxist efforts at the concrete analysis of a concrete social formation, has attracted attention mainly from those with a particular interest in Peru and Latin America. Mariátegui's writings, though, like those of most classical Marxist thinkers, span the widest range of human endeavor, from philosophy to international political developments to art, literature, and culture. In addition, his particular emphasis on the active, creative, and even spiritual aspects of the socialist project has often been obscured by an exposure to the *Seven Essays* to the exclusion of his other writings. This short collection of essays is an attempt to remedy this deficiency by introducing the breadth and depth of his thought to a new generation of English-speaking students of history, philosophy, literature, and radical theory and practice.

Historical Context

Mariátegui was born on June 14, 1894, in Moquegua, a small provincial capital in the Andean foothills of southern Peru. He was the second of three surviving children of an unstable relationship between Francisco Javier Mariátegui, a member of one of Lima's prominent landowning families, and María Amalia Lachira, a poor peasant woman from the nearby sierra. Raised alone by his mother, Mariátegui was left crippled in his left leg by a childhood illness and had to leave school after merely one year of formal education. But the young boy displayed a strong aptitude for intellectual, particularly literary, pursuits, teaching himself to read and write, studying French, and experimenting with poetry of a religious and metaphysical bent. As a young teenager, Mariátegui found work doing odd jobs at *La Prensa*, a Lima newspaper, where he was taken under the wing of a group of anarchist typographers, followers and friends of the noted radical writer Manuel González Prada— one of the first Peruvian intellectuals to adopt the cause of the nation's indigenous peasant population as his own.

The Peru in which Mariátegui matured was in transition from a society dominated by the owners of the large latifundia, descended from the Spanish conquest, to the more modern, dependent capitalism that still characterizes its social relations. The vast majority of Peruvians, the indigenous peasants of the Andean sierra, were exploited by local *gamonales* ("bosses," that is, land-owners) and remained basically unassimilated into the creole and mestizo nation. But the War of Independence against Spain in the early nineteenth century, led by the population of the coastal plains to the exclusion and disinterest of the Native American peoples, opened Peru to trade relations with and economic domination by Great Britain. The development of trade in guano and nitrates and a later cotton boom helped create a small capitalist class, based in the coastal cities, that dynamized commercial relations throughout the country. But this bourgeoisie, based on the international market for raw materials, could only be a minor partner for British and then North American capital, which later came to control the most important sectors of the local economy such as finance, transport, and export-oriented production.

The Peruvian bourgeoisie first appeared on the political front, in opposition to the feudalist landowning interests, as supporters of the Partido Civil, which took power in 1872 with the presidency of Manuel Pardo. Like most similar forces in Latin America, the Pardo government and its Civilista successors carried out some reforms of the backward administrative and educational systems but refused to touch the basic economic and social interests of the landowning class. Peru's defeat by Chile in the Pacific War of 1879 and the resulting loss of the country's nitrate-producing region set back the capitalist class both economically and politically, with power reverting to the military in alliance with the rural landowners. The Civilistas returned to power by 1900 but had meanwhile been forced to compromise both with the feudalists of the sierra and with the ever-increasing power of British and North American capitalists, who had received economic concessions in return for financing the country's foreign debt and were investing in mining and agricultural production on coastal plantations.

The result of these developments was a state that mediated the interests of the comprador capitalist class and the rural landowners, with both subordinate to foreign capital, and with the native peasantry, the young working class, and the urban petty bourgeoisie excluded and manipulated. But by the time of Mariátegui's entrance onto the journalistic scene in 1914, the first stirrings of popular opposition to the rule of this oligarchy were being felt around the country. Local insurrections by indigenous peasants in the sierra

had awakened intellectuals like González Prada and Clorinda Matto de Turner
to the primary importance for the nation's political life of what was to
become known as the "Indian question." The first trade unions among urban workers and the braceros of the coastal plantations had begun agitating
for legalization and the eight-hour day. Thus, the basis was being laid for the
creation of a nationalist, anti-oligarchic political current.

THE EVOLUTION OF A REVOLUTIONARY INTELLECTUAL

Mariátegui's professional writing career began at *La Prensa*, covering the
high society and horse-racing beats under the pseudonym Juan Croniqueur.
His literary aspirations were met by writing poetry and theater pieces, and
he soon became an associate of writers such as César Falcón, Félix del Valle,
and Abraham Valdelomar in founding the new literary review *Colónida*.
Although he later denigrated his early efforts and referred to the period as
his "Stone Age," the Colónida circle was a precursor to a new artistic
generation influenced by nationalists and modernists like González Prada in
their disdain for the academicism and colonialist mentality of the Peruvian
intellectual tradition.

In 1916, Mariátegui began covering the Peruvian parliament for *El Tiempo*,
a new liberal newspaper, and his writing soon displayed a heightened interest
in political affairs and a growing disillusion with the country's ruling elite. His
own entrance on the political scene came inadvertently, when an article he
wrote promoting government spending on education instead of military pro-
curement was met with a physical attack by army officers and became the
center of a public scandal that finally led to the resignation of the minister
of war. In May 1919, Mariátegui and his close friend César Falcón founded
the openly radical newspaper *La Razon*, which sided with a general strike by
Lima's workers for the eight-hour day and the university reform movement
among students at San Marcos University. But the government of Augusto
Leguía, who took power in a military coup during the height of this worker
and student upsurge and compromised with its leaders in a successful effort to
restore order, could not accept the continuing presence of a left-leaning
oppositional press. *La Razon* was shut down in August of that year, and
Mariátegui and Falcón were given the choice between jail and exile, the
latter with a small retainer as government employees. Both chose exile, and
Mariátegui sailed for Europe in October 1919.

Mariátegui's European sojourn was of decisive importance in his ideological
development; arriving a radical journalist of socialist leanings, he was to become a committed Marxist and supporter of the Bolshevik revolution. First
reaching France, Mariátegui spent time among both the militant workers of
the Parisian suburbs, who greatly impressed him with the "religious fervor"

of their political activity, and the leftist intellectuals of Romain Rolland's Clarté group, who were to be a lasting model of social commitment among the intelligentsia. Leaving Paris for reasons of health, he headed south, to Italy, where, as he was to say later, he "married a woman [Anna Chiappe] and some ideas."[1] The ideas were those of the young and vigorous Italian Communist movement, particularly the Ordine Nuovo group headed by Antonio Gramsci. Armando Bazán says that he was told by Mariátegui, his friend and collaborator: "To that point, Marxism had been for me a somewhat confused, ponderous, and cold theory; then I saw its clear light and had a revelation."[2] Many of the "heterodox" elements of Mariátegui's Marxism, moreover, can be traced to the intellectual trends in Italian radical circles of the period, especially the influence of the idealist neo-Hegelianism of Benedetto Croce (a friend of his wife's family), Giovanni Gentile, and Piero Gobetti.

THE BIRTH OF PERUVIAN MARXISM

Mariátegui's time in Europe gave a philosophical basis to his earlier spiritual and emotional commitment to the cause of his country's dispossessed. He returned to Peru in 1923 with the intention of helping to carry these new ideas into practice. In the meantime, the Leguía government had hardened into an authoritarian regime with few of the populist pretenses it had at first adopted, and the popular movement had begun the long and difficult task of institution-building. The political and ideological leadership of this process fell to a group of former student activists around the young intellectual Víctor Raúl Haya de la Torre, who, influenced by Marxist ideas, directed their efforts toward building a broad nationalist and anti-imperialist front of workers, peasants, and intellectuals. The history of Mariátegui's relations with Haya and his fellow activists forms the basic plot of the development of the Peruvian popular movement in the 1920s. In this earliest period, Mariátegui collaborated closely with Haya, with the aim of helping in the practical tasks of building the movement, as well as in its political and ideological self-definition. He was invited to give a lecture series on the international crisis and the European workers' movement at the González Prada Popular University (see "The World Crisis and the Peruvian Working Class" and "Revolutionary and Socialist Agitation in the Eastern World" in this collection), and temporarily edited the movement journal *Claridad* after Haya was forced into exile in October 1923. Meanwhile, Mariátegui returned to writing articles for the liberal press, concentrating on international developments; a collection of these essays, on the Russian revolution, the rise of fascism in Italy, the crisis of European democracy, anti-imperialist movements in Asia, and international trends in literature and art, was published as *La escena contemporánea* (The Contemporary Scene) in 1925.

A recrudescence of his childhood illness in 1924 led to a physical and emotional crisis for Mariátegui. His right leg, which was previously unaffected, had to be amputated, and he was to spend the rest of his life in a wheelchair, forced to endure episodes of extreme pain. For a time he was overwhelmed by depression, but he soon returned to his intellectual labors with renewed commitment. Although he rarely referred to his physical problems, he later wrote in a letter to supporters in Mexico:

> In these years of sickness, of suffering, of struggle, I have invariably gained strength from my optimistic faith in the youth that were repudiating the old politics, among other reasons because they were repudiating *criollo* methods, caudillo-like declamations, and empty and vain rhetoric. I maintain all my reasons to live in order to defend my intellectual positions. I will not compromise with deception. What I have suffered has terribly weakened and anguished me. I don't want to seem pathetic, but I cannot still what I write, feverishly, anxiously, desperately.[3]

It is obvious that Mariátegui's insistence on the importance of revolutionary will, on the heroic aspects of the political struggle, on the voluntaristic and creative side of Marxism, was affected by these personal vicissitudes, as was the deep personal devotion he elicited from his fellow activists.

The major project that Mariátegui envisioned on his return to Peru finally came to fruition in 1926: the publication of a journal directed at his country's vanguard of intellectuals and militants. Baptized *Amauta* (a Quechua word, meaning "wise man" and "teacher"), its goal, in Mariátegui's words, was

> to articulate, illuminate, and comprehend Peru's problems from theoretical and scientific viewpoints. But we will always consider Peru from an international perspective. We will study all the great movements of political, philosophical, artistic, literary, and scientific renewal. Everything that is human is ours. This journal will connect the new men of Peru, first with the other peoples of America, and then with the other peoples of the world.[4]

Articles in *Amauta* ranged from Freudian texts to analyses of international capital, from reviews of modernist Peruvian literature to documents from the Communist International, all attractively displayed alongside sketches by artists such as José Sabogal and Diego Rivera. This unique blend of both the artistic and social avant-gardes was also typical of the discussions at Mariátegui's home on Calle Washington Izqierda in Lima, where poets, union organizers, musicians, and militant students would meet informally to exchange ideas. What united them all was a commitment to revolutionary nationalism, the creation of a new, independent, and self-conscious Peru.

But the most important work published in *Amauta* were the essays that were to become the basis of Mariátegui's *Seven Interpretive Essays on Peruvian Reality.* The Marxism that Mariátegui had adopted in Europe was, as he put it, "a fundamentally dialectical method—that is, a method that bases itself fully on reality, on the facts... not ... a body of principles with the same rigid conclusions for all historical climates and all social latitudes."[5] Thus Mariátegui had begun a study of the Peruvian social formation, not as an academic effort, but with the aim of better understanding the forces at work that could lead to its transformation. His starting point was the indigenous question, "the question of the assimilation into the Peruvian nation of four-fifths of Peru's population."[6] Mariátegui insisted that the continued subjugation of the indigenous masses had an economic basis: "We do not content ourselves to demand the right of the Indian to education, culture, progress, love, and heaven. We begin by categorically demanding his right to the land."[7] While eliminating pre-capitalist relations in the countryside is typically a task of the bourgeois revolution, Mariátegui asserted that the Peruvian capitalist class had been too weak and deformed, because of its position as a comprador for foreign interests, to carry out such a policy. The modern Peruvian state, an alliance between the *latifundistas* and this ineffectual bourgeoisie, could not be expected to resolve the agrarian question in the interests of the indigenous peasantry; therefore, the job would fall to the masses themselves. But, unlike in Western Europe, where the overthrow of feudal relations led to the creation of a large class of smallholding peasants, the collectivist traditions of Incan society had survived the Spanish conquest and remained alive in various forms of cooperative rural labor. Thus, in those parts of the sierra where the *ayllu*—the village community—had not been destroyed during the colonial period or by the slow advance of capitalist property relations, it could become an important force for more radical social transformation in the countryside (note the similarity to Marx's later writings on the Russian *mir*).

MARIATEGUI, THE APRA, AND THE THIRD INTERNATIONAL

This view of Peruvian society as a complex and contradictory combination of three modes of production—communal, feudal, and capitalist—under the domination of the latter and ultimately subordinate to international capital was counterposed to the classic evolutionist and dualist view that saw capitalist social relations as fated to supersede feudalism. This theoretical position had unmistakable political implications and was ultimately responsible for the organizational break between Mariátegui's supporters and the main body of the APRA movement that occurred in 1928. Although sharing many of the same social premises, especially on the indigenous question, Haya de la Torre had come to conclude that the aim of the popular movement should be to stimulate a new stage of autonomous capitalist development, led by the nationalist sectors of the middle class. According to Haya, imperialism in Latin America was actually the first stage of capitalism and was tending to divide Peruvian society into two different modes of production, the backward, national sector dominated by feudalism and the progressive, capitalist sector dominated by foreign interests. Since the working class was too small and weak and the indigenous peasantry too primitive, the urban middle class would have to become the dominant social force and control the negative aspects of imperialist penetration. Nominating himself and his movement for the leading role in this process, Haya decided to convert the APRA from a united front of anti-imperialist workers, peasants, and intellectuals into a continental political party, a self-styled Latin American Kuomintang.

Mariátegui and his supporters reacted quickly to the reformist turn of the Aprista leadership (see "Anniversary and Balance Sheet" in Part III). His internationalist perspective on the development of the world economy left no illusion that an independent Peruvian capitalism could flourish in a world dominated by monopoly and finance capital centered in the imperialist countries; in fact, as capitalist relations spread in Peru, imperialist domination would be even more accentuated. His close study of contemporary developments in both Mexico and China (the democratic revolution was retrogressing in the former; the Kuomintang had turned on the workers' movement in the latter) reinforced his view that "neither the bourgeoisie nor the petty bourgeoisie in power can carry out anti-imperialist politics,"[8] and that only the worker and peasant masses in power could carry out the tasks of the bourgeois revolution, as they had in Russia after October 1917. While still advocating a united front around concrete issues, Mariátegui's supporters in the APRA decided the time had come to organize an independent proletarian party. The Socialist Party of Peru was founded in October 1928 and applied for membership in the Third International.

The very name of this new party indicated Mariátegui's independence from the Stalinist leadership of the Comintern. Although Haya's turn to the right had forced the Third International to break its political collaboration with the APRA (which previously had privileged relations with the Comintern-sponsored anti-imperialist organizations), Stalin's reaction to the disastrous collapse of the alliance between the Kuomintang and the Chinese Communist Party was an incoherent melange of "stagist" strategies and sectarian tactics in the colonial and semi-colonial countries. Mariátegui supported Stalin's position in the Bolshevik Party's internal struggle (although admiring Trotsky's "international sense of the socialist revolution")[9] but differed with Comintern policy for Latin America on three important issues: the nature of the party, the political implications of the indigenous question, and the relationship between anti-imperialism and socialism. All three became subjects of discussion at the first continental meetings of the Latin American Communist movement in 1929 (see Mariátegui's contributions, "Anti-Imperialist Viewpoint" and "The Indigenous Question"). Mariátegui defended the use of the term *socialist*—insisting that the word had not lost its revolutionary meaning in Latin America as it had in Europe after the collapse of the Second International in 1914—and maintained that the Peruvian party should be based on the worker and peasant masses, under proletarian leadership, rather than being an exclusively working-class, Communist party, as the Comintern advocated. He resisted the Comintern's definition of the indigenous question as one of national self-determination, restating his position that the land question was central. And he once again claimed that "anti-imperialism does not and cannot constitute, by itself, a political program for a mass movement capable of conquering state power."[10] While the Comintern argued that the political struggle must go through an anti-imperialist and anti-feudal stage (even while beginning to take a sectarian approach to the APRA and other petty bourgeois national movements), Mariátegui wrote:

> Without ruling out the use of any type of anti-imperialist agitation or any action to mobilize those social sectors that might eventually join the struggle, our mission is to explain to and show the masses that only the socialist revolution can stand as a definitive and real barrier to the advance of imperialism.[11]

Unfortunately for the Latin American and international revolutionary movement, this debate was to be cut tragically short.

Along with organizing the new Socialist Party, Mariátegui was intimately involved in the consolidation of the Peruvian trade union movement. A longtime proponent of trade union unity (see "May Day and the United Front" and "Message to the Workers Congress" in Part III), he was instrumental in the creation of the Peruvian General Workers Confederation (CGTP) in 1929. His publishing house also began a sister journal, *Labor*, directed at the union milieu. But the movement also faced a new wave of repression. Mariátegui had already been interned in a military hospital for approximately a week in 1927 (some sources claim that the U.S. embassy, upset by his article "Yankee Imperialism in Nicaragua," was involved),[12] while forty of his collaborators on *Amauta* were imprisoned, others forced into exile, and the journal suspended until a cry of protest from around Latin America forced the Leguía regime to back down. *Labor* was intended as a biweekly, but only ten issues were published in its first and only year because of constant harassment and censorship. Convinced that *Amauta* was to be permanently suppressed, Mariátegui made plans early in 1930 to move to Buenos Aires and begin publishing there. But at the beginning of March, his old illness flared once again. José Carlos Mariátegui died before his thirty-sixth birthday, on April 16, 1930, mourned by multitudes of Peru's dispossessed as their own revolutionary saint and *amauta*.

THE MARIÁTEGUISTA HERITAGE

The organizational legacy of Mariátegui's labors in Peru proved transitory. Within the year, the Socialist Party submitted to the discipline of the Comintern and changed its name to the Communist Party. Eudocio Ravines, the new party leader, began an internal campaign to "liquidate Amautism"—that is, any political independence from Moscow—and Mariátegui's closest allies left the movement. *Amauta* ceased publication. Applying Stalin's "third period" line, the Communists isolated themselves by condemning the APRA as fascist, and thereby facilitated the repression of both movements. The CGTP was driven underground, and the Peruvian mass movement was crippled. When it began to reassert itself in later decades, the APRA was more dominant and the radical left more marginal than ever. But Mariátegui's reputation as a social thinker grew in these intervening years, and the debate over his legacy intensified, with the APRA, the Communist Party, and other leftists all laying claim to his ideological mantle.

The course of the Cuban revolution, in which a national, anti-imperialist movement found itself obliged to resort to anti-capitalist measures to ensure success in carrying out its revolutionary democratic tasks, showed the actuality of Mariátegui's analysis of class relations in the semi-colonial world and led to a resurgence of interest in his work throughout Latin America. And today, with the failure of neo-liberal capitalism to even begin resolving the economic and social problems of the continent's peoples, the consolidation of new working-class movements like Brazil's Workers Party, and the rising of America's indigenous population from Mexico to Ecuador and beyond, the questions of political strategy broached by Mariátegui are again coming to the fore. The relationship between the democratic and socialist revolutions has become a key issue in debates among Central American revolutionaries, for example, and is implicitly at issue in Brazil and other countries. The Mariáteguist legacy here is complex, but so is the reality it would seek to understand and transform. To some degree, the tasks of the bourgeois revolution remain to be accomplished in nearly every Latin American country, in some (Nicaragua or El Salvador, for example) more than others (Argentina or Uruguay); in most countries, even relatively developed ones like Brazil, it is the land question that is the most important of them. But does this mean that these tasks will be resolved by any social classes other than the workers and peasants themselves? Mariátegui's response is clear:

The capitalist economy of republican Peru, because of the absence of a strong bourgeois class and because national and international conditions have determined the slow advance of the country on the capitalist road, cannot liberate itself from the poisonous vestiges of colonial feudalism under a bourgeois regime in the thrall of imperialist interests and in collusion with *gamonalista* and clerical feudalism.

This process reinforces the country's colonial fate. *The emancipation of the country's economy is only possible through the action of the proletarian masses in solidarity with the international anti-imperialist struggle. Only proletarian action can first stimulate and later realize the work of the bourgeois-democratic revolution, which the bourgeois regime is unable to develop and fulfill* [emphasis added].[13]

But what are the tasks of the workers' and peasants' movement once it takes power in such countries? Mariátegui makes a provocative remark in this regard:

Insufficiently profound and critical minds might suppose that the liquidation of feudalism is a typically and specifically liberal and bourgeois measure, and that to attempt to convert it into a socialist task is to romantically bend the laws of history. These shallow theoreticians oppose socialism with one simplistic criterion as their sole argument—that capitalism has not exhausted its possibilities in Peru. *The partisans of this idea will be astonished to discover that the task of socialism, when it comes to power in the country, depending on the hour and the historical compass to which it must adjust, will to a great degree be the realization of capitalism, or better, the realization of the historical possibilities that capitalism still contains, in the sense that this serves the interests of social progress* [emphasis added].[14]

Does Mariátegui mean to suggest the need for a historical period of capitalist development, led by a socialist party? Not if one considers the whole course of the debate with Haya de la Torre and his position on the impossibility of an independent development of Peruvian capitalism in the imperialist era. But, perhaps, the recent decision of the Cuban government to allow a limited realm for the market, like the Soviet NEP, is a recognition that capitalist social relations cannot be abolished by fiat, but only to the degree practicable "considering the hour and the historical compass." Recent experiences in countries as diverse as Nicaragua and China reveal the potential dangers of such a course, but until revolutionaries in the imperialist countries help change the international balance of forces, we should remain humble before the efforts of revolutionaries in the semi-colonial world to win power and carry out a social transformation in the interests of the masses.

One aspect of Mariátegui's thought that continues to draw attention is his "idealist" emphasis on the spiritual, voluntaristic aspect of political action, exemplified in his admiration for the French syndicalist theoretician Georges Sorel and his ideas on "revolutionary myth." It might at first seem strange that someone so committed to the study of the material, economic basis of society would be open to the influence of a wide variety of idealist thinkers, from Nietzsche to Bergson to Gentile. Some critics, such as Robert Paris, the author of the most comprehensive intellectual biography of Mariátegui, have even flirted with qualifying Mariátegui's work as non-Marxist for these "excesses." But as Michael Löwy has noted,[15] this tendency should be understood as a reaction (similar to that of the young Lukács and Gramsci) to the positivist determinism of the Second International, against which Mariátegui polemicized in the philosophical essays that were published posthumously as *Defense of Marxism*. For example, he writes:

> The voluntarist character of socialism is really no less evident than its determinist foundation, even if it is less understood by critics. To give it its true value, though, it is nevertheless enough to follow the development of the proletarian movement from the actions of Marx and Engels in London at the origin of the First International to the present, dominated by the first experience of a socialist state: the USSR. Every word, every act of Marxists in this process has a resonance of faith, of will, of heroic and creative conviction, whose impulse it would be absurd to seek in a mediocre and passive determinist sensibility.[16]

Why is this so important to Mariátegui, and to us? Because socialism is not a historical inevitability but the conscious act of a revolutionary class movement. As Mariátegui explains:

> Before concluding these lines, I want to say that, along with a realistic sense of history, it is necessary to give the proletarian vanguard a heroic will to create and accomplish. The desire for improvement, an appetite for well-being, is not enough. The defeats and failures of the European proletariat have their origin in the mediocre positivism with which timid union bureaucracies and moderate parliamentary teams cultivated a Sancho Panzaesque mentality and a cowardly spirit among the masses. A proletariat with no greater ideals than a shorter working day and a few cents more in wages will never be capable of a great historical enterprise. And this is why we must elevate ourselves above a vulgar positivism of the belly and above negative, destructive, and nihilist sentiments and interests. The revolutionary spirit is a constructive spirit.[17]

For Mariátegui, the "myth" of the socialist revolution is central to creating this heroic will—an antidote to bourgeois skepticism that takes the role which religion had previously played as a stimulus to bold, historical praxis. Aníbal Quijano, one of contemporary Peru's most important Marxist intellectuals, has pointed out that Mariátegui unites two modes of thinking that European ideology has considered irreconcilable—*logos* and *mythos*.[18] Like the novels of García Márquez, the historical narratives of Eduardo Galeano, and the homilies of the continent's liberation theologists, Mariátegui's writings insist that a scientific and realistic view of the world does not exclude a spiritual and poetic one, and that both are necessary for comprehending and changing the human condition. His own political and personal struggle was a lifelong argument for this position.

Today, the collapse of the USSR, the first, deformed attempt at a transition to socialism, along with the contingent success of neo-liberal assaults on the standard of living of workers, peasants, and the poor, have bred cynicism about the real possibilities of radically transforming capitalist social relations in both Latin and North America. Roberto Fernández Retamar, the Cuban literary critic, broached this issue in a speech welcoming participants to a colloquium, "Mariátegui in the Current Thought of Our America," held during 1994, his centennial year, at the Casa de las Americas in Havana. Retamar recalled Mariátegui's contrast between Ortega y Gasset's references to the "disenchanted soul" of decadent bourgeois civilization and Romain Rolland's "enchanted soul," "the soul of the forgers of a new civilization," the working class.[19] According to Retamar, "We have touched bottom, and it is time to free ourselves from disenchantment . . . And few are as worthy of harboring and spreading this enchanted soul as Mariátegui. . . . He does not interest us as an archeological piece, but as a witness to the necessity and viability of the future."[20]

But, we must ask ourselves, is it the workers' movement in the imperialist countries, so politically weakened, economically vulnerable, and culturally cut off from its roots as a movement for human liberation, that is the archeological piece as we prepare the new millenium? And without a rebirth of this movement, will the masses of the exploited and underdeveloped world be able to find a path to resolving the crisis of an ever more internationalized capitalism that has already lasted more than twenty years and threatens ever greater disasters for the vast majority of humanity? The Peruvian Antonio Cornejo Polar has noted, "Mariátegui is not the end of an era; he is—and here is his active presence—at the founding moment of a process that has not ended."[21] As our reason tells us of the objective difficulties we must transcend to play a role in this process, the tremendous tasks involved, the new challenges we face, our spirit should speak with and of our ancestors, our descendants, and our billions of fellows striving to create a better life out of the raw material that we have at hand. And in the words of José Carlos Mariátegui, socialism in America cannot be "a copy and imitation. It must be a heroic creation. We must give life to a . . . socialism reflecting our own reality and in our own language. Here is a mission worthy of a new generation."[22]

Notes

1. Quoted in Aníbal Quijano, *Introducción a Mariátegui* (Mexico City: Ediciones Era, 1981), pp. 43–44.
2. Armando Bazán, *Mariátegui y su tiempo* [v. 20 of *Obras completas de José Carlos Mariátegui*] (Lima: Editora Amauta, 1959), p. 64.
3. José Carlos Mariátegui, *Correspondencia, 1915–1930* (Lima: Editora Amauta, 1984), p. 135.
4. See "Introducing *Amauta*" in Part III of this collection.
5. See "Message to the Workers Congress" in Part III.
6. See "Nationalism and Vanguardism" in Part III.
7. José Carlos Mariátegui, *Siete ensayos de interpretacion de la realidad Peruana* [v. 2 of *Obras completas de José Carlos Mariátegui*] (Lima: Editora Amauta, 1957), p. 50.
8. See "Anti-Imperialist Viewpoint" in Part IV.
9. See "The Exile of Trotsky" in Part I.
10. See "Anti-Imperialist Viewpoint" in Part IV.
11. Ibid.
12. For example, see Marc Becker, *Mariátegui and Latin American Marxist Theory* (Athens, Ohio: Ohio University Monographs in International Studies, Latin American Series no. 20, 1993), p. 96.
13. See "The Programmatic Principles of the Socialist Party" in Part III.
14. See "Prologue to *Tempest in the Andes*" in Part III.
15. Michael Löwy, ed., *Marxism in Latin America from 1909 to the Present* (Atlantic Highlands, NJ: Humanities Press, 1992), p. xxi.
16. See "Marxist Determinism" in Part V.
17. See "Message to the Workers Congess" in Part III.
18. José Carlos Mariátegui, *Textos basicos*, ed. by Aníbal Quijano (Lima: Fondo de Cultura Económica, 1991), p. ix.
19. See "Man and Myth" in Part V.
20. Roberto Fernández Retamar, "Mariátegui en el pensamiento actual de Nuestra América," in José Carlos and Javier Mariátegui Chiappe, eds., *Anuario Mariateguiano*, v.6 (Lima: Empresa Editora Amauta, 1994), p. 240.
21. Antonio Cornejo Polar, "Apuntes sobre la literatura nacional en el pensamiento crítico de Mariátegui," in Xavier Abril et al., *Mariátegui y la literatura* (Lima: Empresa Editora Amauta, 1980), p. 49.
22. See "Anniversary and Balance Sheet" in Part III.

Chronology*

1894

José Carlos Mariátegui is born in Moquegua, Peru, on June 14. His parents: María Amalia La Chira Ballejos and Francisco Javier Mariátegui Requejo. He has two siblings: Guillermina and Julio César. His father abandons the family when José Carlos is still quite young; to support her children, his mother moves to Lima.

1899

The Mariátegui-La Chira family moves to Huacho, the home of the maternal relatives.

1901

José Carlos starts school.

1902

He has an accident at school and is moved to a hospital in Lima. He suffers through a four-year-long convalescence; his left leg remains fragile, and he cannot continue his studies.

1907

His father, Francisco Javier Mariátegui, dies on November 9, in El Callao.

1909

Mariátegui begins work as a "gofer" at the daily newspaper *La Prensa*.

1910

He becomes a linotypist's assistant and proofreader.

1911

February: His first article appears in *La Prensa*, signed with the pseudonym Juan Croniqueur. He joins the editorial service and helps organize reports from the provinces.

1912

He is entrusted with editing police and lottery news.

---

* Prepared by Alberto Flores Galindo and Ricardo Portocarrero for the anthology *Invitación a la vida heróica*. Corrected and expanded by Ricardo Portocarrero and José Carlos Mariátegui III for the 1994 Lima Exposition, *Mariátegui, 100 Years*. It appears here by permission of José Carlos Mariátegui III.

1913

Mariátegui joins the editorial staff at *La Prensa*.

1914

He begins to write articles on a regular basis for *La Prensa*, on literary and artistic topics. He collaborates on the magazine *Mundo Limeño*.

1915

He begins his collaboration with the horse-racing magazine *El Turf* and the women's magazine *Lulú*, writing social notices, short stories, and poetry.

1916

January: *Las tapadas* (The Veiled Women), a play he has written with Julio de la Paz, debuts. The reviews are unfavorable.

February: He begins a retreat at the Convento de los Descalzos (Convent of the Barefooted). The poems he writes there are published in the magazine *Colónida*.

June: Mariátegui leaves *La Prensa*. The following month he starts at *El Tiempo* as editor and parliamentary reporter, with a column, "Voices," dedicated to critical commentary on national politics.

He is named co-director of *El Turf*, publishes the dramatic poem "La mariscala" (The Marshal's Wife), written with Abraham Valdelomar, and plans a book of poetry, *Tristeza* (Sadness), which is never published.

1917

For a short time, Mariátegui publishes the daily newspaper *La Noche* in contraposition to *El Día*, which was linked to the Pardo government.

He takes a Latin course at the Catholic University, wins the Lima municipal prize given by the Journalists' Circle for his article "The Traditional Procession," and is elected vice president of that organization.

November: The Bolsheviks take power in Russia; Mariátegui is involved in the "Cemetery Scandal" [he and his friends are arrested for dancing with a visiting foreign ballerina in the city cemetery to the strains of Chopin's "Funeral March"].

1918

June: Along with César Falcón and Félix del Valle, he founds *Nuestra Epoca*, a magazine with a socialist orientation. He is attacked by a group of young army officers for his article "Bad Tendencies: The Duty of the Army and the Duty of the State," published in its first issue. He is one of the founders of the Committee for Socialist Propaganda and Organization, which he soon leaves because of internal differences.

1919

Mariátegui leaves *El Tiempo* toward the beginning of the year.

May-August: He publishes the newspaper *La Razon*, which supports the general strike for lowering the cost of subsistence goods, as well as the university reform movement. The newspaper is closed under pressure from the Leguía government because of its oppositional line.

October: Mariátegui is sent to Italy by the Leguía government as a propaganda agent for Peru, a method of concealing his deportation.

November: He arrives in France and meets with Henri Barbusse in Paris. He continues on to Rome.

December: He meets Anna Chiappe at a restaurant in the town of Nervi.

1920

Mariátegui begins writing for *El Tiempo*; his articles are later collected as *Letters from Italy*. He begins his study of Marxism with a systematic reading of the pertinent literature.

July-October: He travels through northern Italy (Turin, Milan, Venice), closely following the Turin strike movement and the factory council phenomenon.

1921

January: As a correspondent for *El Tiempo*, he attends the Livorno Congress of the Italian Socialist Party, where the left wing splits and forms the Italian Communist Party.

February: Mariátegui marries Anna Chiappe; their first child, Sandro Tiziano Romeo, is born in December.

1922

He founds the first Peruvian Communist cell along with César Falcón, Carlos Roe, and Palmiro Machiavello.

April-May: He attends an international conference organized by the League of Nations.

June: He leaves Italy and tours Europe while awaiting his return to Peru. He visits France, Germany, Austria, Hungary, Czechoslovakia, and Belgium and studies the revolutionary movements that have been shaking Europe since the war.

1923

January: Mariátegui embarks for Peru from Belgium on the steamship *Negada*.

March: He returns to Peru, is interviewed by Angela Ramos for the magazine *Variedades*, and plans to edit a newspaper or magazine.

April: He establishes contact with Haya de la Torre and the Popular University through Fausto Posadas, the workers' editor of *La Razon*.

June: He begins his lecture series, "History of the International Situation," at the Popular University.

September: He begins his collaboration with the magazine *Variedades*, writing the column "Figures and Aspects of International Life."
October: Haya de la Torre is deported by the Leguía government. Oscar Herrera becomes rector of the Popular University and Mariátegui the editor of the magazine *Claridad*. He is arrested at an editorial meeting of this periodical, along with a group of professors and students of the Popular University.
November: Announcements appear for a magazine entitled *Vanguard: A Weekly Magazine of Ideological Renovation. The Voice of the New Era*, to be edited by Mariátegui and Félix del Valle. The project was never concretized.

1924

January: Mariátegui concludes his lecture series at the Popular University.
March: Issue 5 of *Claridad* is dedicated to Lenin. Mariátegui is the driving force behind the founding of the *Claridad* Workers Publishing House.
May: He has a severe health crisis; his life is saved by the amputation of his right leg.
September: He begins a collaboration with the magazine *Mundial*, edited by Andrés Avelino Aramburú, writing the column "Polemical Motives" and, later, "Let Us Peruvianize Peru."

1925

Mariátegui is proposed by students for a university chair but is rejected by the rector.
October: He founds Minerva Publishers, which publishes his first book, *The Contemporary Scene*, as part of its Modern Library series.

1926

February: *Books and Reviews*, the organ of Minerva Publishers, appears; it will serve as an economic and circulation base for the journal *Amauta*. With the founding of the first APRA cells, Mariátegui agrees to participate in this united front in Lima.
September: *Amauta*, a monthly journal of ideological definition, first appears.

1927

February–March: Mariátegui polemicizes with Luis Alberto Sanchez over the indigenous question.
June: The Leguía government denounces the existence of a supposed "Communist plot" and initiates repression against worker and intellectual activists. Mariátegui is interned in the San Bartolomé Military Hospital. *Amauta* and Minerva Publishers are shut down. Mariátegui studies the possibility of moving to Buenos Aires or Montevideo.
December: *Amauta* reappears.

1928

April: A break occurs between Mariátegui and Haya de la Torre. Mariátegui makes contact with the Trade Union Secretariat of the Third International through the Spaniard Miguel Contreras. He sends Julio Portocarrero and Armando Bazán to the USSR as delegates to the Fourth Congress of the Profintern (Red International of Trade Unions) in Moscow and the Congress of the Peoples of the East in Baku.

September: Mariátegui defines his socialist orientation in the *Amauta* editorial "Anniversary and Balance Sheet." He begins work on the foundation of the Socialist Party.

October 8: The Socialist Party is formally constituted, with Mariátegui as general secretary.

November: *Seven Interpretive Essays on Peruvian Reality* is published. The workers' biweekly *Labor* begins publication.

1929

February-April: Mariátegui's short novel, *The Novel and Life*, is published in the magazine *Mundial*.

May: The Organizing Committee for a General Confederation of Peruvian Workers is constituted and sends Julio Portocarrero to Montevideo as a delegate to the Constituent Congress of the Latin American Trade Union Conference.

June: Hugo Pesce and Julio Portocarrero are delegates to the First Latin American Communist Conference in Buenos Aires. Mariátegui is named a member of the General Council of the Anti-Imperialist League, a group whose guiding force is the Third International.

September: Mariátegui's house is broken into and searched, this time because of a supposed "Jewish conspiracy." *Labor* is closed.

1930

February: Eudocio Ravines secretly returns to Peru and is named general secretary of the Socialist Party.

March: Mariátegui enters the Villarán Clinic in a medical emergency. He dies on April 16.

PART I
Europe and North America

Mariátegui followed politics in the centers of international capitalism not for the happenstance of his European exile but because he considered that the fate of the colonial and semi-colonial world was in play in these developments. Internationalism was for him not an ideal but a material reality. The European crisis, the Bolshevik revolution, the rise of fascism in Italy, and the growing dominance of North America were the context within which the Peruvian workers' movement faced its own challenges. The following selections include a public lecture offered shortly after his return from Europe and essays written for the liberal press during the following years.

The World Crisis and the Peruvian Working Class*

In this lecture—let's call it a conversation rather than lecture—I am going to limit myself to explaining the program of this series, along with some considerations on the necessity of spreading an understanding of the world crisis among the proletariat. To its disgrace, Peru lacks an educational press that follows the development of this great crisis with attentiveness, intelligence, and ideological conviction. It similarly lacks university professors of the likes of José Ingenieros, who can become impassioned by the ideas of renovation that are currently transforming the world and liberate themselves from the influences and prejudices of a conservative and bourgeois culture and education. It lacks socialist and syndicalist groups with suitable resources of popular culture that could therefore interest the people in a study of the crisis. The only platform for popular education with a revolutionary spirit is this Popular University, now in formation. It therefore falls to it to overstep its modest, initial working plan and present modern reality to the people, explain to them that they are living through one of the most transcendental and great moments of history, and spread the fertile disquiet that is currently moving the rest of the world's civilized peoples.

The working class is not a spectator in this great contemporary crisis; it is an actor. The fate of the world proletariat will be resolved through it. From it will arise, in all probability and with all prescience, the proletarian, socialist civilization that is destined to succeed the declining, decadent, moribund capitalist, individualist, and bourgeois civilization. The proletariat, now more than ever, needs to know what is happening in the world. And it cannot know it through the fragmentary, episodic, homeopathic information of the daily cable, poorly translated and even more poorly edited in the majority of cases, always originating from reactionary agencies charged with discrediting the parties, organizations, and individuals of the revolution and demoralizing and disorienting the world proletariat.

The destinies of all the world's workers are at stake in the European

* Lecture presented at the González Prada Popular University on June 15, 1923.

3

crisis. The development of the crisis, therefore, ought to interest the workers of Peru as it does the workers of the Far East. The main theater of the crisis is Europe, but the crisis of European institutions is the crisis of the institutions of Western civilization. And Peru, like the other peoples of America, revolves in the orbit of this civilization, not only because its countries are politically independent but economically colonized, yoked to the wagon of British, American, or French capitalism, but because our culture is European and our institutions are of a European type. And it is precisely these democratic institutions that we have copied from Europe, and this culture that we have copied from Europe, that are now in a period of definitive and total crisis there. Above all, capitalist civilization has internationalized the life of humanity and created material links among all peoples which establish an inevitable solidarity among them. Internationalism is not merely an ideal; it is a historical reality. Progress unifies and combines the interests, ideas, customs, and regimes of peoples. Peru, like the other American peoples, is therefore not outside the crisis; it is part of it. The world crisis has already reverberated among these peoples. And, of course, it will continue to reverberate. A period of reaction in Europe will also be a period of reaction in America. A revolutionary period in Europe will also be a revolutionary period in America. More than a century ago, when human existence was not as unified, when there were not the means of communication, when nations did not have the immediate and constant contact that they have today, when there was no daily press, when we were still spectators far from European events, the French revolution gave rise to the wars of independence and the appearance of all the republics. This recollection should suffice for us to take account of the rapidity with which the transformation of society will be reflected in American societies. Those who say that Peru, and America in general, are very distant from the European revolution have no notion of modern life, nor even an approximate understanding of history. These people are surprised that the most advanced ideas reach Peru, but are not surprised at the arrival of the airplane, the ocean liner, the wireless telegraph, and the radio—all the most advanced expressions of Europe's material progress. The same reasoning that ignores the socialist movement would have to ignore, for example, Einstein's theory of relativity. And I am sure that it would not occur to even our most reactionary intellectuals—almost all of them are impervious reactionaries— that the study and popularization of the new physics, of which Einstein is the most eminent and greatest representative, should be proscribed.

And if the working class in general must inform itself of the overall aspects of the world crisis, the need is even greater among the socialist, laborite, syndicalist, or anarchist section of the working class, which constitutes its vanguard; among the most combative and conscious, the most militant and prepared section of the working class; among the section of the working class charged with leading great proletarian actions; among that part of the proletariat whose historic role is to represent the Peruvian working class in the current social situation; among that part of the working class which has, in a word, class consciousness, revolutionary consciousness, whatever their particular beliefs. I particularly dedicate my talks to this vanguard of the Peruvian working class. No one needs to study the world crisis more than the vanguard proletarian groups. I do not pretend to come to this free university's open platform to teach them the history of the world crisis, but to study it with them. I am not teaching you the history of the world crisis from this platform, comrades; I am studying it with you. In this study, I only have the modest merit of bringing my personal observations of three and a half years of European life—that is, the culminating three and a half years of the crisis, and of the echoes of contemporary European thought.

I particularly invite the working-class vanguard to study with me the process of the world crisis for various transcendent reasons. I will quickly enumerate them. The first reason is that the revolutionary preparation, revolutionary culture, and revolutionary orientation of this working-class vanguard have been formed on the basis of socialist, syndicalist, and anarchist literature from before the European war, or at least prior to the culminating period of the crisis. It is mostly older socialist, syndicalist, and anarchist books that circulate among us. The classic literature of socialism and syndicalism is somewhat known here; the new revolutionary literature is unknown. Our revolutionary culture is a classic culture, besides being, as you well know, comrades, a very incipient, very inorganic, very disordered, and very incomplete one. Now then, all of this pre-war socialist and syndicalist literature is being revised. And these revisions are not being imposed by the caprice of theoreticians, but by the force of events. This literature, therefore, cannot be used today without taking stock. It is naturally not that it is no longer precise in its principles and foundations, in what of it is ideal and eternal, but that it is often no longer precise in its tactical inspiration, its historical considerations, and in everything related to action, methods, and means of struggle. The task of the workers remains the same; what has necessarily changed because of recent historical events are the paths selected to reach, or even approach, this historical goal. This is why the study of these historic events and their transcendence is indispensable for militant workers in their class organizations.

You know, comrades, that the proletarian forces of Europe have been divided into two great factions: reformists and revolutionaries. There is a reformist, collaborationist, evolutionist International, and a maximalist, anti-collaborationist, and revolutionary International. An intermediary International attempted to arise, but in the end made common cause with the first against the second. There are different shades of opinion in both, but there are clearly and incontrovertibly only two factions: the faction of those who hope to realize socialism by politically collaborating with the bourgeoisie, and the faction of those who hope to realize socialism by conquering political power fully for the proletariat. And the existence of these two factions certainly arises from the existence of two different conceptions, two opposed conceptions, two antithetical conceptions of the current historical moment. One part of the working class believes that the moment is not revolutionary, that the bourgeoisie has not yet exhausted its historical role, that, on the contrary, the bourgeoisie is still strong enough to maintain political power—in short, that the hour of the social revolution has not arrived. The other part of the working class believes that current historical moment is revolutionary, that the bourgeoisie is unable to rebuild the social wealth destroyed by the war and therefore unable to solve the problems of the peace, that the war began a crisis whose only solution is a proletarian, socialist solution, and that the social revolution has begun with the Russian revolution.

There are, then, two proletarian armies because there are two opposed conceptions of the historical moment, two distinct interpretations of the world crisis. The numerical strength of one or the other proletarian armies depends on whether events appear to confirm their respective historical conceptions. This is why the thinkers, theoreticians, and men of learning of both proletarian armies particularly exert themselves to investigate the meaning of the crisis, understand its nature, and discover its significance.

Before the war, two tendencies shared the leadership of the working class: the socialist and the syndicalist tendencies. The socialist tendency was predominantly reformist, social-democratic, and collaborationist. Socialists thought that the hour of social revolution was far off, and struggled for its gradual victory through legalistic activity and governmental, or at least parliamentary, collaboration. Such political activity excessively weakened the revolutionary will and spirit of socialism in some countries. Socialism was considerably bourgeoisified. Syndicalism appeared as a reaction to this bourgeoisification of socialism. Syndicalism opposed the direct action of the unions to the political activity of the socialist parties. The most revolutionary and intransigent spirits among the working class found refuge in syndicalism. But syndicalism also became somewhat collaborationist and reformist. Syndicalism was also dominated by a union bureaucracy without a real revolutionary psychology. And syndicalism and socialism were more or less linked and associated in some countries, like Italy, where the Socialist Party did not participate in the government and kept faithful to other formal principles of independence. Whether mostly belligerent or mostly proximate, depending on the country, there were two tendencies: syndicalists and socialists. The revolutionary literature that has nurtured the sensibility of our proletarian leaderships corresponds almost completely to this period of struggle.

But this situation has changed since the war. The proletarian camp, as we have just noted, is no longer divided into socialists and syndicalists, but into reformists and revolutionaries. We first witnessed a split, a division, in the socialist camp. One section of the socialists has held fast to its social-democratic, collaborationist orientation; the other has followed an anti-collaborationist, revolutionary orientation. And this is the section of socialism that has adopted the name of communism to clearly differentiate itself from the former. The division has occurred in the same manner in the syndicalist camp. One section supports the Social Democrats, the other supports the Communists. The appearance of the European social struggle has thereby changed radically. We have seen many intransigent pre-war syndicalists take the road of reformism. Alternatively, we have seen others follow communism. And among these is reckoned the Frenchman Georges Sorel, no one less than the greatest and most illustrious theoretician of syndicalism, as Comrade Fonkén reminded us recently in a discussion. Sorel, whose death has been a bitter sorrow for France's working class and intelligentsia, gave his full support to the Russian revolution and its people.

Here, as in Europe, the workers must be divided not into syndicalists and socialists—an anachronistic classification—but into collaborationists and anti-collaborationists, reformists and maximalists. But for this classification to occur with clarity and coherence, it is indispensable for the working class to know and understand the general features of this great contemporary crisis. Otherwise, confusion is inevitable.

I share the opinion of those who believe that humanity is living through a revolutionary period. And I am convinced of the imminent collapse of all social-democratic, reformist, evolutionist theses.

Before the war, these theses were explicable because they corresponded to different historical conditions. Capitalism was at its apogee. Production was overabundant. Capitalism could allow itself the luxury of making successive economic concessions to the working class. And its profit margins were such as to allow the formation of a voluminous middle class, a voluminous petty bourgeoisie, which enjoyed a comfortable and commodious lifestyle. The European worker earned enough to eat modestly and, in some countries like England and Germany, was able to satisfy some spiritual needs. There was not, therefore, the environment for the revolution. All this changed after the war. Europe's social wealth has been destroyed to a great degree. Capitalism, responsible for the war, needs to rebuild this wealth at the expense of the working class. And it therefore wants the socialists to collaborate in the government to strengthen democratic institutions, but not to progress along the road of socialist accomplishments. Previously, the socialists collaborated to slowly better the living conditions of the workers. They would now collaborate while renouncing all working-class conquests. To rebuild Europe, the bourgeoisie needs the working class to be reconciled to producing more and consuming less. And the working class resists both and tells itself it is not worthwhile to consolidate the power of a social class responsible for the war and inevitably destined to lead humanity to a still more bloody war. The conditions for collaboration of the bourgeoisie with the working class are of such a nature that collaborationism will necessarily and increasingly lose its now numerous supporters.

Capitalism cannot make concessions to socialism. For the European states to be reconstructed, they need a regime of rigorous fiscal economy, an increase in working hours, a lowering of wages—in a word, the re-establishment of the economic concepts and methods abolished in homage to the will of the proletariat. The working class, logically, cannot consent to this regression. It cannot and does not consent to it. Any possibility for the reconstruction of the capitalist economy is therefore eliminated. This is the tragedy of contemporary Europe. Reaction is canceling the economic concessions made to socialism in Europe. But while, on the one hand, these reactionary policies cannot be either sufficiently energetic or effective to re-establish the spent public treasury, on the other hand, the proletarian united front is slowly being prepared against these reactionary policies. Fearing the revolution, the reaction is therefore not only annulling the economic conquests of the masses, but also attacking their political conquests. We thus see the fascist dictatorship in Italy. But the bourgeoisie is undermining, destroying, and murdering its democratic institutions, and losing all its moral force and ideological prestige.

On the other hand, in the realm of international relations, the reaction is placing foreign policy in the hands of nationalist and anti-democratic minorities. And these nationalist minorities suffuse these foreign policies with chauvinism. And with their imperialist orientations, with their struggle for European hegemony, they prevent the re-establishment of an atmosphere of European solidarity that would allow the states to reach an understanding on a program of cooperation and labor. We have seen the results of this nationalism, these reactionary policies, in the occupation of the Ruhr.

The world crisis is therefore an economic and a political crisis. And it is above all an ideological crisis. The affirmative, positivist philosophies of bourgeois society have for some time been undermined by a current of skepticism and relativism. Rationalism, historicism, and positivism are in irremediable decline. This is undoubtedly the deepest aspect, the gravest symptom of the crisis. This is the most definite and profound index that not only the economy of bourgeois society is in crisis, but fully all of capitalist, Western, European civilization.

Now, the ideologues of the social revolution, Marx and Bakunin, Engels and Kropotkin, lived during the height of capitalist civilization and of historicist and positivist philosophy. Consequently, they could not foresee that the rise of the proletariat would have to occur by virtue of the decline of Western civilization. The proletariat was destined to create a new type of civilization and culture. The economic ruin of the bourgeoisie was also to be the ruin of bourgeois civilization. And socialism was to find itself in need of governing not in a period of plenty, wealth, and abundance, but an era of poverty, misery, and scarcity. The reformist socialists, accustomed to the idea that the socialist regime is a regime of distribution rather than one of production, imagine this to be symptomatic of the fact that the historic mission of the bourgeoisie is not exhausted and that the moment has not yet matured for the realization of socialism. In a report in *La Crónica*, I summoned up a phrase—that the tragedy of Europe is that capitalism can do no longer, and socialism cannot do yet. This phrase, which effectively captures the sense of the European tragedy, is the phrase of a reformist, saturated with an evolutionist mentality, and permeated with the idea of a slow, gradual, and beatific passage from individualist society to collectivist society without convulsions and shocks. And history teaches us that any new social state is formed on the ruins of the preceding social state, and that between the rise of one and the fall of the other, there is logically an intermediate period of crisis.

We are witnessing the disintegration, the agony of a worn-out, senile, decrepit society. And at the same time we are witnessing the gestation, the formation, the slow and disquiet elaboration of a new society. All humanity, all of us with a sincere ideological relationship that connects us to the new society and separates us from the old, ought to fix our gaze profoundly on this transcendent, agitated, and intense period of human history.

Lenin*

The figure of Lenin is clouded by legend, myth, and fable. It moves on a foreign stage that, like all Russian scenes, seems a bit fantastic and Alladinesque. It possesses the mysterious suggestiveness and attributes of Slavic people and things. Other contemporary personalities appear in their day-to-day familiarity, in direct contact with the Western public. Lloyd George, Poincaré, and Mussolini are well known to us. Their practiced faces smile at us in the

---

newspapers from behind their masks. We are abundantly informed of their ideas, their schedules, their menus, their words, their friends. And they are always shown to us in a European context: a hotel, a villa, an automobile, a Pullman car, a boulevard. Lenin, on the other hand, is far from the Western world, in a half-Asian and half-European city. His portrait has the Kremlin as its frame and the East as its backdrop. Nikolai Lenin is not even a name, but a pseudonym. The name of the Bolshevik leader is Vladimir Ilych Ulyanov, much as one might name a protagonist of Gorky, Andreyev, or Korolenko. Even physically, he is a somewhat exotic person: a Mongolian type, Siberian or Tatar. And like the music of Balakirev or Rimsky-Korsakov, Lenin seems to us more Eastern than Western, more Asian than European. (Russia is simultaneously illuminating the world with its Bolshevism, its art, its theater, and its literature. The dramas of Chekov, the statues of Archipenko, and the ideas of the Third International are being synchronically spread, disseminated, and acclimatized in European cities. Traveling promoters of the Russian soul, Stravinsky seduces Paris, Chaliapin conquers Berlin, and Chicherin stirs Lausanne.)

Lenin exercises a strange fascination over the most distant and abstruse peoples. Moscow attracts pilgrims from Persia, China, and India. Moscow is at the moment a fair of motley indigenous costumes and esoteric languages. The fame of Oswald Spengler, Charles Maurras, or General Primo de Rivera is only a Western one. The celebrity of Lenin, though, is fully international. The name of Lenin has penetrated among Afghans, Syrians, Arabs. And it has gained a mythological quality.

Those who have attended assemblies, meetings, and commissions at which Lenin has spoken tell of the religiosity, the fervor, the passion that the Russian leader has inspired. When Lenin rises to speak, feverish, convulsive, and frenetic ovations occur. People cheer, shout, sob.

But Lenin is not a mystical, priestly, or sacerdotal type. He is a terse, simple, crystalline, real, modern man. W. T. Goode, in the *Manchester Guardian*, has sketched him thus:

> Lenin is a man of medium stature, well built, seemingly around 50. At first glance, his features somewhat recall a Chinese type, and his hair and pointed beard have a dark reddish tint. His head is full of hair, his forehead wide and well formed. His eyes and expression are clearly sympathetic. He speaks clearly with a well-modulated voice. In all our conversations, he has never been agitated for a moment. The only genuine impression that I have is of a clear and cold intelligence, a man in total control of himself and his arguments, which he expresses with an extraordinarily suggestive lucidity.

Arthur Ransome, also in the *Manchester Guardian*, has written these physical and psychological facts about the Bolshevik caudillo:

Lenin seems to me a happy man. Returning from the Kremlin to my lodgings, I asked myself what man of his caliber has as happy a temperament as his. I could not think of any. This bald, wrinkled man, turning his chair from side to side, laughing about this and that, ready at any time to give serious advice to whomever interrupts him to ask—well-reasoned advice more powerful than any order—breathes happiness; every wrinkle has been traced by a smile rather than a worry.

This portrait from a British journalist, as circumspect and focused as a Zeiss lens, offers us a healthy and contagiously jocular and placid Lenin, so unlike the sullen, ferocious, and grim Lenin of so many photographs. Neither taciturn, deluded, nor mystic, Lenin is, then, a normal, balanced, sociable man. He is, in addition, well stocked with experience and saturated with modernity. His culture is Western; his intelligence is European. Lenin has lived in England, France, Italy, Germany, and Switzerland. His orientation is neither empiricist nor utopian, but materialist and scientific. Lenin believes that science will resolve the technical problems of socialist organization. He is planning the electrification of Russia. Bertrand Russell, who qualifies this plan as ideological, judges Lenin to be a man of genius.

Lenin's life has been that of an agitator. Lenin was born a socialist. He was born a revolutionary. Coming from a bourgeois family, Lenin nevertheless gave himself to socialism and to revolution from his youth. Lenin is a longtime leader, not only of Russian socialism, but of international socialism. The Second International adopted his and Rosa Luxemburg's motion at the Stuttgart Congress in 1907: "In case war should break out anyway, it is their duty [socialists] to intervene for its speedy termination and to strive with all their power to utilize the economic and political crisis created by the war to rouse the masses and thereby hasten the downfall of capitalist class rule" (*Lenin's Struggle for a Revolutionary International, Documents: 1907–1916* [New York: Monad Press, 1984], p. 35).

This declaration contained the germ of the Russian revolution and the Third International. Faithful to it, Lenin exploited the consequences of the war to lead Russia to revolution. With Lenin at the helm, the Russian revolution will reach its sixth anniversary in November. Lenin's prudent and cautious tactics have avoided the reefs, mines, and tempests of the passage. Lenin is a revolutionary with no lack of confidence, no vacillation, no fear. But he is not a rigid or immobile politician. Rather, he is an agile, flexible, dynamic politician who wisely and constantly revises, corrects, and rectifies his actions, who adapts and conditions them to the march of history. The need to defend the revolution has forced him into some deals, some compromises. On him weighs the responsibility of a general of millions of soldiers who must guard his army from imprudent action through opportune retreats, feints, and maneuvers. The history of Russia in these six years is testimony to his capacity as strategist and leader of multitudes and peoples. Lenin is not an ideologue, but a creator. The ideologue, the originator of a theory, generally lacks the wisdom, perspicacity, and flexibility to realize it. All doctrines, therefore, have their theoreticians and their politicians. Lenin is a politician, not a theoretician. His work as a thinker is a polemical work. Lenin has written many books, and often fleetingly interrupts his work as president of the Council of People's Commissars to reappear at his journalistic platform in *Pravda* or *Izvestia*. But the book, the speech, the article, are for him merely the instruments of propaganda, of the offensive, of struggle. His polemical temperament is characteristically and typically Russian. Lenin is aggressive, harsh, rude, lashing, without manners or euphemism. His dialectic is a dialectic of combat, lacking elegance, rhetoric, or ornamentation. It is not the academic dialectic of a professor, but the naked dialectic of a revolutionary politician. Lenin has maintained a resonant duel with the theoreticians of the Second International: Kautsky, Bauer, Turati. Their argumentation has been more erudite, more literary, more eloquent. But Lenin's discourse has been more original, more warlike, more penetrating.

Lenin is the caudillo of the Third International. Socialism, as is well known, is divided into two groups: the Third International and the Second International, the Bolshevik and revolutionary International and the Menshevik and reformist International. Marxism is the theory of both branches. Their divergence, their disagreement, is therefore not of a programmatic order, but a tactical one. Some attribute to Bolshevism a messianic, miraculous, magical concept of the revolution. They believe that Bolshevism aspires to an instantaneous, violent, sudden transformation of the social order. But Bolshevism and Menshevism are both gradualist. Only Bolshevism is gradualist in a revolutionary way, and Menshevism in a reformist way. Bolshevism maintains that it is impossible to use the current state machinery to reform society, and that it is indispensable to replace it with an adequate machine; that the proletarian state, differing from the bourgeois state in its functions, must also be different in its design. The type of proletarian state created by the Bolsheviks is the soviet state. The Republic of Soviets is the federation of all the local soviets. The local soviet is the organization of manual workers, office workers, and peasants of a commune. There is no duality of powers in the soviet regime. The soviets are, at the same time, administrative and legislative bodies. And they are the organs of the dictatorship of the proletariat. Defending this regime, Lenin says that the soviet is the organ of proletarian democracy, just as the parliament is the organ of bourgeois democracy. Thus, as modern society and feudal society have had their particular forms, their typical instruments, their characteristic institutions, proletarian society will also have to create its own.

And this opposition to parliament is not originally Bolshevik. The crisis of democracy and the crisis of parliament have been on display for several years. And the creation of a type of occupational or syndical parliament, based on the representation of interests rather than the representation of electors, has been suggested. Joseph Caillaux maintains that it is necessary "to maintain parliamentary assemblies, but only leave them political rights, and entrust the complete direction of the economic state to new organs: in a word, to create a synthesis between Western democracy and Russian sovietism." The appearance of the Bolshevik state coincides, then, with a powerful anti-parliamentary evangelism and a growing tendency to give the state a structure that is more economic than political. The parliament is attacked on one side by the revolution, and on the other by reaction. Fascism is essentially anti-democratic and anti-parliamentary. Mussolini took power by extra-parliamentary means. Primo Rivera has just taken the same route. Parliamentary organs have been declared inappropriate for revolution and for reaction.

Lenin and Mussolini, the caudillo of the revolution and the caudillo of reaction, oppose one class dictatorship with another class dictatorship. The clash, the conflict, between these dictatorships disquiets many contemporary thinkers. They foresee that this clash, this class conflict, will reduce civilization to ashes and push the Western world into a new Dark Age. The West distracts itself from this drama with its prizefighters, and anesthetizes itself with alkaloids and jazz. And meanwhile, as Luis Araquistain wrote to Don Ramón del Valle Inclán in July 1920, "Once again a gospel appears in the East, as did Christianity twenty centuries ago."

Trotsky*

Trotsky is not only a protagonist, but also a philosopher, historian, and critic of the revolution. No leader of the revolution, naturally, can be wanting a panoramic and sure vision of its roots and origins. Lenin, for example, was distinguished by a singular ability to sense and understand the direction of modern history and the meaning of its events. But Lenin's penetrating studies touched only on political and economic questions. Trotsky, on the other hand, has also been interested in the consequences of the revolution on philosophy and art.

---

* *Variedades*, April 19, 1924.

Trotsky polemicizes with writers and artists who announce the arrival of a new art, the appearance of a proletarian art. Does the revolution already possess its own art? Trotsky shakes his head. "Culture," he writes, "is not the first phase of happiness; it is a final result." The proletariat presently spends its energies in the struggle to defeat the bourgeoisie and in the work of resolving its economic, political, and educational problems. The new order is still too embryonic and incipient. It finds itself in a formative period. A proletarian art cannot yet appear. Trotsky defines the development of art as the highest testimony to the vitality and value of an epoch. Proletarian art will not be that which describes the episodes of the revolutionary struggle, but rather that which describes the life that emanates from the revolution, its creations, and its fruits. It is not a question, therefore, of speaking of a new art. Art, like the new social order, is passing through a period of trial and error. "The revolution will find its image in art when it is no longer a cataclysm foreign to the artist." The new art will be produced by a new type of humanity. The conflict between the reality that is dying and that being born will last for many years. These will be years of combat and malaise. Only when these years pass, when the new human organization is established and ensured, will the necessary conditions exist for the development of proletarian art. What will be the essential characteristics of this future art? Trotsky formulates some predictions. The future art will be, in his judgment, "irreconcilable with pessimism, skepticism, and all other forms of intellectual exhaustion. It will be full of creative faith, full of an unlimited faith in the future."

This is certainly not an arbitrary thesis. The despair, the nihilism, the morbidity which contemporary literature contains to varying degrees, are characteristic features of an exhausted, worn-out, decadent society. Youth is optimistic, affirmative, and cheerful; old age is skeptical, negative, and quarrelsome. The philosophy and art of a young society will consequently have a different tone than the philosophy and art of a senile society.

Trotsky's thought probes other conjectures and interpretations along this path. Bourgeois cultural and intellectual efforts are mainly directed toward the development of the technique and mechanism of production. Science is principally applied to generate an increasingly complete mechanization. The interests of the ruling class are adverse to the rationalization of production, and are therefore adverse to the rationalization of custom. The preoccupations of humanity are finally utilitarian. The ideal of the era is profit and savings. The accumulation of wealth seems the major purpose of human life. And, indeed, the new order, the revolutionary order, will rationalize and humanize custom. It will resolve the problems that the bourgeois order is unable to solve because of its structure and function. It will allow for the liberation of women from domestic slavery, ensure the social education of children, and free marriage from economic preoccupations. Socialism, so criticized and denounced as materialist, is finally, from this point of view, a recovery, a rebirth of spiritual and moral values crushed by capitalist organization and method. If material ambitions and interests prevailed in the capitalist era, the proletarian era, its nature, and its institutions will find inspiration in ethical interests and ideals.

Trotsky's dialectic leads us to an optimistic vision of the future of the West and of humanity. Spengler announces the total decline of the West. Socialism, according to this theory, is only a stage in the trajectory of a civilization. Trotsky establishes the crisis as one of bourgeois culture alone, the twilight of capitalist society. This culture, this old, detested society, is disappearing; a new culture, a new society is emerging from its bowels. The rise of a new ruling class, its roots much wider and its contents more vital than its predecessor's, will renew and increase the mental and moral energy of humanity. Human progress will then appear divided into the following major stages: antiquity (the regime of slavery); the Middle Ages (the regime of servitude); capitalism (the regime of wage labor); socialism (the regime of social equality). The thirty or fifty years of the proletarian revolution, says Trotsky, will mark a transitional era.

Is the man who theorizes so subtly and profoundly the same man who harangued and reviewed the Red Army? Some people, perhaps, are only acquainted with the martial Trotsky, the subject of so many portraits and caricatures; the Trotsky of the armored train, the minister of war and generalissimo, the Trotsky who threatens Europe with a Napoleonic invasion. And this Trotsky, in fact, does not exist. He is almost exclusively an invention of the press. The real Trotsky, the actual Trotsky, is the one he reveals in his writings. A book always gives a man a more exact and truthful image than a uniform. A generalissimo, especially, cannot philosophize so humanly and humanely. Could one imagine Foch, Ludendorff, or Douglas Haig with Trotsky's mental outlook?

The fiction of the martial Trotsky, the Napoleonic Trotsky, proceeds from a single aspect of the role of the celebrated revolutionary in Soviet Russia: his command of the Red Army. Trotsky, as is well known, first occupied the Commissariat of Foreign Affairs. But the final turn of the Brest-Litovsk negotiations obliged him to abandon this ministry. Trotsky wanted Russia to oppose German militarism with a Tolstoyan attitude: to reject an imposed peace and cross one's arms, defenseless, before the adversary. Lenin, with more political sense, preferred capitulation. Moved to the Commissariat of War, Trotsky was charged with organizing the Red Army. In this task, Trotsky demonstrated his capacity as organizer and realizer. The Russian army had dissolved. The fall of czarism, the progress of the revolution, and the end of the war had led to its destruction. The Soviets lacked the means to reconstitute it. Scarcely any war materiel remained. The monarchist officers and general staff could not be utilized because of their obvious reactionary spirit. For the moment, Trotsky tried to take advantage of the technical aid of the Allied military missions, exploiting the interest of the Entente in regaining the aid of Russia against Germany. But the Allied missions wanted the fall of the Bolsheviks above all else. If they pretended to ally with them, it was to better undermine them. Among the Allied missions, Trotsky found only one loyal collaborator: Captain Jacques Sadoul of the French ambassadorial staff, who finally joined the revolution, seduced by its ideals and its people. The Soviets, in the end, had to expel the Entente's diplomats and military staff from Russia. And, mastering all difficulties, Trotsky came to create a powerful army that victoriously defended the revolution from the attacks of all its enemies, external and internal. The initial nucleus of this army were two hundred thousand volunteers from the vanguard and the Communist youth. But, in the riskiest period for the Soviets, Trotsky commanded an army of more than five million soldiers.

And, like its former generalissimo, the Red Army is a new instance in the world's military history. It is an army that senses its role as a revolutionary army and never forgets that its purpose is the defense of the revolution. Its spirit, therefore, excludes any specifically warlike, imperialist sentiment. Its discipline, organization, and structure are revolutionary. Perhaps while the generalissimo was writing an article on Romain Rolland, the soldiers were invoking Tolstoy or reading Kropotkin.

The Exile of Trotsky*

Trotsky exiled from Soviet Russia: here is an event to which international revolutionary opinion cannot become easily accustomed. Revolutionary optimism never admitted the possibility that this revolution would end, like the French, condemning its heroes. But what in good sense should not have been expected is that the task of organizing the first great socialist state would be fulfilled with unanimous agreement, without debate or violent conflicts, by a party of more than a million impassioned militants.

Trotskyist opinion has a useful role in Soviet politics. It represents, if one

---

* *Variedades*, February 23, 1929.

wishes to define it in two words, Marxist orthodoxy, confronting the over-flowing and unruly current of Russian reality. It exemplifies the working-class, urban, industrial sense of the socialist revolution. The Russian revolution owes its international, ecumenical value, its character as a precursor of the rise of a new civilization, to the ideas that Trotsky and his comrades insist upon in their full strength and import. Without vigilant criticism, which is the best proof of the vitality of the Bolshevik Party, the Soviet government would probably run the risk of falling into a formalist, mechanical bureaucratism.

But, to this point, events have not proven Trotskyism correct from the point of view of its ability to replace Stalin in power with a greater objective capacity to realize the Marxist program. The essential part of the Trotskyist opposition's platform is its critical part. But in the estimation of those elements who might plot against Soviet policies, neither Stalin nor Bukharin is very far from subscribing to most of the fundamental concepts of Trotsky and his adepts. The Trotskyist proposals and solutions, on the other hand, do not have the same solidity. In most of what relates to agrarian and industrial policies and the struggle against bureaucratism and the NEP spirit, Trotskyism tastes of a theoretical radicalism that has not been condensed into concrete and precise formulas. On this terrain, Stalin and the majority, along with having the responsibility for administration, have a more real sense of the possibilities.

The Russian revolution, which, like any great revolution, advances along a difficult path that it clears with its own impetus, has not yet known easy or idle days. It is the work of heroic and exceptional men, and for this very reason has only been possible through the greatest and most tremendous creative tension. The Bolshevik Party, therefore, neither is nor can be a peaceful and unanimous school. Lenin imposed his creative leadership until shortly before his death, but not even with this extraordinary leader's immense and unique authority were violent debates unusual inside the party. Lenin gained his authority with his own strength; he later maintained it through the superiority and perspicacity of his thought. His points of view always prevailed because they best corresponded to reality. Many times, though, they had to defeat the resistance of his own lieutenants of the Bolshevik old guard.

Lenin's death, which left vacant the post of creative leader with immense personal authority, would have been followed by a period of profound disequilibrium in any party less disciplined and organic than the Russian Communist Party. Trotsky stood out from all his comrades because of the brilliant distinctiveness of his personality. But he not only lacked a solid and long-standing connection with the Leninist team. His relationship with the majority of its members had been quite uncordial before the revolution. Trotsky, as is well known, had an almost individual position among Russian revolutionaries until 1917. He did not belong to the Bolshevik Party, whose leaders, even Lenin himself, polemicized bitterly with him more than once. Lenin intelligently and generously appreciated the value of collaborating with Trotsky, who himself—as the volume of his writings on the revolution's leader attests—unreservedly and unjealously respected an authority consecrated by the most inspiring and enthralling work of revolutionary consciousness. But if almost all the distance between Lenin and Trotsky could be erased, the identification between Trotsky and the party itself could not be equally complete. Trotsky could not count on the full confidence of the party, as much as his performance as people's commissar merited unanimous admiration. The party machinery was in the hands of members of the old Leninist guard, who always felt themselves a bit distant from and alien to Trotsky, who, for his part, was not able to fully join them in a single bloc. Moreover, Trotsky, it seems, does not possess the special talents of a politician as Lenin did to the greatest degree. He does not know how to gather men; he is not acquainted with the secrets of managing a party. His singular position—equidistant from Bolshevism and Menshevism—during the years between 1905 and 1917, besides disconnecting him from the revolutionary team that prepared and realized the revolution with Lenin, must have disaccustomed him to the concrete practice of a party leader.

As long as the mobilization of all revolutionary energies against the threats of reaction continued, Bolshevik unity was ensured by the pathos of war. But once the work of stabilization and normalization began, the discrepancies between individuals and tendencies had to manifest themselves. The lack of an exceptional personality like Trotsky would have reduced the opposition to more modest terms. In this case, it would not have come to a violent schism. But with Trotsky at the command post, the opposition quickly took an insurrectionary and combative tone to which the majority and the government could not be indifferent.

Trotsky, moreover, is a man of the cosmopolis. Zinoviev, at another moment during a Communist congress, accused him of ignoring and neglecting the peasant. He has, in any case, an international sense of the socialist revolution. His notable writings on the transitory stabilization of capitalism are among the most alert and sagacious criticisms of the era. But this very international sense of the revolution, which gives him such prestige on the world scene, momentarily robs him of his power in the practice of Russian politics. The Russian revolution is in a period of national organization. It is not a matter, at the moment, of establishing socialism internationally, but of realizing it in a nation that, while a nation of 130 million inhabitants that overflows onto two continents, does not yet constitute a geographical and historical unit. It is logical that in this stage, the Russian revolution is represented by men who more deeply sense its national character and problems.

Stalin, a pure Slav, is one of these men. He belongs to a phalanx of revolutionaries who always remained rooted in the Russian soil, while Trotsky, Radek, and Rakovsky belong to a phalanx that passed the larger part of their lives in exile. They were apprenticed as international revolutionaries in exile, an apprenticeship that has given the Russian revolution its universalist language and its ecumenical vision. For now, alone with its problems, Russia prefers more simply and purely Russian men.

The Russian revolution finds itself in a necessary period of prudence. Trotsky, personally disconnected from the Stalinist team, is an excessive figure on the stage of national achievement. One imagines him destined to carry the socialist gospel in triumph through Europe, with Napoleonic energy and majesty, at the head of the Red Army. It is not as easy to conceive him filling the modest role of minister in normal times. The NEP condemns him to return to his belligerent position as polemicist.

Mussolini and Fascism*

Fascism and *Mussolini* are two consubstantial and intimately connected words. Mussolini is the animator, leader, and *duce maximo* of fascism. Fascism is the platform, tribune, and vehicle of Mussolini. To explain a part of this episode of the European crisis, we will quickly summarize the history of the *fasci* and their caudillo.

Mussolini, as is well known, is a politician who came out of the socialist movement. Within socialism, he had neither a centrist nor a moderate position, but rather an extremist and incandescent one. His role was in consonance with his temperament, because Mussolini is, spiritually and organically, an extremist. His post is at the extreme left or the extreme right. From 1910 to 1911, he was one of the leaders of the socialist left. In 1912, he directed the expulsion from the socialist camp of Bonomi, Bissolati, Cabrini, and Podrecca, four deputies who were partisans of ministerial collaboration, and took over the directorship of *Avanti*. Then 1914 and the war arrived. Italian socialism demanded Italian neutrality. Mussolini, naturally disquiet and belligerent, rebelled against the pacifism of his co-religionists. He proposed the intervention of Italy into the war. Initially, he gave his interventionism

---

* Published in *La escena contemporánea* (1925).

a revolutionary cast. He maintained that to extend and exacerbate the war was to hasten the European revolution. But, actually, in his interventionism beat a warlike psychology that could not be reconciled with the Tolstoyan and passive attitude of neutrality. In November 1914, Mussolini abandoned the directorship of *Avanti* and founded *Il Populo d'Italia* to support the attack on Austria. Italy joined the Entente. And Mussolini, the propagandist of intervention, became a soldier of intervention also.

Then came victory, armistice, and demobilization. And with these came a period of unemployment for the interventionists. D'Annunzio, nostalgic for action and epic, undertook the Fiume adventure. Mussolini created the *fasci di combatimento*: *haces* or bundles of fighters. But the moment in Italy was revolutionary and socialist. The war had been bad business for Italy. The Entente had assigned it a meager share of the booty. Oblivious to the contribution of Italian arms to the victory, they had stubbornly cheated them of possession of Fiume. Italy, in short, ended the war with a sense of discontent and disenchantment. Elections took place in this atmosphere, and the socialists won 155 seats in the parliament. Mussolini, a candidate in Milan, was noisily defeated by socialist votes.

But these sentiments of deception and national depression were propitious to a violent nationalist reaction. And these were the root of fascism. The middle class is particularly receptive to the most passionate patriotic myths. And the Italian middle class, moreover, felt themselves distant from and adversarial to the proletarian socialist class. It did not pardon their neutralism. It did not pardon their high salaries, state subsidies, and social legislation that the fear of revolution had secured during and after the war. The middle class regretted and suffered the fact that the working class, neutralist and even defeatist, became the beneficiaries of a war they had not wanted and whose results they minimized, belittled, and disdained. This ill-temper in the middle class found a home in fascism. Mussolini thereby attracted the middle class to his *fasci di combatimento*.

Some socialist and syndicalist dissidents enrolled in the *fasci*, bringing their experience and skill in organizing and winning over the masses. Fascism was not yet a programmatically and consciously reactionary and conservative sect. Its propaganda had subversive and demagogic aspects. Fascism, for example, howled against the nouveau riches. Its principles—tendentially republican and anti-clerical—were full of the intellectual confusion of the middle class, which, instinctively discontented and disgusted with the bourgeoisie, is vaguely hostile to the working class. The Italian socialists committed the error of not using their political arms wisely to change the spiritual attitude of the middle class. But, even worse, they accentuated the enmity between the working class and the petty bourgeoisie, who were treated disdainfully and mocked by some priestly theoreticians of revolutionary orthodoxy.

Italy entered into a period of civil war. Frightened by the chance of revolution, the bourgeoisie armed, supplied, and solicitously encouraged the fascists. It pushed them toward the fierce persecution of socialism, the destruction of the revolutionary unions and cooperatives, and the crushing of strikes and insurrections. Fascism thereby became a large and veteran militia. It finally became stronger than the state itself. And then it demanded power. The fascist brigades conquered Rome. Mussolini, in his "black shirt," rose to power, compelled the majority of parliament to obey, and inaugurated a fascist regime and a fascist era.

Many stories have been written about Mussolini, but little history. Because of his political belligerence, an objective and clear definition of his personality and image is almost impossible. Some definitions are exaggeratedly poetic and obliging; others are rancorous and propagandistic. At times, Mussolini is known through anecdotes and snapshots. It is said, for example, that Mussolini is the inventor of fascism. Some think that Mussolini "created" fascism. Mussolini is indeed an experienced agitator, an expert organizer, a dizzily active type. His activities, dynamism, and potential greatly influence the fascist phenomenon. During the electoral campaign, Mussolini spoke in three or four cities on the same day. He used the airplane to leap from Rome to Pisa, Pisa to Bologna, Bologna to Milan. Mussolini is a volatile, dynamic, verbose, and extremely Italian type, singularly endowed to agitate the masses and excite the multitudes. And he was the organizer, the animator, the *condottiere* of fascism. But he was not its creator, and it was not his invention. He extracted a political movement from a state of mind, but he did not model this movement in his own image and likeness. Mussolini did not give a spirit or program to fascism. On the contrary, fascism gave spirit to Mussolini. His consubstantiation, his ideological identification with the fascists, obliged Mussolini to exonerate himself, to purge himself of the last residues of socialism. Mussolini had to assimilate and absorb the anti-socialism and chauvinism of the middle class to organize it into the ranks of the *fasci di combatimento*. And he had to define his politics as reactionary, anti-socialist, and anti-revolutionary. The case of Mussolini differs in this way from that of Bonomi, Briand, and other ex-socialists. Bonomi and Briand were never forced to explicitly break with their socialist origins. To the contrary, they have assumed a minimal socialism, a homeopathic socialism. Mussolini, on the other hand, has come to say that he is embarrassed by his socialist past, as a mature man is embarrassed by his adolescent love letters. And he has leaped from the most extreme socialism to the most extreme conservatism. He has not attenuated or lessened his socialism; he has abandoned it totally and integrally. His economic course, for example, is averse to political interventionism, statism, and fiscal policy. It does not accept the transactional type of capitalist and entreprenurial state; it tends to restore the classic type of tax-collecting and police state. Today's viewpoints are diametrically opposed to yesterday's. Mussolini was as convinced then as he is now. What was the mechanism or process of his conversion from one theory to the other? It is not a question of a mental phenomenon; it is an irrational phenomenon. The motor force for this change in ideological attitude was not an idea; it was an emotion. Mussolini has not been freed of his socialism, either intellectually or conceptually. For him, socialism was not an idea, but an emotion, in the same way that fascism is not in itself an idea, but an emotion. Let us note a psychological and physiognomic fact: Mussolini has never been a cerebral, but rather an emotional type. In politics, in the press, he has not been a theoretician or a philosopher, but a rhetorician and a leader. His language has not been programmatic, principled, or scientific, but rather passionate and emotional. Mussolini's most flaccid speeches have been those in which he has attempted to define the derivation and ideology of fascism. The fascist program is confused, contradictory, heterogeneous, containing liberal and syndicalist concepts mixed pell-mell. Better yet, Mussolini has not given fascism a true program; he has given it a plan of action.

Mussolini passed from socialism to fascism, from revolution to reaction, by an emotional route, not a conceptual one. All historical apostasies have probably been spiritual phenomena. Mussolini, yesterday's revolutionary extremist, today's reactionary extremist, reminds us of Julian. Like this emperor, the character of Ibsen and Merezhkovsky, Mussolini is a disquieted, theatrical, deluded, superstitious, and mysterious being who has felt himself chosen by Destiny to decree the persecution of the new gods, and restore to their altar the dying, old gods.

The Decline of England*

The surest and most visible decline of the moment—although the elegant criticism of Don José Ortega y Gasset has not yet taken note of it—is the decline of England. Perhaps Spengler's famous *Untergang des Abendlandes* (Decline of the West) is politically summarized in Leon Trotsky's *Decline of England*. The German professor's thesis undoubtedly seems more manageable and verifiable to bourgeois intellectuals than that of the Russian revolutionary.

* *Variedades*, May 21, 1927.

But the reason for this is that Spengler's thesis expresses a philosophy of history, while Trotsky's is a translation of the dialectic of the revolution. We have a thousand concrete proofs of England's descent. The most recent, irrefutable, and authentic are, first, the loss of the Hankow concession, militarily occupied by the Chinese revolutionaries in a grave offense to Britain's majesty, and, second, the raid at the offices of the Arcos Company and the Soviet commercial delegation in London. The first event represents a great material and moral defeat for Britain's colonial empire in Asia. The second proclaims the bankruptcy of decorum and fair play in Britain's official conduct in Europe. The two events constitute two different symptoms of the decline of Great Britain, one internal, the other external. The process of invading an office normally protected by diplomatic immunity, sequestering its papers, and searching its male and female employees has all the appearances of a Bolshevik and revolutionary proceeding. And its incorporation into the technique of England's police is of great importance, since it indicates a break with a leading resort of British conduct.

But these are only the most obvious and material signs of England's decline. We find deeper signs of this phenomenon in its contemporary history. England apparently or, rather, materially reached its greatest strength and expansion when the peace treaties were signed to end the great war. But, actually, the bases of British greatness had begun to appear seriously undermined before this. The decline of Great Britain began the moment that liberalism, parliamentarism, and evolutionism, which had been adopted by humanity in a more or less orthodox manner under British hegemony, entered into crisis. And Great Britain lost its economic and technical primacy once electricity and oil revolutionized industry and transportation. British industry, and therefore the British Empire, rested on coal. Thus, to the degree that oil and electricity have replaced coal in industry and transportation, British omnipotence has been undermined. The struggle for oil between Great Britain and the United States thus presents itself as the most important competition between the two great industrial and capitalist countries.

The revision of the most characteristic ideas of the nineteenth century is actually a revision of English ideas. During the era of its absolute predominance, Great Britain had been the provider of humanity's fundamental ideas and objects. The principles of anthropology, sociology, and other substantive sciences have had a British origin and cast, and have spiritually and intellectually reinforced and extended Great Britain's political rule. Darwinism, for example, which has dominated the world's scientific thought for so long, and which I have already qualified as a typical product of the British mentality and genius, has nurtured and sustained an integral evolutionism that, among other things, has tended to justify the triumph and rule of the English people over other peoples. The unilinearism of the English school of sociology, which attributes the same historical process to all societies, also has the elements of a theory aiming to confirm English superiority.

Great Britain has maintained special privileges over the leading ideas in the sciences of greatest political importance. It has not shown the same predominance in the other sciences. In more than a few cases, it has abandoned them to other Western peoples. And the same has occurred in the industrial field. It reserved to itself the role of purveyor of substantive merchandise. Ceding hegemony to France in women's fashion was not of importance; rather, it monopolized the technique and materials of men's clothing. No conviction is as widespread and deeply rooted internationally as that of the superiority of English cashmere. The rule of Great Britain has been, above all, the rule of coal and cashmere. For some time now, England has carded and spun the world's wool to knit the network of its rule. And the Western and "civilized" man of this era has been the man who dresses and thinks in the English manner.

All this colossal scaffolding is now collapsing. Evolutionism is undergoing a cruel revision in all its aspects. The English idea—peculiar to Saxon imperialism—of the absolute and incontestable superiority of the white man is irreparably debilitated. Parliament no longer maintains its authority, even in England itself, where the class struggle is sapping its classic function. The cardinal principles and most important products of Great Britain must confront growing competition under increasingly disadvantageous conditions.

Bernard Shaw is probably one of the Englishmen who has most lucidly taken account of the British crisis. But Shaw himself is not able to fully free himself of all English superstitions. His socialism is fundamentally a Fabian socialism, that is, a socialism of liberal texture.

The Destiny of North America*

All the arguments between French neo-Thomists and German racists as to whether the defense of Western civilization falls to the Latin and Roman spirit or the German and Protestant one find their meaninglessness incontestably documented in the Dawes plan. The payment of German repara-

---

* *Variedades*, December 17, 1927.

tions and the Allied debt have put the fate of Europe's economy, and therefore its politics, into the hands of the United States. The financial recovery of the European states is impossible without Yankee credit. The spirit of Locarno, the security pacts, etc., are merely names for the guarantees demanded by North American finance for its copious investments in the public finances and industry of the European states. Fascist Italy, which so arrogantly announces the restoration of Rome's power, forgets that its agreements with the United States put its currency at the mercy of this creditor.

Capitalism, which displays a lack of confidence of its own strength in Europe, appears limitlessly optimistic concerning its destiny in North America. And this optimism rests simply on its good health. It is the biological optimism of youth, displaying an excellent appetite and untroubled that the hour of arteriosclerosis must come. In North America, capitalism still has possibilities for growth that the war's destruction has left late and lamented in Europe. The British Empire still maintains a formidable financial organization, but, as the problem of its coal mines proves, its industry has lost the technical level that earlier ensured its primacy. The war has converted it from the creditor to the debtor of North America.

All these facts indicate that capitalist society now finds its seat, its axis, its center in North America. Yankee industry is the best equipped for large-scale production at the lowest cost; its banks, to whose coffers flow the gold cornered by North America in wartime and post-war commerce, guarantee with their capital the conquest of the markets that its products must absorb at a time of incessant growth of its industrial capacity. The illusion, if not the reality, still remains that it is a system of free competition. Its government, education, and laws conform to the principles of an individualistic democracy, in which any citizen can freely aspire to have a hundred million dollars. While the members of the working class and middle class in Europe sense themselves more and more enclosed within their class boundaries, in the United States they believe that fortune and power are still accessible to all those with the ability to win them. And this is the measure of the existence of the psychological factors that distinguish the development of capitalist society.

The North American phenomenon, for its part, has nothing arbitrary about it. North America was from its beginnings predestined to the greatest capitalist achievement. In England, despite its extraordinary power, capitalist development has not succeeded in removing all feudal remnants. Aristocratic privileges have not ceased to weigh upon its politics and economy. The English bourgeoisie, content to concentrate its energies in industry and commerce, did not concern itself with contesting the aristocracy for its land. Its control of the land had to encumber the exploitation of the subsoil. But the English bourgeoisie did not want to sacrifice its landlords, who were destined to maintain their exquisitely refined and decorative pedigrees. This is why it only now seems to be discovering its agrarian problem. Only now, with its industries in decline, does it miss a prosperous and productive agriculture on the lands where the aristocracy has its hunting preserves. North American capitalism, in the meantime, has not had to pay any feudal dues, either monetarily or spiritually. On the contrary, it emanates freely and vigorously from the first intellectual and moral seeds of the capitalist revolution. The New England pioneer was a Puritan expelled from the European homeland for a religious rebellion that constituted the first assertion of the bourgeoisie. The United States thus grew as a manifestation of the Protestant Reformation, considered the purest and first spiritual manifestation of the bourgeoisie, that is, of capitalism. In its era, the founding of the North American republic signified the definitive consecration of this event and of its consequences.

Waldo Frank writes:

> The first permanent colonies on the Eastern seaboard were grounded upon conscious purposes of wealth. Their revolution against England in 1775 was one of the first clear-cut struggles between bourgeois capitalism and the old feudality. The triumph of the colonies which gave birth to the United States marked the triumph of the capitalistic state. And from that day to this, America has had no tradition, no articulation outside of the industrial revolution which threw it into being (*Our America* [New York: Boni and Liveright, 1919], p. 14).

And this very Frank recalls Charles A. Beard's famous and concise judgment of the Constitution of 1789:

> The Constitution was essentially an economic document based upon the concept that the fundamental private rights of property are anterior to government and morally beyond the reach of popular majorities (*An Economic Interpretation of the Constitution of the United States* [New York: Macmillan, 1961], p. 324).

No material or moral obstacle has troubled the energetic and free flourishing of North American capitalism, unique in the world in that its origin combined all the historical factors of the perfect bourgeois state, without the impediment of aristocratic and monarchical traditions. Upon their arrival in the virginal land of America, from which they expunged all indigenous vestiges, the Anglo-Saxon colonizers laid the foundations of the capitalist order.

The Civil War also constituted a necessary assertion of capitalism, liberating the Yankee economy from the sole snake-in-the-grass of its infancy—slavery. With slavery abolished, the capitalist phenomenon finds its path absolutely clear. The Jew—so connected to the development of capitalism, as studied by Werner Sombart, not only by the spontaneous utilitarian application of his expansive and imperialistic individualism, but above all by the radical exclusion from all "noble" activity to which he was condemned by the Middle Ages—joined the Puritan in the business of building the most powerful industrial state and the most robust industrial bourgeoisie.

Ramiro de Maeztu—who occupies a much more solid ideological position than the neo-Thomist philosophers of reaction in France and Italy when he recognizes New York as the real antithesis of Moscow, thus assigning to the United States the task of defending and continuing Western civilization as a capitalist civilization—generally understands quite well, within the context of his bourgeois apologetics, the moral elements of North America's riches and power. But he reduces them almost completely to their Puritan or Protestant elements. The Puritan ethic, which sanctifies wealth, regarding it as a sign of divine favor, is at bottom a Jewish ethic, whose principles the Puritans assimilated through the Old Testament. The doctrinal bond between Puritanism and the Jew has been established for a long time, and the Anglo-Saxon capitalist experience only confirms it. But Maetzu, the fervent panegyrist of industrial "Fordism," must avoid it, as much in deference to Mr. Ford's clamorings against the "Jewish International" as for his adherence to the malice with which all the world's "nationalist" and reactionary movements view the Jewish spirit, suspected of a terrible concurrence with the socialist spirit because of their common ideal of universalism.

To the extent that the role of the United States as the impresario of European capitalist stabilization, whether fascist or parliamentary, becomes clear, the dilemma "Rome or Moscow" will cede place to the dilemma "New York or Moscow." The two poles of contemporary history are Russia and North America, capitalism and communism, both universalist, although quite differently and oppositely: Russia and the United States, the two people that are most opposed in doctrine and in politics, and, at the same time, the two closest peoples, as the supreme and highest expression of Western activism and dynamism. Some years ago, Bertrand Russell was already pointing out the strange similarity between the captains of Yankee industry and the Marxist functionaries of the Russian economy. And that tragically Slavic poet, Alexander Blok, saluted the dawn of the revolution with these words: "Here is the star of the new America."

Yankeeland and Socialism*

The spectacle of North American power inspires impressionistic and super-ficial critics to accord the most unlimited credit to the prospect of a Yankee recipe for a capitalist renaissance that would forever frustrate Marxism's temp-tation of the working masses. After reading Henry Ford's book, writers co-piously provisioned with literature and philosophy but little informed in economic matters frequently claim on the front pages of great newspapers that socialism is a school or theory already superseded by the wondrous experience of North American capitalism. Drieu La Rochelle, for example, a talented artist, when venturing a review of the contemporary scene, writes things such as:

> The theories that are still discussed in socialist and communist milieus arose in the England of 1780, the France of 1830, the Germany of 1850, countries experiencing the invasion of the machine, like today's Russia. But despite these novelistic theories, the Russians know to look toward large-scale North American capitalism, which, in turn, knows that it is only a stage on a road to elsewhere. Ford and Lenin are two powers approaching each other, exchanging verbal blows, along the same dark corridor.

The author of *Mesure de la France*, as a good Frenchman and European, does not feel that the defense of Western civilization is falling to the United States. He sees it, to the contrary, as the mission of a European confedera-tion presided over by France. But, for the moment, he trusts much more in Mr. Ford than in Poincaré and Henry Massis to be captain of the bourgeoi-sie and the strategist of capitalism.

Meanwhile, a study of the actual factors of North American prosperity teaches us that Yankee capitalism has not yet confronted the crisis that faces European capitalism, so that it is premature to speak of its ability to over-come it successfully.

Until recently, North American industry drew the components of its growth from the very vitality of the United States. But since its production has exceeded the necessities of Yankee consumption, the conquest of external markets has become the inevitable condition of this process. The accumula-tion of most of the world's gold in Yankee coffers has created the problem

---

* *Variedades*, December 31, 1927.

of exporting capital. It is now not enough for the United States to place its excess of production; it also needs to place its excess of gold. The country's industrial development cannot absorb its financial resources. Before the war, Yankee industry was a good investment for European money. As is well known, the war's profits allowed Yankee industry to become fully independent of European banking. The United States was transformed from a debtor nation into a creditor nation. During the period of post-war economic crisis and revolutionary turmoil, the United States had to abstain from all new loans. The European countries had to systematize the condition of their debt to North America before soliciting any credit from New York banks. As to investment in private enterprise itself, the threat of Communist revolution, to which Europe seemed pushed by misery, counseled greater prudence among North American capitalists. The United States thus employed all of its influence to direct Europe into the Dawes plan. It only attained this after Poincaré's policies suffered their failure in the Ruhr in 1923. Since then, with the conditions for the payment to the Yankee treasury of German reparations as well as the Allied debt having been stipulated, Yankeeland has opened numerous credits to Europe. It has lent to states to stabilize their exchange rates; it has lent to private industry for the reorganization of their plants and businesses. A good number of European shares and titles have passed into Yankee hands. But these investments have their limit. North American capital cannot dedicate itself to supplying funds to European industry without the danger that its production will dispute those markets that the United States now dominates. On the other hand, these investments tie the Yankee economy to the fate of the European economy. The Dawes plan and its consequent arrangements and financial conventions have inaugurated a period of capitalist—and democratic—stabilization in Europe, which the apologists of reaction entertain themselves by describing as an exclusively fascist task. But Europe, as evidenced by the latest economic conference, has not yet found its equilibrium.

Trotsky has made a singularly penetrating and objective examination of the situation of Yankee capitalism. The Russian leader observes:

Gold "inflation" is just as dangerous for [an] economy in its own way as currency inflation. One can die not only of anemia, but also of plethora. If there is too great a quantity of gold, no new revenues can be derived from it, the interest on capital is lowered and thereby the further expansion of production is made inexpedient and even irrational. To produce and to export for the sake of locking one's gold in cellars is equivalent to throwing one's goods into the sea. Consequently, as time goes on, America's need to expand grows greater and greater; that is, she must invest her surplus resources in Latin America, Europe, Asia, Australia, Africa. The more this happens, all the more does the economy of Europe and other parts of the world become integrated with that of the United States ("Europe and America," a speech delivered on February 15, 1926, and reprinted in *Fourth International*, 1943, translated by John G. Wright).

If it would suffice for the United States to resolve its internal productive problems to ensure indefinite growth for its capitalism, then the golden predictions and rosy hopes of Henry Ford might constitute a serious probability of the effacement of Marxist theory. Through the work of historical forces superior to the will of its own people, North America has embarked on a vast imperialist adventure which it cannot renounce. Spengler, in his famous book of a few years ago on the decline of the West, maintained that the last stage of a civilization is an imperialist one. His German patriotism made him hope that this imperialist mission would fall to Germany. Lenin, some years previously in perhaps the most fundamental of his books, anticipated Spengler in considering Cecil Rhodes as a representative of the imperialist spirit, giving us a Marxist definition of the phenomenon, understood and grasped as an economic phenomenon. With his brilliant conciseness, he wrote:

Economically, the main thing in this process is the displacement of capitalist free competition by capitalist monopoly. Free competition is the basic feature of capitalism, and of commodity production generally; monopoly is the exact opposite of free competition, but we have seen the latter being transformed into monopoly before our eyes, creating large-scale industry and forcing out small industry, replacing large-scale by still larger-scale industry, and carrying concentration of production and capital to the point where out of it has grown and is growing monopoly: cartels, syndicates, and trusts, and merging with them, the capital of a dozen or so banks, which manipulate thousands of millions. At the same time the monopolies, which have grown out of free competition, do not eliminate the latter, but exist above it and alongside it, and thereby give rise to a number of very acute, intense antagonisms, frictions, and conflicts. Monopoly is the transition from capitalism to a higher system.

If it were necessary to give the briefest possible definition of imperialism, we should have to say that imperialism is the monopoly stage of capitalism. Such a definition would include what is most important, for, on the one hand, finance capital is the bank capital of a few very big monopolist banks, merged with the capital of the monopolist associations of industrialists; and, on the other hand, the division of the world is the transition from a colonial policy which has extended without hindrance to territories unseized by any capitalist power, to a colonial policy of monopolist possession of the territory of the world, which has been completely divided up (*Imperialism, the Highest Stage of Capitalism*, in V. I. Lenin, *Selected Works: One-Volume Edition* [New York: International Publishers, 1971], pp. 232–233).

The United States empire, by virtue of these policies, assumes all the responsibilities for capitalism. And, at the same time, it inherits all its contradictions. And it is precisely from the latter that socialism gains its power. The destiny of North America can only be contemplated on a world scale. And, on this level, North American capitalism, while still vigorous and prosperous internally, ceases to be a national and autonomous phenomenon and becomes the culmination of an international phenomenon, subordinated to an inevitable historical fate.

PART II
The Anti-Imperialist
Struggle

Along with the Russian revolution, the rise of anti-colonial movements from China and India to Ireland and Central America marked a turning point in the international situation during and after the First World War. Mariátegui was attracted to the Third International and its unconditional support for these independence movements, despite their national and bourgeois-democratic goals. As he pointed out, it was the popular masses who were most committed to these struggles, while the feudal and bourgeois forces were inclined to compromise with the imperial powers. Most of the essays in this section were written in the early to mid-1920s; Mariátegui's analysis of later developments in China (the Kuomintang attack on the left in 1927) reinforced his views on the need for the working class to maintain its political independence in this process.

Revolutionary and Socialist Agitation in the Eastern World*

Tonight's subject is the revolutionary and nationalist ferment in the East. I have already explained the connection that exists between the European crisis and the revolt of the East. Some European statesmen seek the remedy for the West's economic malaise in a more methodical, more scientific, and more intense exploitation of the Eastern world. They have the bold plan of extracting from the colonial nations those resources necessary for the recovery and restoration of the capitalist nations. Let the braceros of India, Egypt, Africa, or colonial America produce the money needed to concede better wages to the braceros of England, France, Germany, the United States, etc. European capitalism dreams of making the European workers its partner in the business of exploiting the colonial peoples. Europe intends to rebuild its wealth, squandered during the war, with the tribute of the colonies. Western capitalism has not succeeded in resigning the Western proletariat to miserable and impoverished living conditions. It takes into account that the European proletariat does not want the economic obligations of the war to fall upon itself. And for this reason it is undertaking the colonial enterprise of reorganizing and extending the exploitation of the Eastern peoples. European capitalism is attempting to stifle Europe's social revolution by distributing among European workers the profits obtained by exploiting the colonial workers. Let the three hundred million inhabitants of Western Europe and the United States enslave the billion and a half inhabitants of the rest of the world. The program of European and North American capitalism reduces itself to this—the enslavement of the underdeveloped and uncultured majority for the benefit of the world's developed and cultured minority. But this plan is too simplistic to be carried out. Various factors oppose its realization. For many years, Europe has preached the right of peoples to freedom and independence. The last war was carried out by England, France, the United States, and Italy in the name of freedom and democracy against imperialism and conquest. Many African and Asian soldiers fought alongside European

*Lecture presented at the González Prada Popular University on September 28, 1923.

soldiers for these myths and these principles. And these myths and principles, of which Allied and North American capitalism have made such imprudent and excessive abuse, have taken root in the East. India, Egypt, Persia, and southern Africa, invoking European ideas, today demand the recognition of their right to rule themselves. Asia and Africa wish to emancipate themselves from the tutelage of Europe in the name of the ideology and doctrine that Europe has taught and preached to them. In addition, there is another psychological motive for the revolt of the East. Until the war, the Eastern peoples had a superstitious respect for European societies, for Western civilization, the creators of so many marvels and repositories of such a culture. The war and its consequences have undermined and weakened much of this superstitious respect. The peoples of the East have seen the peoples of Europe fight, claw, and devour each other with such cruelty, such fury, and such perfidy that they no longer believe in their superiority and progress. More than its material authority over Asia and Africa, Europe has lost its moral authority. It still has sufficient arms to impose itself, but its moral arms are fewer each day.

Moreover, the moral consciousness of the Western countries has advanced too far for policies of conquest and oppression to be defended and accepted by the popular masses. Earlier, the proletariat had not posed an effective and committed opposition to the colonialist and imperialist policies of their governments. English, French, and German workers were more or less indifferent to the fate of Asian and African workers. Socialism was an international theory, but its internationalism ended at the borders of the West, at the boundaries of Western civilization. The socialist and syndicalist spoke of liberating humanity, but in practice they were only interested in Western humanity. The Western workers tacitly considered the enslavement of colonial workers to be natural. In the end, Western men, educated in the prejudices of Western civilization, saw the workers of the East as barbarians. All of this was natural and just. Western civilization was then too proud of itself. One did not speak of Western civilization and Eastern civilization, but simply of civilization. The ruling culture did not accept the coexistence of two civilizations, did not accept the equality of civilizations—none of the ideas that historical relativism now presumes. At the borders of Western civilization began Egyptian barbarism, Asian barbarism, Chinese barbarism, Turkish barbarism. Everything that was not Western, everything that was not European, was barbarian. It was therefore natural and logical that in this atmosphere of ideas, Western socialism and the Western proletariat also had turned internationalism into a mainly European doctrine. Only the European and North American workers were represented in the First International. The vanguards of the South American workers and others incorporated into the orbit of the European world, the Western world, joined the Second International. But the Second International remained an International of the Western workers, a phenomenon of European civilization and society. All of this was natural and proper, moreover, because socialist theory, proletarian theory, constituted a creation, a product, of European and Western civilization. I have already said, while summarily discussing the crisis of democracy, that socialist and proletarian theory is the child of capitalist and bourgeois society. Bourgeois society developed and matured in the midst of medieval and aristocratic society. Similarly, proletarian society is currently developing and maturing in the midst of bourgeois society. The social struggle, therefore, does not have the same character among the peoples of the West and the peoples of the East. Among the peoples of the East, even slave regimes still survive. The problems of the Eastern peoples are different from those of the peoples of the West. And socialist theory, proletarian theory, is a fruit of the problems of the Western peoples, a method to resolve them. The solution appears where the problem exists. The solution cannot be attempted where the problem does not yet exist. In the Western countries, the solution has been outlined because the problem exists. Socialism, syndicalism, the theories that inspired the European multitudes, therefore left the Eastern multitudes indifferent. For this reason, there was not an international solidarity of the exploited multitudes, but a solidarity of the socialist multitudes. This was the meaning, the extent, the reach of the old Internationals, the First and Second Internationals. And hence the working masses of Europe would not energetically combat the colonization of the working masses of the East, so distant from their own customs, sentiments, and aims. This state of mind has now been changed. Socialists are beginning to understand that the social revolution must not be a European revolution, but a world revolution. The leaders of the social revolution sense and understand capitalism's maneuver, seeking in the colonies the resources and means to avoid or delay the revolution in Europe. And they are making efforts to combat capitalism, not only in Europe, not only in the West, but in the colonies. The tactics of the Third International find inspiration in this new orientation. The Third International encourages and promotes the rising of the peoples of the East, although this rising lacks a proletarian and class character and is above all a nationalist rising. Many socialists have polemicized with the Third International precisely about this colonial question. Without understanding the decisive character that the emancipation of the colonies from capitalist domination has for the social revolution, these socialists have objected to the cooperation that the Third International has lent to the political emancipation of the colonies. Their reasons are these: that socialism should support only socialist movements, and that the rebellion of the Eastern peoples is a nationalist one. It is not a proletarian insurrection, but a bourgeois one. The Turks, the Persians, the Egyptians, are not struggling to inaugurate socialism in their countries, but to become politically independent from England and Europe. The proletarians among these peoples are fighting and agitating, intermingled and jumbled with their bourgeoisies. There is no social war in the East, but political wars, wars of independence. Socialism has nothing in common with these nationalist insurrections that do not tend to liberate the proletariat from capitalism, but to liberate the Indian, Persian, or Egyptian bourgeoisie from the English bourgeoisie. Some socialist leaders who do not appreciate and consider all the historical value, all the social value, of the rising of the East say and maintain this. At the memorable Halle Congress, Zinoviev, in the name of the Third International, defended its colonial policies from the attacks of Hilferding, the socialist leader and current finance minister. Zinoviev said at this opportunity:

> The Second International was limited to white men; the Third does not divide men by color. If we want a world revolution, if we want to liberate the proletariat from the chains of capitalism, we must not think solely of Europe. We also ought to direct our gaze to Asia. Hilferding will scornfully say: "These Asians, these Tatars, these Chinese!" Comrades, I say to you: a world revolution is impossible if we do not plant ourselves in Asia, too. Four times more people live there than in Europe, and these people are oppressed and abused like ourselves. Should we approach them, move them toward socialism, or shouldn't we? If Marx said that a European revolution without England would seem like a tempest in a teapot, we say, German comrades, that a proletarian revolution without Asia is not a world revolution. And this has great importance to us. I am a European too, like yourselves, but I feel that Europe is a small part of the world. We realized in the Moscow Congress what has been lacking until now in the working-class movement. We have sensed what is necessary to accomplish the world revolution. And this is the awakening of the oppressed masses of Asia. I confess to you—when I saw hundreds of Persians and Turks sing the Internationale with us in Baku, I felt tears in my eyes. And I was hearing the breath of the world revolution.

And this is why the Third International neither is nor has wanted to be an exclusively European International. Attending the founding congress of the Third International were delegates of the Chinese Workers Party and the Korean Workers Union. Persians, Turkestanis, Armenians, and delegates of other Eastern peoples have attended the following congresses. And on August 14, 1920, that great Congress of the Peoples of the East to which Zinoviev alluded met in Baku, attended by the delegates of twenty four Eastern peoples. The foundations of an International of the East were established at this congress—not a socialist International, but a uniquely revolutionary and insurrectionary one.

Under the pressure of these events and ideas, these very reformist socialists, these very democratic socialists, so full of old Western prejudices, have become much more interested than before in the colonial question. And they have begun to recognize the need for the proletariat to seriously concern itself with fighting the oppression of the East and supporting the right of these peoples to rule themselves. This new attitude of the Socialist parties restrains and constrains the great capitalist nations from employing the power of armed expeditions against the peoples of the East. And thus we saw last year that England, challenged in Turkey by Mustafa Kemal, could not respond to this threat with military operations. The English Labour Party initiated furious agitation against sending troops to the East. The English dominions, Australia, and the Transvaal declared their will to refuse their consent to an attack on Turkey. The English government saw itself obliged to compromise with Turkey, to give way to Turkey, which in other times it would have smashed pitilessly. Similarly, three years ago, we saw the Italian working class resolutely oppose Italy's occupation of Albania. The Italian government was forced to withdraw its troops from Albanian soil and sign a friendship treaty with tiny Albania. These events reveal a new international situation. This new situation can be summarized by three observations: 1) Europe lacks the material authority to subjugate the colonial peoples; 2) Europe has lost its old moral authority over these peoples; 3) the moral conscience of the European nations does not allow the capitalist regime a brutally oppressive and conquistador policy against the East in this era. In other words, the historical conditions, the necessary political conditions exist for the East to rise, for the East to win its independence, for the East to liberate itself. Just as the peoples of America won their independence at the beginning of the last century because the world situation was propitious, opportune for their liberation, now the peoples of the East are shaking off the political rule of Europe because the world situation is propitious, opportune for their liberation.

East and West*

The revolutionary tide has not only affected the West. The East is also convulsed, restive, stormy. One of the most current and transcendent realities of modern history is the political and social transformation of the East.

---

*Published in *La escena contemporánea* (1925).

This period of agitation and expectancy in the East coincides with a period of unusual and mutual eagerness of the East and the West to get acquainted, study, and understand each other.

In its haughty youth, Western civilization treated the Eastern peoples with disdain and contempt. The white man considered his rule over the man of color to be necessary, natural, and just. He used the words *Eastern* and *barbarian* identically. He thought that only what was Western was civilized. The exploration and colonization of the East was never the responsibility of intellectuals, but of merchants and warriors. The Westerners unloaded their merchandise and their machine guns in the East, but not their instruments or aptitude for research, interpretation, and spiritual conversion. The West was preoccupied with consummating the material conquest of the Eastern world, but did not attempt its moral conquest. And thus the Eastern world maintained its sensibility and psychology intact. The millenarian roots of Islam and Buddhism remain fresh and vital today. The Indian still wears his old khaddar. The Japanese, the Easterner most permeated with Westernisms, still maintains something of his samurai nature.

But today, when the relativist and skeptical West senses its own decadence and foresees its coming decline, it feels the need to explore and better understand the East. Moved by a new and feverish curiosity, Westerners are passionately investigating Asian customs, history, and religions. Thousands of artists and thinkers are drawing texture and color for their thought and art from the East. Europe is avidly stockpiling Japanese paintings and Chinese sculpture, Persian dyes and Indian rhythms. It is becoming inebriated with the orientalism distilled in Russian art, fantasy, and life. And it confesses an almost morbid desire to orientalize itself.

The East, in turn, is now permeated with Western thought. European ideology has liberally infiltrated its way into the Eastern soul. An ancient Eastern development, despotism, is in agony, undermined by this infiltration. China, now republicanized, is renouncing its traditional wall. The democratic idea, having grown decrepit in Europe, is reappearing in Asia and Africa. The Goddess of Liberty is the most eminent goddess in the colonial world at the very moment when Mussolini declares her disowned and abandoned by Europe ("The demagogues have killed the Goddess of Liberty," the blackshirts' *condottiere* has declared). The Egyptians, the Persians, the Indians, the Filipinos, the Moroccans wish to be free.

Europe is harvesting, among other things, the fruits of its wartime sermonizing. The Allies used demagogic and revolutionary language to incite the world against the Austro-Germans. They emphatically and noisily proclaimed the right to independence of all peoples. They presented the war against Germany as a crusade for democracy. They proposed new international law. This propaganda profoundly excited the colonial peoples. And once the war ended, these colonial peoples announced their desire to emancipate themselves in the name of European ideas.

The theories of Marx have penetrated into Asia, imported by European capital. Socialism, which at first was a phenomenon of Western civilization alone, currently is extending its historical and geographical radius. The first workers' Internationals were exclusively Western institutions. Only the proletariats of Europe and America were represented in the First and Second Internationals. On the other hand, delegates from the Chinese Workers Party and the Korean Workers Union assisted at the founding conference of the Third International in 1920. Persian, Turkestani, and Armenian delegations have taken part in the following congresses. A revolutionary congress of Eastern peoples took place in August 1920 in Baku, sponsored and promoted by the Third International. Twenty-four Eastern peoples were represented at the congress. Some European socialists, Hilferding among them, reproach the Bolsheviks for their understanding of organized nationalist movements. Polemicizing with Hilferding, Zinoviev responded: "A world revolution is impossible without Asia. Four times more people live there than in Europe. Europe is a small part of the world." The social revolution has a historical need of the uprising of the colonial peoples. Capitalist society tends to renew itself through the more methodical and intensive exploitation of its political and economic colonies. And the social revolution must incite the colonial peoples against Europe and the United States to reduce the number of vassals and tributaries of capitalist society.

The new moral conscience of Europe also conspires against European domination over Asia and Africa. There are now many millions of people in Europe of pacifist affiliation who are opposed to any act of war, any inhuman actions against the colonial peoples. Europe is therefore obliged to negotiate, sign agreements, and give way before these peoples. The Turkish example is quite illustrative in this regard.

A vigorous will to independence is thus appearing in the East at the same time that the capacity to coerce and stifle it is weakening in Europe. In short, the historically necessary conditions for the liberation of the East are appearing. More than a century ago, an ideological revolution came from Europe to our peoples in America. And, inflamed by its own bourgeois revolution, Europe could not escape the process of American independence engendered by this ideology. Similarly, Europe, now undermined by a social revolution, cannot militarily repress insurrection by its colonies.

And in this serious and pregnant moment of human history, it seems that something of the Eastern soul is transmigrating to the West, and something of the Western soul is transmigrating to the East.

The Chinese Revolution*

Let us attempt a summary interpretation of current events in China. It is impossible to be disinterested in the destiny of a nation that occupies such a principal position in time and space. China weighs too greatly in human history for its deeds and its people not to captivate us.

The theme is vast and labyrinthine. Events tumultuously and confusedly pile upon events on this vast stage. The elements for study and judgment of which we dispose are scarce, partial, and at times unintelligible. Our petulant country, so little studious and attentive, knows almost nothing of China except the coolie and a few herbs, products, and superstitions (our only Sinophile is, perhaps, Don Alberto Carranza). Nevertheless, China is much nearer to us spiritually and physically than Europe. The cast of our people's psychology is more Asian than Western.

Another of the great modern revolutions is occurring in China. A powerful will of renewal has been convulsing this old and skeptical empire for thirteen years. The revolution has neither the same goal nor the same program in China as in the West. It is a bourgeois and liberal revolution. Through it, China is quickly moving toward democracy. Thirteen years is a very short time. Capitalist and democratic institutions in Europe have needed more than a century to reach their full development.

Until its first contacts with Western civilization, China had maintained its ancient political and social forms. Chinese civilization, one of history's oldest, had already reached the end of its trajectory. It was an exhausted, mummified, paralyzed civilization. The Chinese spirit, more practical than religious, oozed skepticism. The contact with the West was more a shock than a contact. The Europeans entered China with a brutal and rapacious spirit of depredation and conquest. For the Chinese, it was an invasion of barbarians. This pillage kindled a bitter and ferocious reaction in the Chinese psyche against Western civilization and its eager agents. It provoked a xenophobic sensibility, as well as the Boxer Rebellion, which brought upon China a punitive military expedition by the Europeans. This belligerence maintained and stimulated a mutual incomprehension. China was visited by very few Westerners of the stripe of a Bertrand Russell, and many of the stripe of a General Waldersee.

---

*Variedades, October 4, 1924.

But the Western invasion did not bring to China only its machine guns and merchandise, but also its machinery, technique, and other instruments of its civilization. Under their influence, the Chinese economy and mentality began to change. A loom, a locomotive, a bank implicitly contain all the seeds of democracy and its consequences. At the same time, thousands of Chinese left their country, which was previously closed and diffident, to study in European and American universities. There they acquired the ideas, inquietude, and emotions that have taken everlasting possession of their intellect and psychology.

The revolution thus appears as a task of adapting Chinese politics to a new economy and consciousness. For some time now, the old institutions have not corresponded to the new methods of production and new forms of living. China is already too populated with factories, banks, machines, ideas, and things that do not accord with a primitive patriarchalist regime. Industry and finance need a liberal and even agitated atmosphere to develop. Their interests can depend neither on Asiatic despotism nor Buddhist, Taoist, or Confucian mandarin ethics. A people's economy and politics must function in solidarity.

Currently, the democratic currents in China are struggling against absolutist remnants. The interests of the big and petty bourgeoisie are fighting against the interests of the feudal class. The actors of this struggle are military caudillos, *tuchuns*, like Chang Tso-lin or minister Wu P'ei-fu. But, in truth, they are simple instruments of greater historical forces. The Chinese writer F. H. Djen remarks in this regard:

> It can be said that the manifestation of the popular spirit has until now had only a relative value, since its lieutenants, its champions, have consistently been military chiefs, among whom one can always suspect personal ambitions and dreams of glory. But it should not be forgotten that we are not far from an era in which the same was true in the great Western states. The personalities of the political actors, the intrigues sown by this or that foreign power, should not keep us from seeing the decisive political power, which is the popular will.

Let us make use of a little chronology to illustrate these ideas. The Chinese revolution began formally in October 1911, in the province of Hupeh. The Manchu dynasty found itself undermined by the liberal ideas of the new generation and disqualified to continue representing national sentiment because of its conduct in the face of the European repression of the Boxer Rebellion. It could therefore not withstand a national resistance, nor could it pose a serious opposition to the insurrectionary wave. The republic was proclaimed in 1912. But the republican tendency was only powerful among the population of the South, where the conditions of landed property and industry favored the spread of the liberal ideas sown by Dr. Sun Yat-sen and the Kuomintang Party. The forces of feudalism and mandarinism prevailed in the North. The government of Yüan Shih-k'ai, republican in form but monarchist and *tuchun* in essence, arose from this situation. Yüan Shih-k'ai and his followers came from among the old dynastic clientele. His policies tended toward reactionary goals. A period of tension arose between these two bands. Yüan Shih-k'ai finally declared himself emperor. But his empire turned out to be quite fleeting. The people rose against his ambition and forced him to abdicate.

After this episode, the history of the Chinese republic was a succession of reactionary attempts, quickly combated by the revolution. Efforts at restoration were invariably frustrated by the persistence of a revolutionary spirit. Different *tuchuns* passed through the Beijing government: Chang Huin, Tuan Ch'i-jui, etc. The opposition between the North and South grew during this period. A complete secession finally occurred. The South separated from the rest of the empire in 1920, and a republican government headed by Sun Yat-sen was established in Canton, the principal metropolis and historical center of revolutionary ideas. Canton—the antithesis to Beijing—where economic life had acquired a style analogous to that in the West, was home to the most advanced ideas and people. Some of the workers' unions remained under the influence of the Kuomintang Party, but others adopted socialist ideology.

The factional war continued in the North. Liberalism remained in arms against all attempts to restore the past. General Wu P'ei-fu, an enlightened caudillo, became the interpreter and repository of the people's vigilant republican and nationalist sentiment. Chang Tso-lin, military governor of Manchuria, a *cacique* and *tuchun* in the old style, embarked upon the conquest of Beijing, in whose government he wished to place Liang Shi Y. But Wu P'ei stopped and inflicted a tremendous defeat upon him near Beijing in May 1922. This event, followed by the proclamation of Manchuria's independence, ensured his rule over the greater part of China. A proponent of Chinese unity, Wu P'ei-fu then worked to realize this idea, re-establishing relations with one of the leaders of the South, Ch'en Chiung-ming. Meanwhile, Sun Yat-sen, who was accused of ambitious schemes and whose liberalism in any case seemed quite diminished, flirted with Chang Tso-lin.

At the moment, Chang Tso-lin and Wu P'ei-fu are struggling once again. Japan, which hopes for a government subservient to its wishes, favors Chang. Behind the scenes, the Japanese are playing a principal role in Chinese affairs. Japan has always found support in the Anfu Party and among the feudal interests. The popular and revolutionary current has been opposed to it. Thus the victory of Chang Tso-lin would only be one more reactionary episode that a new development would soon annul. The revolutionary upsurge can only ebb with the realization of its goals. The military chiefs move on the surface of the revolutionary process. They are the external symptom of a situation struggling to find its own form. Either pushing them or opposing them, the forces of history are in action. Thousands of intellectuals and students are propagating a new agenda in China. The students, agitators par excellence, are the leaven of a China in birth.

The process of the Chinese revolution is finally tied to the fluctuating direction of Western politics. China needs to organize itself and develop a minimum degree of freedom on the international level. It must be the master of its own ports, customs, wealth, and administration. It still depends too much on foreign powers. The West subjugates and oppresses it. The Washington agreement, for example, has been nothing but an effort to establish the spheres of influence and rule of each power in China.

Bertrand Russell, in his *The Problem of China*, says that the Chinese situation has two solutions: the transformation of China into a military power capable of imposing respect upon foreigners or the inauguration of a socialist era throughout the world. The first solution is not only detestable, but absurd. Military power cannot be improvised in this era. It is a consequence of economic power. The second solution, on the other hand, today seems less distant than during the bitter, reactionary days in which Bertrand Russell wrote his book. The chances of socialism have improved since then. It is enough to recall that the friends and co-religionists of Bertrand Russell today are in the government of England. They still do not really govern, however.

Gandhi*

This gentle and pious man is one of the most important personages of modern history. His thought not only influences 320 million Indians; it moves the whole of Asia and echoes throughout Europe. Romain Rolland, who, discontented with the West, turns toward the East, has devoted a book to him. The European press curiously explores the biography and the story of this apostle.

The main chapter of Gandhi's life begins in 1919. The post-war period put Gandhi at the head of his people's movement for emancipation. Until

---

*Published in *La escena contemporánea* (1925).

then, Gandhi had faithfully served Great Britain. He collaborated with the English during the war. India made an important contribution to the Allied cause. England had promised to concede it the rights of its other "dominions." With the conflict over, England went back on its word and the Wilsonian principle of peoples' self-determination. It superficially reformed its administration of India, according the Indian people a secondary and innocuous role. It responded to Indian resentment with warlike and bloody repression. Facing such perfidious treatment, Gandhi changed his attitude and abandoned his illusions. India arose against Great Britain and demanded autonomy. The death of Tilak had placed the leadership of the nationalist movement in the hands of Gandhi, who exercised a great religious influence over his people. Gandhi accepted the obligation of leading his compatriots, and led them to the strategy of non-cooperation. He opposed armed insurrection. In his opinion, the means should be as decent and moral as the ends. It was the resistance of the spirit and of love that must oppose British arms. Gandhi's evangelical words inflamed the mysticism and fervor of the Indian soul. The Mahatma gradually escalated his strategy. Indians were urged to desert the schools and universities, the administration and the courts, to weave their khaddars with their own hands, and to reject British goods. Gandhian India poetically turned to the "music of the spinning wheel." English textiles were burned in Bombay as damned and satanic works. The tactic of non-cooperation led to its ultimate conclusion: civil disobedience, the refusal to pay taxes. India seemed on the verge of a definitive rebellion. Some violence occurred. Gandhi, angered by this failing, suspended the order for civil disobedience and mystically submitted to penance. His people had not yet been educated to the use of *satyagraha*, the love-force, the soul-power. The Indians obeyed their leader. But this retreat, ordered at the moment of greatest tension and ardor, weakened the revolutionary wave. The movement was consumed and spent itself without a struggle. There were some defections and some dissent. Gandhi's arrest and trial came at the right moment. The Mahatma relinquished the leadership of the movement before its decline.

The Indian National Congress of December 1923 marked the decline of Gandhianism. The revolutionary tendency of non-cooperation prevailed at this meeting, but it was confronted by a rightist or revisionist tendency that, in opposition to the Gandhian tactic, proposed participation in reformist councils created by England to domesticate the Indian bourgeoisie. At the same time, a new revolutionary current of socialist inspiration appeared in this assembly, now emancipated from Gandhianism. This current's program, led from Europe by nuclei of Indian students and emigrés, proposed India's complete separation from the British Empire, the abolition of feudal landed property, the suppression of indirect taxation, the nationalization of the mines, railroads, telegraphs, and other public services, state intervention in the management of industry, modern labor legislation, etc. Later, this split continued to widen. The two big factions displayed their class content and physiognomy. The revolutionary tendency was followed by the proletariat, which, harshly exploited without the aid of protective legislation, suffered most from English domination. The poor, the humble, were faithful to Gandhi and the revolution. The industrial proletariat organized itself into unions in Bombay and other Indian cities. The rightist tendency, on the other hand, was based among the rich castes, the Parsees, merchants, and landlords.

Thus, the strategy of non-cooperation, sabotaged by the Indian aristocracy and bourgeoisie, contradicted by economic reality, slowly failed. The boycott of English textiles and the return to the lyric spinning wheel could not prosper. Manufacturing by hand could not compete with mechanized manufacturing. The Indian people, moreover, had an interest in not creating resentment among the English working class by adding to a cause for their unemployment with the loss of a large market. They could not forget that the Indian cause needs the support of the English Labour Party. On the other hand, functionaries who had been dismissed in large measure returned to their posts. In short, all forms of non-cooperation were relaxed.

When MacDonald's Labour government amnestied and freed him, Gandhi found the Indian nationalist movement divided and diminished. A short time before, the majority of the National Congress, in an extraordinary meeting in Delhi in September 1923, had declared itself favorable to the Swaraj Party, led by C. R. Das, whose program agreed to demand the rights of the British "dominions" for India and was preoccupied with obtaining solid and secure guarantees for Indian capitalism.

Currently, Gandhi neither leads nor controls the political orientation of the greater part of Indian nationalism. Neither the right, which wishes to collaborate with the English, nor the far left, which urges insurrection, obeys him. The number of his supporters has decreased. But if his prestige as a political leader has declined, his prestige as ascetic and saint has not stopped growing. A journalist tells of how pilgrims of different Asian races and regions gather as the Mahatma retires to his home. Gandhi receives all who call at his door without ceremony or protocol. Surrounding his house live hundreds of Indians, happy to feel attached to him.

This is the natural tendency of the Mahatma's life. His work is more religious and moral than political. In a dialogue with Rabindranath Tagore, the Mahatma has declared his intention to introduce religion into politics. The theory of non-cooperation is full of ethical preoccupations. Gandhi is actually not the caudillo of India's freedom, but the apostle of a religious movement. Indian autonomy interests and moves him only secondarily. He feels no rush to attain it. Above all, he wishes to purify and elevate the Indian soul. While his outlook is nurtured, in part, by European culture, the Mahatma repudiates Western civilization. He opposes its materialism, its impurity, its sensuality. Like Ruskin and Tolstoy, whom he has read and loves, he detests the machine. For him, the machine is the symbol of "satanic" Western civilization. He therefore does not wish mechanization and its influence to be accepted in India. He understands that the machine is the agent and motor of Western ideas. He feels that the Indian psychology is not suited for a European education, but he dares to hope that India, having collected itself, can elaborate a morality that can be used by other people. Indian from head to toe, he thinks that India can prescribe its own discipline to the rest of the world. His goals and actions, when they pursue fraternization between Hindus and Moslems or the redemption of the untouchables, the pariahs, have a vast political and social transcendence. But their inspiration is essentially religious.

Gandhi classifies himself as a "practical idealist." And Henri Barbusse considers him a true revolutionary. He says that "to our mind, this term refers to those who, having conceived a different order in opposition to the established political order, dedicate themselves to the realization of this ideal plan by practical means," and adds that "the utopian is not a true revolutionary, no matter how subversive his motives." This definition is excellent. But Barbusse also believes that "if Lenin had found himself in Gandhi's place, he would have spoken and acted like him." And this hypothesis is arbitrary. Lenin was an achiever and a realist. He was unquestionably a practical idealist. It has not been proven that the path of non-cooperation and non-violence is the only one for the emancipation of India. Tilak, the previous leader of Indian nationalism, did not disdain the method of insurrection. Romain Rolland argues that Tilak, whose genius he praises, would have been able to come to an understanding with the Russian revolutionaries. Yet Tilak was no less Asian or Indian than Gandhi. Better founded than Barbusse's hypothesis is the opposing one, that Lenin would have worked to take advantage of the war and its consequences to liberate India and, in any case, would not have restrained those Indians on an insurrectionary path. Gandhi, governed by a moralistic temperament, has, at times, not felt the same need for freedom as has his people. His strength, in the meantime, has depended on the fact that he has offered the Indians a solution for their slavery and hunger, more than on his religious preaching.

The theory of non-cooperation contained many illusions. One of these was the medieval illusion of reviving a vanquished economy in India. The spinning wheel is powerless to resolve the social question of any people. Gandhi's argument—hasn't India lived like this before?—is too anti-historical and ingenuous. As skeptical and distrustful as his attitude toward progress might be, a modern man instinctively rejects the idea that one can go backward. Once the machine has been acquired, it is difficult for humanity to renounce its use. Nothing can contain the infiltration of Western civilization into India. Tagore is fully correct in this aspect of his polemic with Gandhi. "Today's problem is international. No people can seek safety by separating itself from the others. They will be saved together or disappear together."

These accusations against Western materialism are exaggerated. Western man is not as prosaic and rude as some contemplative and ecstatic souls suppose. Socialism and syndicalism, despite their materialist conception of history, are less materialist than they appear. They base themselves on the interests of the majority, but they tend to ennoble and dignify life. Westerners are mystical and religious in their own way. Isn't the revolutionary spirit a religious spirit? It is said in the West that religiosity has been displaced from heaven to earth. Its motives are human and social, not divine. They belong to terrestrial, not celestial, existence.

The renunciation of violence is more romantic than violence itself. India will never force the English bourgeoisie to restore its freedom by moral arms alone. Honest British judges will recognize the integrity of the apostles of non-cooperation and *satyagraha* as many times as necessary, but they will continue condemning them to six years in jail. Unfortunately, a revolution is not made by fasting. Revolutionaries throughout the world must choose between suffering violence or utilizing it. If they do not wish spirit and intelligence to be the subject of force, they must resolve to make force the subject of intelligence and spirit.

Ireland and England*

The question of Ireland is still alive. De Valera, the caudillo of the Sinn Feiners, is again agitating the Irish scene. Ireland is not pacified. Since 1922, its right to live autonomously within the orbit and the moral, military, and international confines of Great Britain has been recognized. But this independence is not enough for all the Irish. They wish to feel free of all British coercion and tutelage. They cannot resign themselves to their own internal administration; they also aspire to their own foreign policy. This sentiment

---

Variedades, October 25, 1924.

must be quite deep when neither compromises nor defeats manage to domesticate or destroy it. It is impossible for a people to struggle so hard for an arbitrary aspiration.

Luis Araquistain once wrote that Catholic and conservative Ireland would be less democratic and liberal outside of Great Britain. Thus keeping it in its empire and oppressing it a bit served the interests of democracy and freedom. This paradoxical and simplistic judgment corresponded quite well to the mentality of a democratic writer and Allied sympathizer, as Araquistain then was. But an attentive examination of the matter did not confirm this; it contradicted it. The rich and conservative classes of Ireland have been generally content with home rule. The proletariat, on the other hand, has declared itself republican, revolutionary, and more or less "Fenian," as always, and has demanded the country's unconditional autonomy. Araquistain prejudged the question before deepening his study of it.

Nevertheless, the reference to Irish Catholicism, while apparently putting him on the right track, imprecisely captured only a part of the reality. The conflict between Catholicism and Protestantism is actually more than a metaphysical quarrel, something more than a religious schism. The Protestant Reformation tacitly contained the essence, the germ, of the liberal ideal. Protestantism and liberalism appeared simultaneously and in solidarity with the first elements of the capitalist economy. It is not by mere chance that capitalism and industrialism have had their principal seat among the Protestant peoples. The capitalist economy has reached its full development only in England and Germany. And the peoples of Catholic faith in these nations have instinctively maintained rural and medieval tastes and habits. Bavaria, for example, is peasant. Only with difficulty has large-scale industry acclimatized to its soil. The Catholic nations have experienced the same phenomenon. France—which cannot be judged only by the cosmopolitanism of Paris—is predominantly agricultural. Its population is *très paysanne*. Italy loves the agricultural life. Its demography has pushed it on the road of industrial labor. Milan, Turin, and Genoa have become great capitalist centers for this reason. But some remnants of the feudal economy survive in southern Italy. And while the modernist movement was an attempt to rejuvenate Catholic dogma in the northern Italian cities, the Italian South has never seen any heterodox crisis or heretical disquiet. Protestantism thus appears in history as the spiritual leaven of the capitalist process.

But now that the capitalist economy, having reached its full development, is entering into a period of decline, now that a new economy is developing in its bowels and fighting to replace it, the spiritual elements of its development are slowly losing their historical value and belligerent sensibility. Isn't it symptomatic, or at least new, that the different Christian churches are beginning to approach each other? For some time now, the possibility has been discussed of uniting all the Christian churches into one, and it has been said that the causes of their enmity and competition have weakened. Free inquiry frightens Catholics much less than in the days of the struggle against the Reformation. And, meanwhile, free inquiry seems less combative, less disturbing than before.

It is therefore not the clash between Catholicism and Protestantism, so mitigated by centuries and events, which impedes a cordial relationship between Ireland and England. The adherence to Catholicism in Ireland has a basis in nationalist passion. For Ireland, its Catholicism and its language are, above all, a part of its history, a proof of its right to autonomously control its own destiny. Ireland defends its religion as one of the factors that differentiates it from England and bears witness to its own national physiognomy. For all these valid reasons, an objective observer cannot distinguish in this conflict merely a reactionary Ireland and a democratic and evolutionist England.

England has used its extensive means of propaganda wisely, to persuade the world of the hyperbole and exorbitance of Irish rebelliousness. It has artificially inflated the Ulster question to present it as an insuperable obstacle to Irish independence. But despite these efforts—history is not mystified—it has been unable to hide the evidence, the reality, of the Irish nation, forcibly and militarily obliged to live in conformity with the interests and laws of the British nation. England has been powerless to assimilate the Irish people, powerless to weld them to its empire, powerless to break their unadulterated national sensibility. The martial methods that it has employed to reduce Ireland to obedience have bred in its soul an obstinate will to resist. The history of Ireland since the invasion of its territory by the English is the history of intransigence: passive and latent at times, warlike and violent at others. In the last century, British domination was threatened by three great insurrections. Later, around 1870, Issac Butt fostered a movement to obtain home rule for Ireland. This tendency prospered. Ireland seemed to content itself with a discreet autonomy and abandon the demand for complete freedom. It was thereby able to win a part of English opinion to favorably consider this new and moderate demand. Irish home rule gained many partisans in Great Britain. It finally became a project, an intent, of the majority of the English people. But the world war came, and Irish home rule was forgotten. Irish nationalism regained its insurrectionary character. This situation produced the rising of 1916. Treated belligerently by England, Ireland prepared itself for a definitive battle. The moderate nationalists, supporters of home rule, lost the leadership and control of the movement for autonomy. The Sinn Feiners replaced them. The Sinn Fein tendency, created by Arthur Griffith, was born in 1906. Its activities were theoretical and literary in the early years; but, gradually modified by political and social factors, it attracted to its ranks the most energetic soldiers of Irish independence.

In the 1918 elections, the nationalist party won only six seats in the English parliament. The Sinn Fein Party gained seventy-three. The Sinn Fein deputies decided to boycott the British chamber and found an Irish parliament. This was a formal declaration of war on England, which then refloated its project for Irish home rule. Finally accepted by the British parliament, it conceded autonomy to Ireland as a dominion. The Sinn Feiners remained in arms nevertheless. Led by De Valera, their great agitator and leader, the Irish people were not content with home rule. But England succeeded in dividing Irish opinion. A split in the nationalist movement began to develop. Toward the end of 1921, England and Ireland finally sought a formula for accommodation. Once again in English history, the tendency to compromise won out. The Irish autonomists and the British government reached an agreement in December 1921 that gave Ireland its current constitution. The Sinn Fein Party split. The majority—sixty-four deputies—voted in the Irish chamber in favor of compromise with England; De Valera's minority—fifty-seven deputies—voted against. The antagonism between the two groups was so deep as to cause a civil war. The partisans of the pact with England won, and De Valera was jailed. Now, free once more, he is returning to the business of agitating and motivating his people to revolution.

These romantic Sinn Feiners will never be defeated. They represent the persistent desire for Ireland's freedom. The Irish bourgeoisie has capitulated before England, but a part of the petty bourgeoisie and the proletariat have remained faithful to their national demands. The struggle against England thus acquires a revolutionary meaning. The national sentiment is confounded and identified with a class sentiment. Ireland will continue fighting for its freedom until it conquers it completely. Only when they realize their ideal will it lose its present importance to the Irish.

The only thing that can one day reconcile and unite the English and the Irish is that which seemingly separates them. World history is full of such paradoxes and contradictions, which are really neither so contradictory nor so paradoxical.

Yankee Imperialism in Nicaragua*

Those who are ignorant of the circumstances and spirit of United States policy in Central America might certainly consider the reasons with which Mr. Kellogg claims to excuse the invasion of Nicaraguan territory by Yankee troops. But those who recall the development of these policies in the last twenty or twenty-five years can better understand, undoubtedly, the absolute consistency of this armed intervention into the domestic affairs of Nicaragua with the notorious purposes and practice of these expansionist policies.

It was many years ago that the United States first laid eyes on Nicaragua, and on many opportunities, with similar pretexts, it has laid hands upon her formal autonomy.

When President Zelaya governed the country, Roosevelt, the "big game hunter," notified Nicaragua of the United States' intention to convert San Juan into an interoceanic canal and establish a naval base in the Gulf of Fonseca. But this plan, with its clearly imperialist intent, naturally met with sharp resistance from Nicaraguan public opinion. President Zelaya could make no concession to the North American government in this matter. The United States could only obtain a friendship treaty from its overseer of Nicaraguan politics. But then, with the protection of Yankee rifles, its agents devoted themselves to the task of organizing a revolt among those who could produce a government obedient to the imperialists of the North.

This objective was definitively reached with the formation of the government of Adolfo Díaz, an unconditional servant of Yankee capitalism. When its stability seemed seriously threatened, American troops intervened, then as now, in defense of a regime that was vigorously repudiated by public sentiment. And the United States got the treaty it craved from the Díaz government.

The prime minister who signed this treaty, Chamorro, inherited power. North American interests remained well protected for some years. But popular sentiment, in constant ferment, finally drove out this agent of Yankee imperialism. Since then, the United States, or better, its government, has felt the need to intervene again in Nicaragua. The president that North American

---

Variedades, January 22, 1927.

guns are trying to dominate is Adolfo Díaz Sacasa, the legal vice president, who represents the constitution and vote of Nicaragua after the resignation of the president.

It is quite easy for the American press to represent the people of Central America as being in a constant state of revolutionary ferment. It is certainly much more difficult for it to hide from the world's view the major role of the Yankees in this turbulent agitation. The United States has an interest in keeping Central America divided and inflamed. The necessary confederation of the small Central American republics finds its greatest enemies in North America. When such a confederation was attempted six years ago, Yankee machinations were charged with its frustration. Nicaragua, whose government was at that point completely in the thrall of Yankee politics, constituted the center and home of this imperialist maneuver against the free union of Central American states.

The accentuation of North American expansionism at this time is perfectly logical. Europe currently finds itself in a period of "capitalist stabilization." It is therefore reorganizing its ruined empire in Africa, Asia, etc. On the other hand, the United States is being forced to assert its predominance over its own markets, transport routes, and centers of raw materials because of its natural drive toward industrial and financial growth. If North American capitalism is not able to expand its domain, it will enter a period of unpardonable crisis. The United States already suffers from the consequences of its plethora of gold and its agricultural and industrial overproduction. Its banks and industry need to imperiously ensure bigger markets for itself. The awakening of China, which is reacting resolutely against foreign domination after so many years of moral collapse, puts in danger one of the arenas in which Yankee imperialism is struggling to gradually displace British and Japanese imperialism. More than ever, the United States needs to turn toward the American continent, where the war has helped to partially uproot the previously omnipotent influence of England.

These reasons preclude Latin American opinion from considering the conflict in Nicaragua as one that is foreign to its interests. It therefore unreservedly declares its solidarity with Nicaragua, represented and defended by the constitutional government of Sacasa.

And even more than the misdeeds of Yankee imperialism itself, the betrayals of those Central American chiefs who place themselves at its service find themselves condemned by the continent's judgment.

PART III
Peruvian Reality

Mariátegui considered that the question of the indigenous peoples and the land was at the center of Peruvian politics, but his own writings on Peru span the realm of economic, social, political and cultural issues; four of his famous *Seven Interpretive Essays on Peruvian Reality* concern what Marxists classify as problems of the "superstructure"—education, religion, regionalism, and literature. The essays in this section, presented in a modified chronological order, reflect this breadth of concerns. The final three are of particular interest as reflections of Mariátegui's most mature thought: "Anniversary and Balance Sheet" is an *Amauta* editorial announcing the split with Haya de la Torre and the APRA (see the introduction to this collection), "Programmatic Principles of the Socialist Party" is his proposals for the program of the newly founded Socialist Party of Peru, and "The Indigenous Question" is a document presented to a 1929 meeting of Latin American Communist trade unions.

The Economic Factor in Peruvian History*

The interpretive essays on the history of the republic that slumber on the shelves of our libraries generally coincide in their disdain for or ignorance of the economic basis of all politics. This suggests our people have an obstinate inclination to explain Peruvian history only romantically or novelistically. All eyes look for the protagonist in every episode and act. No effort is made to understand the interests or passions that the person represents. Mediocre chiefs and vulgar leaders of *criollo* politics are taken for the makers and motivators of a reality of which they have been modest and dull instruments. The *criollo*'s mental laziness is easily habituated to doing without the plot of Peruvian history; he contents himself with a knowledge of its *dramatis personae*.

The study of the phenomena of Peruvian history languishes for a lack of realism. Belaúnde, with an excessive optimism, believes that our nation's thinking has been particularly positivist for a long time. He calls positivist the university generation that preceded his own. But we must rectify his judgment in large part, considering that this university generation adopted the flimsiest and most ethereal part of positivism—its ideology—and not the most solid and valid—its method. We have not had even one positivist generation. Adopting an ideology is not wielding its most superfluous commonplaces. One must distinguish the ideas of a philosophical current or school from its phraseology.

Thus, even simply speculative criticism should be pleased with the increasing favor found by historical materialism among our new generation. This ideological direction should be fertile, even if it only serves to help the Peruvian mentality adapt itself to the perception and understanding of the economic factor.

Nothing is more obvious than the impossibility of understanding the phenomena that dominate the process of formation of the Peruvian nation without the aid of economics. Economics probably does not explain the totality of a phenomenon and its consequences. But it explains its roots. This is at least clear in our epoch, an epoch that, if it seems ruled by any logic, is undoubtedly ruled by the logic of economics.

---

*Mundial, August 14, 1925.

The conquest destroyed an economic and social formation in Peru that had been born spontaneously from Peru's land and people and had been fully nourished by an indigenous sensibility of life. During the colonial period, the complex work of creating a new economy and a new society began. Spain, too absolutist, rigid, and medieval, was unable to have this process completed under its control. The Spanish monarchy aspired to keep all the keys to the nascent colonial economy in its own hands. The development of the colony's young economic forces demanded the breaking of this link.

This was the primary cause of the revolution of independence. The ideas of the French revolution and the United States' Constitution found a climate favorable to their spread in South America because there was already an existing bourgeoisie, though embryonic, which could and had to be infected by the revolutionary sensibility of the European bourgeoisie because of its own economic needs and interests. Hispanic America's independence would certainly have never been won if there were not a heroic generation responsive to the emotion of its epoch, with the ability and will to carry out a true revolution among its peoples. Independence presents itself in this regard as a heroic enterprise. But this does not contradict the thesis of the economic foundation of the revolution for independence. The leaders, caudillos, and ideologues of this revolution were neither prior nor superior to the economic premises and causes of these events. The intellectual and emotional factors were not previous to the economic factor.

The economic factor similarly contains the key to all the other phases of the republic's history. In the early days of independence, for example, the struggle of factions and military chiefs appears as a consequence of the lack of an organic bourgeoisie. In Peru, the revolution meets with the elements of a less defined, more backward bourgeois order than among other Hispanic-American peoples. For this order to function more or less embryonically, a vigorous capitalist class had to be constituted. While this class was organizing itself, governmental power was at the mercy of the military caudillos. These caudillos, heirs to the rhetoric of the independence revolution, at times found temporary support in mass demands—stripped of their ideology—to conquer or maintain their power against the conservative and reactionary sensibility of the descendants and successors of the Spanish *encomenderos*. Castilla, for example, the most interesting and representative of these military chiefs, effectively raised the banner of abolishing the taxation of indigenous peoples and the servitude of Blacks. Naturally, once in power, he needed to adapt his program to a political situation dominated by the interests of the conservative caste, which he indemnified with state funds for the damage caused them by the emancipation of the slaves.

The Castilla government, moreover, marked the stage of the solidification of a capitalist class. Government concessions and profits from guano and saltpeter created capitalism and a bourgeoisie. And this class, which soon organized itself as the Civilistas, moved quickly toward the complete conquest of power. The war with Chile interrupted its ascendancy. The conditions and circumstances of the early years of the republic were re-established for a period. But the economic evolution of the post-war period gradually opened the road for them again.

The war with Chile also had an economic basis. The Chilean plutocracy, which coveted the profits of Peruvian traders and the treasury of their government, prepared themselves for conquest and plunder. An incident in the economic realm also provided the pretext for aggression.

It is impossible to understand Peruvian reality without searching for and discovering the economic factor. The new generation perhaps does not understand this in a very precise way. But it senses it quite energetically. It realizes that the fundamental problem of Peru, that of the Indian and the land, is most of all a problem of the Peruvian economy. The existing Peruvian economy, the existing Peruvian society, maintains the original sin of the conquest, the sin of having been brought forth and formed without and against the Indian.

May Day and the United Front*

Throughout the world, May Day is a day of revolutionary proletarian unity, a day that unites all organized workers in an immense international united front. On this day, the words of Karl Marx resound, unanimously observed and respected: "Workers of the world, unite!" On this day, all the barriers that differentiate and separate the proletarian vanguard into various groups and schools spontaneously fall.

May Day does not belong to a single International; it is the day of all the Internationals. Socialists, communists, and anarchists of all shades mingle and lose themselves this day in a single army marching toward the final conflict.

El Obrero Textil, May 1, 1924.

This day, in short, is affirmation and proof that the proletarian united front is possible and practical, and that its realization is opposed by no existing interest or exigency.

This international day invites many thoughts. But for the Peruvian workers, the most current, the most opportune, concerns the necessity and possibility of the united front. Some secessionist attempts have occurred recently. And it is urgent that they be understood and restrained so that they may not prosper, undermining and consuming the nascent working-class vanguard of Peru.

My attitude, since my incorporation into this vanguard, has always been that of a convinced supporter, a fervent propagandist, of the united front. I remember having declared this in one of the initial lectures of my series on the history of the world crisis. Responding to the first signs of resistance and apprehension from some old and sectarian anarchists, more preoccupied with rigid dogmas than effective and fruitful action, I said from the rostrum of the Popular University that "we are still too few to divide ourselves. We will not dispute over labels or titles."

I have since repeated these or similar words, and I will not tire of repeating them. The class movement is still too incipient, too limited among us to think of dividing and splitting. Before the possibly inevitable moment for division, we need to carry out many common actions and much solidarity work. We must take many long journeys together. It is our duty, for example, to promote class consciousness and a class sensibility among the majority of the Peruvian proletariat. This is equally the task of socialists and syndicalists, communists and anarchists. We all have the duty of sowing the seeds of renovation and spreading class ideas. We all have the duty of separating the proletariat from the "yellow" unions and fake "representative institutions." We all have the duty to struggle against reactionary attacks and repression. We all have the duty to defend the proletarian platforms, press, and organizations. We all have the duty to support the demands of the enslaved and oppressed indigenous race. In fulfilling these historic and elementary duties, our paths will meet and join, whatever our final goals.

The united front does not negate the individuality or the affiliation of any groups of which it is composed. It does not mean the entanglement or the amalgamation of all their ideas into a single idea. It is a contingent, concrete, practical action. The program of the united front exclusively considers the immediate reality, over and above all abstractions and utopias. Praising the united front, then, does not mean praising ideological confusionism. Within the united front, each and all should maintain their own affiliations and their own strategies. Each and all should work for their own beliefs. But all should feel themselves united by class solidarity, connected by the struggle against the common adversary, linked by the same revolutionary will and the same renovatory passion. To form a united front is to carry out an act of solidarity in regard to a concrete problem and an urgent necessity. This does not mean renouncing the theories that each party holds or the position that each occupies in the vanguard. A variety of tendencies and a diversity of ideological currents are inevitable in this immense human legion that is called the proletariat. The existence of tendencies and well-defined and distinct groups is not an evil; it is on the contrary a sign of an advanced period in the revolutionary process. What matters is that these groups and tendencies know how to act in concert while confronting the concrete reality of the day. Let them not purify themselves byzantinely by reciprocal excommunications and expulsions. Let them not alienate the masses from the revolution with the spectacle of dogmatic quarrels among its supporters. Let them not employ their weapons nor squander their time by injuring each other, but in combating the social order, its institutions, its injustices, and its crimes.

Let us sincerely try to sense the historical links that unite all the people of the vanguard to each other, to all the supporters of renovation. The examples that arrive daily from abroad are innumerable and magnificent. The most recent and moving of these examples is that of Germaine Berthon. Berthon, an anarchist, skillfully shot her revolver at an organizer and leader of the white terror to revenge the assassination of Jean Jaurès. The noble, elevated, and sincere spirits of the revolution thus sense and respect the historical solidarity of their efforts and their works, above and beyond all theoretical barriers. The privilege of incomprehension and sectarian egotism belongs to the mean-spirited and visionless, to the dogmatic mentalities that hope to petrify and immobolize life into a rigid formula.

Fortunately, the proletarian united front is the obvious choice and desire of our proletariat. The masses demand unity. The masses desire faith. And this is why their spirit rejects the corrosive, dissolvent, and pessimistic voice of those who deny and doubt, and seeks the optimistic, sincere, youthful, and fruitful voice of those who affirm and believe.

Feminist Demands*

The first signs of feminist restlessness are reverberating through Peru. Some feminist cells and nuclei now exist. The proponents of ultra-nationalism will probably think, "Here is another exotic, foreign idea that is being grafted onto the Peruvian mentality."

Let us calm these apprehensive people a bit. We should not see feminism as an exotic or foreign idea. We need to see it simply as a human idea—an idea that is characteristic of a civilization, peculiar to an epoch—and therefore, an idea with the right to citizenship in Peru, as in any other part of the civilized world.

Feminism has appeared in Peru neither artificially nor arbitrarily. It has appeared as a consequence of the new forms of women's intellectual and manual labor. The women with a real connection to feminism are the women who work, the women who study. The feminist idea flourishes among women with intellectual or manual professions: university professors, working women. It finds a propitious environment for growth in university classrooms, which attract more and more Peruvian women, and in the trade unions, where women from the factories join and organize themselves with the same rights and duties as the men. Apart from this spontaneous and organic feminism, which recruits its adherents among the different categories of women's work, there exists here, as elsewhere, a feminism of dilettantes, some a bit pedantic, others a bit mundane. Feminists of this type turn feminism into a simple literary exercise, a mere fashionable sport.

No one should be surprised that all women do not unite in a single feminist movement. Feminism necessarily has various shades and diverse tendencies. We can distinguish three fundamental tendencies, three substantive shades of feminism: bourgeois feminism, petty bourgeois feminism, and working-class feminism. Each of these feminisms formulates its demands in a distinctive manner. The bourgeois woman, as a feminist, solidarizes with the interests of the conservative class. The working-class woman combines her feminism with the faith of the revolutionary multitudes in the future society. The class struggle—a historical fact, not a theoretical assertion—is reflected on the plane of feminism. Women, like men, are reactionaries, centrists, or revolutionaries. They consequently cannot fight the same battle together. In

---

Mundial, December 19, 1924.

the current human panorama, class differentiates individuals more than sex. But this multiplicity of feminisms does not result from the theory itself. It depends, rather, on its practical deformations. Feminism as a pure idea is essentially revolutionary. The ideas and attitudes of women who consider themselves both feminist and conservative thus lack internal coherence. Conservatism works to maintain the traditional organization of society. This organization denies women the rights that women wish to gain. Bourgeois feminists accept all the consequences of the prevailing order except those opposed to women's demands. They tactically maintain the absurd thesis that the only reform society needs is feminist reform. The protest of these feminists against the old order is too exclusive to be valid.

It is true that the historical roots of feminism are found in the liberal sensibility. The French revolution contained the first seeds of the feminist movement. The question of the emancipation of women was then laid out in precise terms for the first time. Babeuf, the leader of the Conspiracy of Equals, was a proponent of feminist demands. Babeuf harangued his friends in this way:

> Do not force silence on this sex, which does not deserve to be disdained. Rather, cultivate the better part of yourselves. If women count for nothing in your republic, you will make them lovers of the monarchy. Their influence will be such that they will restore it. If, on the contrary, they count for something, you will make of them Cornelias and Lucretias. They will give you Brutuses, Gracchi, and Scaevolas.

Polemicizing with anti-feminists, Babeuf spoke of "this sex that men's tyranny has always sought to humble, this sex that has never been useless in a revolution." But the French revolution did not wish to accord women the equality and freedom proposed by such Jacobin or egalitarian voices. The Rights of Man, as I once wrote, could better be called the Rights of the Male Sex. Bourgeois democracy has been an exclusively masculine democracy.

Born of the liberal womb, feminism has not been put into effect during the development of capitalism. It is now, when the historical trajectory of democracy is reaching its end, that women are gaining the political and legal rights of men. And it is the Russian Revolution that has explicitly and categorically granted to women the equality and freedom that Babeuf and the egalitarians demanded in vain from the French revolution more than a century ago.

But if bourgeois democracy has not implemented feminism, it has involuntarily created the moral and material conditions and premises for its realization. It has given women value as an element of production, as an economic factor, making increasingly extensive and intensive use of their labor. Work radically changes the female mentality and spirit. By virtue of her labor, woman gains a new idea of herself. Formerly, society destined woman to marriage or concubinage. It now principally destines her to work. This fact has changed and elevated the position of women in life. Those who impugn feminism and its progress with sentimental or traditionalist arguments claim that women should be educated only for the home. But, in practice, this means that women should be educated only for the role of female and mother. The defense of the poetry of the home is actually a defense of woman's servitude. Instead of ennobling and dignifying the role of women, it diminishes and lowers it. A woman is something more than a female and a mother, just as a man is something more than a male.

The type of woman that a new civilization will produce must be substantially different from that formed by a currently declining civilization. In an article on women and politics, I examined some aspects of this theme in the following way:

> The troubadours and lovers of feminine frivolity have no lack of reasons to be upset. The type of women created by a century of capitalist refinement is condemned to decadence and decline. An Italian writer, Pitigrilli, classifies this type of contemporary woman as a sort of elegant breeder.
>
> And this elegant breeder will continue to disappear bit by bit. To the degree that the collectivist system replaces the individualist system, feminine extravagance and elegance will fade. Humanity will lose some elegant breeders, but it will gain many women. The dress of the woman of the future will be less expensive and sumptuous, but the condition of this woman will have more dignity. And the center of female life will be displaced from the individual to the social. Fashion will finally not consist of imitating a modern Madame Pompadour dressed in a Paquín. Perhaps it will be the imitation of a Madame Kollontai. A woman, in short, will cost less but will be worth more.

This subject is quite vast. This short article merely aims to point out the nature of the first manifestations of feminism in Peru and to attempt a very quick and summary interpretation of the physiognomy and spirit of the international feminist movement. Men who are sensitive to the great passions of the epoch should feel neither foreign nor indifferent to this movement. The woman question is a part of the human question. Feminism seems to me, moreover, a more interesting and more historic subject than the wig. While feminism is a subject, the wig is merely an anecdote.

Education and the Economy*

I

The question of education cannot be understood properly without being considered as an economic and social question. The mistakes of many reformers have resided in their abstractly idealist method and their exclusively pedagogical theories. Their projects have ignored the intimate connection between the economy and education, and they have pretended to change the latter without understanding the laws of the former. They have thus been able to reform things only to the degree that economic and social laws have allowed.

The educational debate between classicists and modernizers has been no less governed by capitalist development than the political debate between conservatives and liberals. The programs and systems of public education have depended on the interests of the bourgeois economy. The realistic or modern orientation, for example, has been imposed, above all, by the necessities of industrialization. Not by chance is industrialism the particular and substantive phenomenon of this civilization that, dominated by its consequences, demands from its schools more technicians than ideologues and more engineers than rhetoricians. When Rabindranath Tagore, looking on Western civilization with Eastern eyes, discovers that it has made man a slave of the machine, he has not reached an exaggerated conclusion.

II

But these consequences of capitalism have not generally provoked any effort by intellectuals with the real purpose of re-establishing an equilibrium between the moral and the material. Intellectuals, in their majority, have played the game of reaction. They have only mastered opposing the present in the name of the past. Imbued with a conservative spirit and an aristocratic mentality, they have directly or indirectly supported the very ideas of the heirs or successors of the feudal regime. They have subscribed to the old and simple idealist recipe: classical studies.

And the decadent European bourgeoisie sought a remedy for its problems in this recipe, without considering that it was adopting a thesis contrary to

---

Mundial, May 29, 1925.

its own historical role. It wed classical education with practical education. It differentiated the education of its politicians and literati from that of its engineers and businessmen. Politics and literature, unable to govern the economy, were thus corrupted by rhetoricians and humanists, whose labor has been one of the most active agents of the modern crisis, which is characterized precisely by a series of contradictions between politics and economics.

Georges Sorel, in one of the chapters of his book *The Decline of the Ancient World*, denounced the parasitism of literary genius as one of the most serious causes of the corruption of the learned classes. "The parasitism of literary genius," he wrote, "continues to fester in Europe, and it does not seem that it will disappear. Its form may change, but it is fed by a very powerful tradition that boasts of very old and very particular educational principles."

Modern experience with classical studies in no way supports the thesis or, better yet, the dogma that attributes to it a privileged role in forming idealistic and superior souls. The idealism it engenders is a reactionary idealism, an idealism contrary or alien to the direction of history, which therefore lacks all value as a force for human renovation and advancement. The lawyers and literati coming from humanities faculties have almost always been much more immoral than the engineers from the science faculties and institutes. And the practical and theoretical activities of the latter have followed the direction of the economy and civilization, while the practical, theoretical, or esthetic activities of the former have frequently resisted them, to the benefit of the most vulgar conservative interests and sentiments. On the other hand, the value of science as a stimulant to philosophical speculation can neither go unrecognized nor be disdained. This society's atmosphere and ideas most certainly owe more to science than to the humanities. Ultimately, classicism has not looked to Greece as much as to Rome. In Latin countries, or self-styled Latin countries, it has particularly struggled to maintain the cult of Roman rhetoric and law. And the new Hispanic-American generation, to which these articles are directed, finds in Italy an exact and precise explanation of what Romanism specifically represents in our era. The theory and practice of Italian fascism are thoroughly inspired by Roman history. It even supposes itself predestined to revive the Roman Empire.

The conservative nature of classicism in education has been obvious for some time. The left has always been consciously or instinctively opposed to an undue restoration of classical studies. Rather than originating in a clear revolutionary orientation, this opposition actually arose more from an optimistic positivism, today discredited and in decline, that sees science as the solution to all human problems.

Among socialist thinkers, Georges Sorel has undoubtedly best understood the mechanism of the conservative influence of classical studies. Sorel formulated his idea in this way:

The child does not know how to observe, or observes poorly; it is therefore necessary to instill the habit of observation, and this ought to be the principal preoccupation of the teacher. Because of this natural imperfection, we have a constant tendency to misunderstand principles, to allow ourselves to be deceived by false arguments, to content ourselves with vulgar and anti-scientific explanations. But a classical education develops these natural defects to an enormous degree, and we can look forward to a condition I call a state of ideological disassociation, in which we have lost all sense of the reality of things. When education is directed toward a practical end, when it has as its purpose to train us to occupy a place in economic life, such a deplorable result cannot occur in a complete manner. Ideological disassociation not only makes sophisms easily acceptable, but keeps us from exercising any criticism of our intellectual operations; it is thereby quite favorable to an inversion of elective functions that allows us to justify all our actions. It develops a monstrous egoism that subordinates all considerations to the desires of our appetites and has us appreciate the resources put at our disposition as a weak tribute rendered to our talents. In the economic realm, we can demand a portion socially equal to our labor. But because of ideological disassociation, we leave the economic realm; we claim a share in relation to our talent—that is, we aspire to take from production the part we appreciate to be related to the worth of our genius.

III

The supporters of classics base nearly all their theory on a rigid and dogmatic foundation. They claim that classical philology and rhetoric are the sole creators of idealism and the best discipline for the intelligence. But these assertions are absolutely unproven. Respectable modern educators who cannot be accused of revolutionary sectarianism refute them for valid reasons supported by their professional observations. Albert Girard, president of the Compagnons of the New University, writes the following in a polemic with the extremist partisans of Latin:

Undoubtedly this is an excellent discipline, but who can prove that others are not equally valid? The inferior results of the section without Latin are put forward. But, in the first place, some excellent students are to be found there, and if they are now rarer than before, isn't this because the better ones are pushed toward the Latin sections? Who knows what would occur with equitable recruitment? While in this case the modern section is revealed as inferior, we must still ask if this isn't due to methods of teaching living languages that are still quite far from perfect. The modern section has yet to reach the consummation of its educational possibilities, either through recruitment or method. Do we have the right thereby to hastily decide against it? This is scientifically impossible. Nothing proves that one cannot exercise the faculties of the spirit by analogous means and thereby realize one of the conditions for cultural unity.

Those educators in Germany who have created a new type of secondary school, the Deutsche Oberschule, agree with these essentially technical viewpoints. "The partisans of this type of school judge that Greco-Latin culture has no educational privilege, that German youths can find in the very country in which they were born, in a more direct, more popular, and more democratic manner, a culture equal to that of any other establishment of secondary education" (*Educational Reform in Germany* by M. P. Roques).

IV

The unity of the economy and education is concretely revealed in the ideas of the only educators who have truly proposed renovating the schools. Pestalozzi, Froebel, etc., who have truly worked for renovation, have taken into account that modern society tends above all to be a society of producers. Their concept of education is substantially modern. The Labor School expresses a workers' sensibility. The capitalist state has held back from fully adopting and activating it. It has limited itself to incorporating "educational manual labor" into primary education—which is class education. It is in Russia where the Labor School has been raised to the first plane in educational politics.

In Germany, the tendency to test it found its principal support during the socialist ascendancy of the revolutionary period.

Singularly illustrative and symptomatic is the fact that this reform has originated in the field of primary education. This fact clearly shows us that secondary and university education, dominated by the spirit of its rhetoricians, still constitute an unfavorable terrain for any attempt at renovation and are still insensitive to the new economic reality.

The modern concept of the school places manual labor and intellectual labor in the same category. The vanity of rancid humanists, fed by Romanism and elitism, cannot accept this leveling. Despite the repugnance of these men of letters, the Labor School is the genuine product and a fundamental idea of a civilization created by labor and for labor.

V

How does this question stand in our America? The people of this continent who think and speak with such little originality on American problems already show a certain frivolous inclination to recommend to us the principles of the Bérard and Gentile reforms. A vote demanding the extension of the restoration of Latin in secondary instruction formed a part of the incoherent and disoriented deliberations of this section of the last Pan-American Scientific Congress. In short, we fear that the leaders of public education in our America, not satisfied with the experience of methods inherited from Spain that have so effectively obstructed the development of the Hispanic-American economy, consider it necessary to inject a little classicism of the Bérard or Gentile type into the chaotic and inorganic educational programs of these peoples.

But the new men of Hispanic America should not turn their backs on reality. Our America needs more technicians than rhetoricians. The development of the Hispanic-American economy demands a practical and realistic orientation in education. Classicism will not create better mental and moral aptitudes (this idea is finally a new reactionary superstition). It will, on the other hand, sabotage the formation of greater industrial and technical capabilities.

Nationalism and Vanguardism[*]

In Political Ideology

I

The assertion that the most Peruvian, most national aspect of modern Peru is the sensibility of the new generation will possibly amuse some recalcitrant conservatives of incontestable good faith. It is nevertheless one of the easiest truths to demonstrate. That conservatism neither can nor knows how to understand this is perfectly explicable. But it neither diminishes nor obscures the evidence.

To understand how the new generation feels and thinks, a faithful and serious critic would undoubtedly begin by inquiring into its demands. This would consequently inspire him to establish that the major demands of Peru's vanguardists are those of the Indian. This fact will tolerate neither mystification nor conscious equivocation.

[*]*Mundial*, November 27 and December 4, 1925.

Translated into a language intelligible to all, conservatives included, the indigenous question presents itself as the question of four million Peruvians. Expressed in unquestionably orthodox nationalist terms, it presents itself as the question of the assimilation into the Peruvian nation of four-fifths of Peru's population. Who can deny the Peruvian nature of an idea and a program that proclaims with such vehement courage its eagerness and will to resolve this problem?

II

The disciples of the monarchist nationalism of *Action française* probably adopt Maurras's formula: "All that is national is ours." But their conservatism is far from defining what is national and Peruvian. Both theoretically and practically, the conservative *criollo* comports himself as an heir to the colony and a descendent of the conquest. For all our lovers of the past, the nation begins in the colonial period. Emotionally if not theoretically, the indigenous peoples are pre-national. Conservatism can conceive of and admit only one Peruvian nature: that formed on the Spanish or Roman model. This sense of *Peruanidad* has serious consequences for the theory and practice of the very nationalism that it inspires and engenders. The first is that it limits the history of the Peruvian nation to four centuries. And four centuries of tradition must appear quite insignificant to any nationalism, even the most modest and deluded. No stable nationalism appears in our era as a development of only four centuries of history.

To shoulder a more respectable and illustrious antiquity, reactionary nationalism invariably resorts to the artifice of annexing not only the whole past and glory of Spain, but also the whole past and glory of the Latin world. The roots of its nationality are thus Hispanic and Latin. Peru, as represented by these people, does not descend from the autochthonous Incan empire; it descends from a foreign empire that imposed its laws, religion, and language four centuries ago.

Maurice Barrés, in a phrase that our reactionaries undoubtedly hold as an article of faith, said that the fatherland is the land and its dead. No nationalism can do without the land. This is the drama of what the spirit and interests of the conquest and the colonial period, along with their appeal to an imported ideology, represent in Peru.

III

In opposition to this spirit, the vanguard proposes the reconstruction of Peru on an Indian foundation. The new generation is recovering our true past, our true history. Our antiquarians content themselves with the fragile, courtly memories of the viceroyalty. Vanguardism, on the other hand, seeks more truly Peruvian and more remotely ancient materials for its work. And its *indigenismo* is neither literary speculation nor a romantic pastime. Nor is it an *indigenismo* that, like many others, reduces itself to an innocuous apologia for the Incan empire and its splendors. In place of a Platonic love for the Incan past, the revolutionary *indigenistas* show an active and concrete solidarity with today's Indian.

This *indigenismo* does not indulge in fantasies of utopian restorations. It perceives the past as a foundation, not a program. Its conception of history and its events is realistic and modern. It neither ignores nor slights any of the historical facts that have modified the world's reality, as well as Peru's, in these four centuries.

IV

The supposition that our youth is seduced by foreign mirages and exotic theories certainly flows from a superficial interpretation of the relationship between nationalism and socialism. Nowhere in the world is socialism an anti-national movement. It might seem so in the empires. In England, France, the United States, etc., the revolutionaries denounce and fight the imperialism of their own governments. But the function of the socialist idea differs among the politically or economically colonized peoples. While in no way denying any of its principles, socialism acquires a nationalist attitude among these peoples by force of circumstance. Those who follow the process of the Moroccan, Egyptian, Chinese, Indian, and other nationalist movements can easily explain this completely logical aspect of revolutionary praxis. They will observe the essentially popular character of such agitation from its origin. Western imperialism and capitalism always encounter minimal resistance, if not complete submission, from the conservative classes and ruling castes of the colonial peoples. The demands for national independence receive their impulse and energy from the popular masses. This phenomenon can be fully and precisely studied in Turkey, where a quite vigorous and auspicious nationalist movement has operated in recent years. Turkey has been reborn as a nation through the merit and labor of its revolutionary people, not its conservatives. The same historical impulse that expelled the Greeks from Asia Minor, inflicting a defeat on British imperialism, evicted the caliph and his court from Constantinople.

One of the most interesting phenomena and broadest movements of our epoch is precisely this revolutionary nationalism, this revolutionary patriotism. The idea of the nation, as an internationalist has said, is the incarnation of the spirit of freedom in certain historical periods. In Western Europe, where it is now most dated, it began and developed as a revolutionary idea. It now has this value among all those peoples exploited by a foreign imperialism who are struggling for their nation's freedom.

In Peru, those who represent and interpret *Peruanidad* are those who conceive of it as an affirmation and not a negation, who work to return the nation to those who were conquered and subdued by the Spaniards, to those who lost it four centuries ago and have not yet regained it.

In Literature and Art

I

Those who have no wish to venture into other realms will easily see the national sense and value of all positive and authentic vanguardism in the field of literature and art. The most national of any literature is always the most profoundly revolutionary. This is very logical and clear.

A new school, a new literary or artistic tendency, seeks its foundation in the present. If it does not find it, it inevitably dies. On the other hand, old schools, old tendencies, are content to represent the spiritual and formal remnants of the past.

Therefore, conceiving the nation as a static reality can only be imagined a national spirit and inspiration among the imitators and enthusiasts of an old art, not the creators or inventors of a new art. A nation lives much more in the precursors of its future than in the survivals of its past.

We can demonstrate and explain this thesis with some concrete facts. Excessively general or abstract assertions run the danger of appearing sophistic or, at the least, insufficient.

II

I have already had the occasion to maintain that the Italian futurist movement can only be recognized as a spontaneous gesture of Italy's genius, and that the iconoclasts who proposed to cleanse Italy of its museums, ruins, and relics, all its venerable objects, were at heart moved by a profound love for Italy.

The study of the biology of Italian futurism inevitably leads to this conclusion. Futurism represented a moment of Italian consciousness, not as a literary and artistic mode, but as a spiritual attitude. Futurist artists and writers, rising loudly and immoderately against vestiges of the past, were affirming the right and ability of Italy to renew and surpass itself in literature and art.

Having fulfilled this mission, futurism ceased being a movement sustained by Italy's purest and highest artistic values, as it had been at first. But the emotional state that it aroused has subsisted. And the fascist phenomenon, whose roots are so purely national according to its apologists, was in part prepared by this emotional state. Futurism became fascist because art does not rule politics and, in particular, because it was the fascists who conquered Rome. But it would just as easily have become socialist if the proletarian revolution had been victorious. And in this case, its lot would have been different. Instead of definitively disappearing as a movement or artistic school (which has been its fate under fascism), futurism would have enjoyed a dynamic renaissance. Fascism, after having exploited its motivation and spirit, has obliged futurism to accept its reactionary principles, that is, to repudiate itself theoretically and practically. The revolution, though, would have stimulated and promoted its will to create a new art in a new society.

This has been the fate of futurism in Russia, for example. Russian futurism had been more or less a twin of the Italian movement. Continuous and intimate relations existed between the two futurisms. And just as Italian futurism followed fascism, Russian futurism subscribed to the proletarian revolution. Russia is the only country in Europe where futurist art has been elevated to the category of official art, as Guillermo de Torre has said with satisfaction.

This victory has not been obtained in Russia at the cost of a renunciation. Futurism in Russia remains futurism. It has not allowed itself to be domesticated as in Italy. It continues to consider itself an agent of the future. While futurism in Italy no longer has a single great poet in full command of their iconoclastic and futuristic belligerence, in Russia, Mayakovsky, the troubadour of the revolution, has attained more enduring triumphs in this craft.

III

But to more exactly and precisely establish the national character of all vanguardism, let us turn to our America. The new poets of Argentina constitute an interesting example. All of them are nurtured by a European esthetic. All, or almost all, have traveled in one of those cars of the Grand European Express that for Blaise Cendrars, Valery Larbaud, and Paul Morand are undoubtedly the vehicles of European unity, as well as indispensable elements of a new literary sensibility.

Yet, notwithstanding this infusion of cosmopolitanism, notwithstanding their ecumenical conception of art, the best of these vanguardist poets are still the most Argentine. The *Argentinidad* of Girondo, Güiraldes, Borges, etc., is no less evident than their cosmopolitanism. Argentine literary vanguardism is called "Martín Fierroism." Anyone who has read *Martín Fierro*, the periodical of this nucleus of artists, will have found there both the most authentic Gaucho accents and the most recent echoes of Europe's ultra-modern art.

What is the secret of this ability to feel both international and native events? The answer is simple. The artist's personality, human personality, is only fully realized when it knows itself superior to all limits.

IV

We observe the same phenomenon in Peruvian literature, although with less intensity. As long as Peruvian literature maintained a conservative and academic character, it could not be truly and profoundly Peruvian. Until recently, our literature has only been a modest colony of Spanish literature. Its transformation in this regard, as well as in others, begins with the Colónida movement. The case of Valdelomar is one in which a cosmopolitan sentiment and a national one are united and combined. The snobbish love of European fashions and things neither stifled nor diminished Valdelomar's love for the rustic and humble things of his land and his village. On the contrary, it possibly helped rouse and exalt it.

And now the phenomenon is being underscored. Perhaps what attracts and moves us in the poet César Vallejo is the indigenous foundation, the autochthonous basis, of his art. Vallejo is quite Indian and very much ours. The fact that we esteem and understand him is not a product of chance. Nor is it the exclusive result of his genius. It is one more proof that, in these cosmopolitan and ecumenical journeys for which we are so reproached, we are increasingly discovering ourselves.

Introducing *Amauta**

This journal does not represent a group in the intellectual arena. It represents, rather, a movement, a spirit. A current of renewal, ever more vigorous and well defined, has been felt for some time now in Peru. The supporters of this renewal are called vanguardists, socialists, revolutionaries, etc. History has not christened them definitively at this point. Some formal discrepancies, some psychological differences, exist between them. But beyond what differentiates them, all these spirits contribute to what groups and unites

---

Amauta, September 1926.

them: their will to create a new Peru in a new world. The perspicacity and coordination of the most willful of these elements is gradually progressing. The intellectual and spiritual movement is becoming organic. With the appearance of *Amauta*, it enters the stage of definition.

Amauta has had a normal gestation. It is not arising suddenly from my determination alone. I returned from Europe with the proposition of founding a journal. Painful personal vicissitudes did not allow me to do this. But this time has not passed in vain. My efforts have been joined by those of other intellectuals and artists who think and feel as I do. Two years ago, this journal would have been an excessively personal voice. Now it is the voice of a movement and a generation.

The first result that we writers of *Amauta* propose to attain is to better understand and harmonize with each other. The work of this journal will solidarize us more. At the same time as it attracts other positive elements, it will alienate some wavering and disillusioned elements who now flirt with vanguardism but will make haste to abandon it once a sacrifice is demanded of them. *Amauta* will sift the members of the vanguard, both activists and sympathizers, until the wheat is separated from the chaff. It will produce or precipitate a polarization and concentration.

It is unnecessary to expressly state that Amauta is not a free tribune open to all spiritual currents. We who are founding this journal cannot imagine an agnostic culture and art. We are moved by a belligerent, polemical force. We make no concessions to the generally false concept of the toleration of ideas. For us, there are good ideas and bad ideas. In the prologue to my book *The Contemporary Scene*, I wrote that I am a man with an affiliation and a faith. I can say the same of this journal, which rejects everything contrary to its ideology, as well as everything that does not bear any ideology.

We have more solemn words to introduce *Amauta*. I would like to forbid rhetoric in this journal. Programs seem absolutely useless to me. Peru is a country of titles and ceremonies. We are finally creating something with content—that is, with spirit. On the other hand, *Amauta* has no need of a program; it has need only of a destiny, a goal.

The title will probably worry some people. This is due to the excessive, fundamental importance that titles have for us. The strict meaning of the word does not matter in this case. The title only refers to our adherence to *la raza* and simply reflects our homage to Incaism. But the word *Amauta* specifically gains a new meaning with this journal. We will create it again.

The goal of this journal is to articulate, illuminate, and comprehend Peru's problems from theoretical and scientific viewpoints. But we will always consider Peru from an international perspective. We will study all the great movements of political, philosophical, artistic, literary, and scientific renewal. Everything that is human is ours. This journal will connect the new men of Peru, first with the other peoples of America, and then with the other peoples of the world.

I will add no more. One would have to be quite dense not to see that a historic journal is being now born in Peru.

Message to the Workers Congress*

Considering its means, the first Lima Workers Congress fulfilled its essential purpose, creating the Local Workers Federation, the cell, nucleus, and cement of the organization of Peru's working class. Its spontaneous program, apparently modest, was limited to this step. The development and work of the Local Workers Federation during these five years show that, through this assembly, the vanguard workers of Lima, after uncertain attempts, have been able to finally find their way.

The second congress has duly arrived. It was delayed a bit, but it would be improper to reproach its organizers for this fact. And its goals, logically, are new and specific. It is now a question of taking another step forward, and this must be done resolutely and surely.

The experience of five years of union work in Lima should be reviewed and utilized. Proposals and debates that would have been premature and inopportune in 1922 can now be undertaken with the proper elements for judgment gathered during this period of struggle. The discussion of orientation, of praxis, is never as sterile as when it rests exclusively upon abstractions. The history of the last years of the world crisis, so full of considerations and lessons for the proletariat, demands a realistic analysis by its leaders. They must strip themselves of old dogmas, discredited prejudices, and archaic superstitions.

Marxism, of which everyone speaks but with which very few are acquainted and, especially, understand, is a fundamentally dialectical method—that is, a method that bases itself fully on reality, on the facts. It is not, as some erroneously suppose, a body of principles with the same rigid conclusions for all historical climates and all social latitudes. Marx drew his method from

---

*Amauta, January 1927.

the very entrails of history. In each country, among each people, Marxism operates and acts on the environment, on the medium, without neglecting any of its patterns. This is why, after more than a half-century of struggle, its strength appears greater and greater. Russian Communists, British Labourites, German Socialists, etc., all equally claim to be Marxist. This fact alone prevails against all objections to the validity of the Marxist method.

Revolutionary syndicalism, whose greatest teacher is Georges Sorel—also less known by our workers than his qualifiers and mediocre repetitors, paraphrasers, and falsifiers—in no way denies the Marxist tradition. On the contrary, it completes and extends it. Revolutionary syndicalism, in its impulse, its essence, and its ferment, constitutes precisely a rebirth of the revolutionary spirit, that is, the Marxist spirit, provoked by the reformist and parliamentary degeneration of the Socialist parties (the Socialist parties, not socialism). Georges Sorel felt himself similarly alienated from the domesticated socialists in parliament as from the incandescent anarchists of riots and sporadic violence.

The revolutionary crisis opened by the war has fundamentally changed the terms of ideological debate. The opposition between socialism and syndicalism no longer exists. The old revolutionary syndicalism has grow old and degenerate in the very country where it claimed to be the most purely and faithfully Sorelian—in France—just like the old parliamentary socialism against which it reacted and rebelled. One section of this syndicalism is now as reformist and bourgeoisified as the socialist right with which it tenderly collaborates. Everyone knows that the post-war crisis split the CGT (the French General Labor Confederation) into two factions, one of which works alongside the Socialist Party, while the other marches with the Communist Party. Old union leaders, who a short while ago filled their mouths with the names of Pelloutier and Sorel, now cooperate with the most domesticated reformist politicians of socialism.

The new situation has thus brought on a new rupture, or better, a new division. The revolutionary spirit is not represented by those who represented it before the war. The terms of the debate have totally changed. Georges Sorel, before his death, had the opportunity to salute the Russian Revolution as the dawn of a new age. One of his last works is his "Defense of Lenin."

To repeat the commonplaces of pre-war syndicalism in response to an essentially different situation is to stubbornly defend an attitude that has been transcended. It means acting with absolute neglect of the accelerated and convulsive historical developments of recent years, especially when the commonplaces repeated are not those of real Sorelian syndicalism, but those of a bad Spanish or, rather, Catalonian translation. (If there is something to learn from Barcelona's anarchistic syndicalism, it is undoubtedly the lesson of its failure.)

Our programmatic debate, therefore, should not lose itself in theoretical digressions. Union organization has no need of etiquettes, but of spirit. I have already said in *Amauta* that this is a country of labels, and I wish to repeat it here. To lose one's way in sterile debates of principles among a proletariat where principles have such weak roots will only serve to disorganize the workers, when it is properly a question of organizing them. The theme of the congress ought to be *proletarian unity*. Theoretical differences do not keep us from agreeing on a program of action. The workers' united front is our goal. In the effort to create it, the vanguard workers have the duty to set an example. On today's work shift, nothing divides us; everything unites us.

The union should only demand the acceptance of *class principle* from its affiliates. Therefore, there is room in the union for reformist socialists and syndicalists, for communists and anarchists. The union is fundamentally and exclusively a *class organ*. Its *praxis*, its *tactics*, depend on the current that predominates internally. And there is no reason to distrust the instincts of the majority. The masses always follow the creative, realistic, certain, and heroic spirits. The best prevail when they know to truly be the best.

There is therefore no real difficulty to be understood about the program of the workers' organization. Rather, they are all byzantine discussions about remote goals. The workers' vanguard has concrete questions in view: the national organization of the working class, solidarity with the demands of the indigenous peoples, the defense and development of institutions of popular culture, cooperation between day laborers and peasants on the haciendas, the development of the workers' press, etc.

These are the questions that should mainly preoccupy us. Those who provoke splits and dissidence in the name of abstract principles, while contributing not at all to the study and solution of these concrete problems, consciously or unconsciously betray the proletarian cause.

It falls to the Second Workers Congress to lay the bases for a general confederation of labor to unite all the republic's unions and workers' associations that adhere to a class program. The goal of the first congress was local organization; the goal of the second, as far as possible, should be national organization.

It is necessary to mold class consciousness. Organizers know well that the majority of the workers have only a guild or trade sensibility. This spirit should be widened and educated until it becomes a class sensibility. The first thing that must be overcome and conquered is the anarchistic, individualistic, egoist spirit that, besides being profoundly anti-social, merely constitutes the exhaustion and degeneration of the old bourgeois liberalism. The second thing to overcome is the spirit of guild, of profession, of caste.

Class consciousness is not found in empty, noisy declarations (which is why it is supremely comic, for example, to hear protestations of raving, extremist internationalism from a person stuffed full of literary revolutionism who often, in his conduct and practical vision, has not been liberated from the sentiments and motives of the steeple or the town hall).

Class consciousness is found in solidarity with all the basic demands of the working class. And it is found in discipline. There is no solidarity without discipline. No great human labor is possible without fellowship carried as far as sacrifice by the people who endeavor to perform it.

Before concluding these lines, I want to say that, along with a realistic sense of history, it is necessary to give the proletarian vanguard a heroic will to create and accomplish. The desire for improvement, an appetite for well-being, is not enough. The defeats and failures of the European proletariat have their origin in the mediocre positivism with which timid union bureaucracies and moderate parliamentary teams cultivated a Sancho Panzaesque mentality and a cowardly spirit among the masses. A proletariat with no greater ideals than a shorter working day and a few cents more in wages will never be capable of a great historical enterprise. And this is why we must elevate ourselves above a vulgar positivism of the belly and above negative, destructive, and nihilist sentiments and interests. The revolutionary spirit is a constructive spirit. And the proletariat, just as the bourgeoisie, has its dissolvent, corrosive elements that unconsciously work toward the dissolution of its own class.

I will not discuss the program of the congress in detail. These welcoming lines are not guidelines, only opinions, the opinion of an intellectual comrade attempting to fulfill his disciplined duty without facile demagogic declarations and with an honest sense of his responsibility.

Prologue to *Tempest in the Andes**

After having given us a schematic outline of the history of the Tawantinsuyu in his works *De la vida inkaika* (On Incan Life) and *Del ayllu al imperio* (From the *Ayllu* to the Empire), Luis E. Valcárcel with this book offers us a

---

*Preface to Luis E. Varcárcel, *Tempestad en los Andes* (Lima: Ed. Minerva, 1927).

dynamic vision of the indigenous present. This book announces "the coming of a world," the appearance of the new Indian. It therefore cannot be an objective critique or neutral analysis; it must be a passionate affirmation, an exalted protest.

Valcárcel sees the indigenous renaissance clearly because he believes in it. A germinating historical movement cannot be understood in its full transcendence except by those who are struggling for its fulfillment. The socialist movement, for example, is only fully understood by its militants. The same is not true for an already realized movement. The phenomenon of capitalism has not been understood and explained as fully and precisely by anyone as by socialists.

The role of Valcárcel in this work, if we judge it as Unamuno might, is not that of professor, but of prophet. He does not propose merely to register those facts that announce or signal the formation of a new indigenous consciousness, but to translate their intimate historical meaning, thereby helping this indigenous consciousness to encounter and be revealed to itself. In this case, as in perhaps no other, interpretation becomes creation.

Tempest in the Andes is not presented as a work of doctrine or theory. Valcárcel feels the revival of the Quechua race. This resurrection is the theme of his work. One does not prove that a people is alive by reasoning or theorizing, but by showing it to be alive. This is the procedure followed by Valcárcel, who, rather than documenting the extent and the route of the indigenous renaissance, is preoccupied with showing us evidence of its reality.

The first part of *Tempest in the Andes* has a political intonation. Valcárcel puts the emotions and the ideals of the Incan resurgence into his vehement prose. It is not the Incan Empire that is reviving; it is the Incan people, who, after four centuries of slumber, have once again started on the march toward their destiny. Commenting on Valcárcel's first book, I wrote that neither the conquests of Western civilization nor the vital consequences of the colonial and republican periods could be renounced.[1] Valcárcel recognizes these limits to his longing.

The second part of the book, a collection of pictures, full of color and movement, presents us with indigenous rural life. Valcárcel's prose assumes a fondly bucolic accent when he evokes, with simple images, the rustic enchantment of farming in the sierra. The vehement pamphleteer reappears in his description of the "mestizo villagers," outlining the sordid portrait of a parasitic, obsolete, diseased, alcoholic, and worm-eaten people in whom the qualities of both the Spaniard and the Indian have degenerated in an unfavorable mixture.

In the third part, we assist at the characteristic episodes of the Indian drama. The landscape is the same, but its colors and voices are different. The georgic sierra of the planting, the harvest, and the *Kaswa* becomes the tragic sierra of the *gamonal* and the *mita*. The brutal despotism of the *latifundista*, the *kelkere*, and the policeman weigh down on the peasant *ayllu*.

In the fourth section, the sierra rises, pregnant with hope. It is no longer a race united in resignation and renunciation that lives here. A strange wind sweeps the villages and fields of the sierra. The "new Indians" appear: here, the teacher and agitator; there, the laborer, the shepherd—different than before. The Adventist missionary is not extraneous to their arrival, but Valcárcel accompanies an appreciation of his work with a prudent reserve, for one reason: as Alfredo Palacios warns, these missions can assume the role of outpost for Anglo-Saxon imperialism. The "new Indian" is not a mythic, abstract being, only given life by the prophet's faith. We feel him alive, real, and active by the end of this "movie of the sierra," which is how the author himself defines his book. What distinguishes the "new Indian" is not education, but spirit (literacy does not redeem the Indian). The "new Indian" waits. He has a goal. This is his secret and his power. The rest is peripheral. I, too, have recognized him in more than one messenger of the race that has come to Lima. I recall the unexpected and impressive type of agitator that I met four years ago in the person of the Indian Ezequiel Urviola, from Puno. This encounter was the strongest surprise that Peru had reserved for me on my return from Europe. Urviola represented the first spark of a fire to come. Tubercular and hunchbacked, he succumbed after two years of indefatigable work. It does not matter today that Urviola no longer lives. It is enough that he did. As Varcárcel says, the sierra today is pregnant with Spartacuses.

The "new Indian" explains and indicates the true nature of *indigenismo*, which in Valcárcel has one of its most passionate evangelists. Faith in the indigenous resurgence does not proceed from a process of the material "Westernization" of the land of the Quechua. It is not the civilization or the alphabet of the white man that is lifting the soul of the Indian. It is the myth, the idea of the socialist revolution. The hope of the indigenous people is absolutely revolutionary. This very myth, this very idea, is the decisive agent in the awakening of other failing ancient peoples and races: Hindus, Chinese, etc. Today, as never before, world history tends to be guided by the same compass.

Why should the Incan people, who constructed the most developed and harmonious communist system, be the only group insensitive to the world's emotions? The close relationship between the indigenous movement and the world's revolutionary movements is too obvious to document. I have already said that I came to an understanding and realization of the importance of the indigenous people through socialism. The case of Valcárcel precisely confirms my personal experience. A man with a broad intellectual background, influenced by his traditionalist tastes, guided by different sorts of influences and studies, Varcarcel resolves his *indigenismo* politically, through socialism. In this book he tells us, among other things, that "the indigenous proletariat awaits its Lenin." A Marxist's language would be no different. The indigenous program lacks historical concreteness as long as it remains on a philosophical or cultural plane. To gain this concreteness—that is, to acquire reality, corporeity—it must become a political and economic program. Socialism has taught us to pose the indigenous question in new terms. We have stopped considering it abstractly as an ethnic or moral problem, and now recognize it concretely as a social, economic, and political problem. And we therefore feel that, for the first time, we have clarified and demarcated the issue.

Those who have not yet broken out of the context of their liberal bourgeois education and, basing themselves on an abstract and literary position, continue to confuse themselves with the racial aspects of the problem forget that it is fundamentally dominated by politics, and therefore by economics. They employ a pseudo-idealist language to obfuscate reality, which lies hidden behind its attributes and consequences. To the revolutionary dialectic they oppose an absurd and confused criticism, according to which the solution to the indigenous question does not lie in reform or political action, since their immediate effects would not influence a complex multitude of customs and vices that can only be transformed through a slow and regular evolution.

History, fortunately, resolves all doubts and dispels all ambiguities. The conquest was a political act. It brusquely interrupted the autonomous development of the Quechua nation, but did not imply a sudden substitution of native laws and customs by those of the conquerors. Nevertheless, this political act opened a new period in all arenas of life, both spiritual and material. This change of regime was enough to untie the life of the Quechua people from its moorings. Independence was another political act. It did not result in a radical transformation of the economic and social structure of Peru, but it nevertheless inaugurated another period in our history. If it did not better the condition of the indigenous peoples in practice, because it barely touched the colonial economic infrastructure, it changed their legal position and cleared the way for their political and social emancipation. If the Republic did not continue down this path, the responsibility for this omission lies exclusively with the class that took advantage of the work of the liberators, which was so potentially rich in creative principles and values.

The indigenous question no longer allows for the mystification to which it has been subjected by a mob of lawyers and literati who are consciously or unconsciously tied to the interests of the *latifundistas*. The moral and material misery of the indigenous race too clearly appears as a simple consequence of the economic and social regime that has weighed upon it for centuries. This regime, the successor to colonial feudalism, is called *gamonalismo*.

Under its rule, one cannot seriously speak of the redemption of the Indian. The term *gamonalismo* does not only designate a social and economic category that includes the *latifundistas* and large landowners. It signifies a phenomenon. *Gamonalismo* is not represented only by the *gamonales* themselves. It includes an extensive hierarchy of functionaries, intermediaries, agents, parasites, etc. The literate Indian himself becomes an exploiter when he puts himself at the service of *gamonalismo*. The key factor in this phenomenon is the hegemony of the giant semi-feudal landowners in the politics and machinery of the state. Consequently, it is this factor that must be acted upon if we wish to radically attack this evil, which some insist upon contemplating only in its episodic or subsidiary manifestations.

The liquidation of *gamonalismo*, or of feudalism, could have been carried out by the republic in the context of its liberal and capitalist principles. But for reasons I have already discussed in other studies, these principles have not effectively and fully directed our historical process. Sabotaged by the very class that was charged with applying them, they have been powerless for more than a century to redeem the Indian from a servitude that is absolutely at one with its feudal counterpart. Now that these principles are in crisis around the world, it would be useless to wait for them to suddenly acquire an unexpected creative vitality in Peru.

Revolutionary or even reformist thought can no longer be liberal, but must be socialist. Socialism appears in our history not by chance, imitation, or fashion, as superficial minds suppose, but as a historical necessity. On the one hand, we who profess socialism logically and coherently propose the reorganization of the country on a socialist basis. And maintaining that the economic and political regime we are combating has gradually become a force for the colonization of the country by foreign capitalist imperialists, we proclaim that, at this moment in our history, it is impossible to be truly nationalistic or revolutionary without being a socialist. On the other hand, in Peru, there is not, and there has never been, a progressive bourgeoisie with a national sensibility that declares itself liberal and democratic and bases its politics on the postulates of its theory. With the sole exception of the traditionally conservative elements, there is no one in Peru who, with greater or lesser sincerity, does not claim for himself a certain dose of socialism.

Insufficiently profound and critical minds might suppose that the liquidation of feudalism is a typically and specifically liberal and bourgeois measure, and that to attempt to convert it into a socialist task is to romantically bend the laws of history. These shallow theoreticians oppose socialism with one simplistic criterion as their sole argument—that capitalism has not exhausted its possibilities in Peru. The partisans of this idea will be astonished to discover that the task of socialism, when it comes to power in the country, depending on the hour and the historical compass to which it must adjust, will to a great degree be the realization of capitalism, or better, the realization of the historical possibilities that capitalism still contains, in the sense that this serves the interests of social progress.

Valcárcel, who does not start from any ideological a priori (as might be said of myself or those elements of the younger generation known to be closest to me), discovers this same path through the natural and spontaneous work of probing and studying the indigenous question. The work he has written is not one of theory and criticism. It is somewhat evangelical, even apocalyptic. One will not find here the exact principles of the revolution that will restore the indigenous race to its place in the history of the nation. But here are its myths. And since the elevated spirit of Georges Sorel, reacting against the mediocre positivism that had infected the socialists of his era, discovered the perennial value of myth in the creation of great popular movements, we have known well that this is an aspect of the struggle we must not neglect or underestimate, while being fully realistic.

Tempest in the Andes has arrived at the right moment. Its voice will move all sensitive consciences. It is a passionate prophecy announcing a new Peru. And it matters not that for some it is facts that create prophecy, and for others, prophecy that creates facts.

Note

1. Here is exactly what I wrote (*Mundial*, September 1925): "Valcárcel goes too far, which almost always happens when one gives free reign to the imagination. Western civilization is neither as exhausted or rotten as Valcárcel supposes. Nor once it has acquired its experience, technique, and ideas can Peru mystically renounce such valid and precious instruments and return with bitter intransigence to its old agrarian myths. The Conquest, with all its evil, was an historical deed. The Republic, as it exists, is an historical reality. Abstract mental speculations and pure spiritual concepts have little or no power against historical facts. The history of Peru is but a piece of human history. A new reality has been created in these four centuries. Torrents from the West have created it. It is a weak reality; but it is, in any case, a reality. It would be overly romantic to choose to ignore it."

Principles of National Agrarian Policy*

As an appendix or complement to the study on the land question in Peru that I concluded in the last issue of *Mundial*, I consider it opportune to outline, in accord with the premises of my studies, the features which agrarian policies inspired by the proposition of organically solving this problem would have under the prevailing historical conditions. This outline is necessarily limited to a body of general conclusions, which excludes from consideration any particular or qualifying aspect of the question, focusing on its general design.

The formal and doctrinal starting point of a socialist agrarian policy can be none other than a law on the nationalization of the land. But, in practice, this nationalization ought to be adapted to the necessities and concrete conditions of the country's economy. The principle itself suffices in any case. We have already seen how the liberal principles of the constitution and the civil code have been insufficient to inaugurate a liberal, that is, a capitalist economy, and how the forms and institutions of a feudal economy still exist today despite these principles. It is possible to carry out a policy of nationalization without incorporating the respective principle in a pure form in the constitution, if such a law is not totally revised. The Mexican example can be consulted to best advantage in this regard. Article 27 of the Mexican Constitution establishes the state's doctrine of land ownership:

> The ownership of the lands and waters inside the borders of the national territory belongs in the first instance to the Nation, which has had and has the right of transmitting their dominion to individuals, constituting private property.
>
> Expropriations can only be carried out for reasons of public utility and with compensation.
>
> The Nation at all times will have the right to impose on private property those conditions which public interest dictates, such as regulating the use of those elements of nature liable to appropriation, carrying out an equitable distribution of the public wealth, and attending to its conservation. With this purpose, the necessary measures will be prescribed for the division

---

Mundial, July 19, 1927.

of the latifundia, for the creation of new centers necessary for the development of agriculture, and to avoid the destruction of those elements of nature and the damage that property can allow to the detriment of society. The villages, settlements, and communities that lack land and water or do not have a sufficient quantity for the needs of their population will have the right to endow themselves with such, taking them from contiguous properties, while respecting smallholdings. Therefore, the endowments of lands that have been made until now in conformity with the decree of March 6, 1915, are hereby confirmed. The acquisition of the particular properties necessary to obtain the aforementioned objectives will be considered of public utility.

In contrast to the formally liberal but practically *gamonalista* politics of our first century, a new agrarian policy must principally direct itself to the development and protection of the indigenous "community." The *"ayllu,"* the basic unit of the Incan state that still survives despite the attacks of feudalism and *gamonalismo*, summons yet enough vitality to gradually convert itself into the basic unit of a modern socialist state. State action, such as Castro Pozo correctly proposes, should be directed toward the transformation of the agricultural communities into production and consumption cooperatives. The assignment of land to the communities should naturally be carried out at the expense of the latifundia, excepting smallholders from expropriation as in Mexico, and even medium-sized landowners if there is the requisite amount of "royal land" under state control. The extent of available lands allows for reserving the amount necessary for their progressive apportionment in continuous relation to the growth of the communities. This single measure will ensure the demographic growth of Peru to a greater degree than any currently possible "immigrationist" policies.

Agricultural credit, which can stimulate agriculture in the direction most convenient to the needs of national agriculture solely when controlled and guided by the state, will constitute the best resource for communal production within this agricultural policy. The National Agricultural Bank will give preference to the operations of cooperatives, which will also be aided by the state's technical and educational units to improve the working of the land and the industrial education of its members.

The capitalist exploitation of the lands where agriculture is mechanized can be maintained as long as it continues to be the most efficient method and does not lose its progressive capacity. But it must remain subject to strict state control in everything concerning the observance of labor legislation and public health, as well as financial participation in its profits.

Smallholding has possibilities and reasons for development in the coastal and mountain valleys, where there are economically and socially favorable conditions for its growth. The coastal sharecropper, once his habits and traditions of indigenous socialism have been uprooted, represents the small farmer in formation or transition. As long as there is insufficient water for irrigation, there is no reason to divide the coastal lands dedicated to mechanized cultivation and subject to modern technique. A policy of dividing the lands to the benefit of the smallholder should in no case submit to proposals that do not aim at greater productivity.

The confiscation of uncultivated land and the irrigation or improvement of common land will place expanses at the disposition of the state that should be preferentially allotted for colonization by technically trained cooperatives.

Lands that are not directly exploited by their proprietors—those which belong to unproductive, large absentee owners—should pass into the hands of their tenants in those cases where the exploitation of the land is carried out with modern industrial technology and efficient installations and capital, within the context of state ownership and rights of usufruct.

The state should organize agricultural education for its maximum diffusion among the rural masses through rural primary school and practical agricultural schools, etc. The education of the children of the countryside should have a clearly agricultural character.

I do not think it necessary to ground these conclusions, which are solely proposed to sketch some of the concrete features of an agrarian policy that corresponds to the country's present historical conditions, in the current rhythm of the continent's history. I only wish it not be said of my critical examination of Peru's agrarian question that it set forth only negative conclusions or intransigent, doctrinaire proposals.

Anniversary and Balance Sheet[*]

With this issue, *Amauta* reaches its second birthday. It was at the point of collapse after the ninth issue, before its first anniversary. Unamuno's warning—"a journal that ages, degenerates"—could have been the epitaph of a resonant but ephemeral work. But *Amauta* was not created to remain an

---

[*]*Amauta*, September 1928.

episode, but to be history and to make it. If history is the creation of people and ideas, we can face the future with hope. People and ideas are our strength. The first obligation of any work of the type that *Amauta* has attempted is this: to last. History is endurance. A single scream is worthless, no matter how loud its echo; what is useful is constant, continuous, persistent evangelizing. The perfect, absolute, abstract idea, indifferent to facts, to moving, changing reality, is worthless; what is useful is the germinal, concrete, dialectical, operative idea, rich in potential and capable of movement. *Amauta* is not a diversion, nor the game of pure intellectuals. It professes a historical ideal, affirms an active and popular faith, and is obedient to a contemporary social movement. In the struggle between two systems, between two ideas, it would not occur to us to be spectators, nor to invent a third way. Originality, taken to the extreme, is a literary and anarchic preoccupation. On our banner, we inscribe a single, simple, and great word—socialism (and with this slogan, we affirm our absolute independence from the ideas of a petty bourgeois and demagogic Nationalist Party).

We have wanted *Amauta* to have an organic, autonomous, distinctive, national development. For this reason, we began by seeking a title in the Peruvian tradition. *Amauta* could be neither a plagiary nor a translation. We took an Incan word to create it anew, so that Indian Peru and indigenous America would feel that this journal was its own. And we presented *Amauta* as the voice of a movement and a generation. In these two years, *Amauta* has been a journal of ideological definition that has gathered in its pages the proposals of those with the merit of sincerity and competence who have wished to speak in the name of this generation and this movement.

The work of ideological definition seems to us to have been fulfilled. In any case, we have already heard such categorical and diligent opinions being expressed. Any debate is open to those who speak, not to those who remain silent. *Amauta*'s first act has finished. In the second act, it no longer needs to call itself a journal of the "new generation," the "vanguard," or the "left." To be faithful to the revolution, it is enough to be a socialist journal.

"New generation," "new spirit," "new sensibility": all these terms have grown old. The same must be said for these other slogans: "vanguard," "left," "renovation." They were new and good in their moment. We have used them to establish provisional demarcations for contingent reasons of topography and orientation. Today, they are already too generic and ambiguous. Gross counterfeits are being passed under these titles. The new generation will only be really new to the degree that it finally knows to be adult, creative.

The very word *revolution*, in this America of so many small revolutions, quite lends itself to ambiguity. We must rigorously and intransigently rehabilitate it. We must restore its strict and exact meaning. The Latin American revolution will be nothing more or nothing less than a stage, a phase of the world revolution. It will be, simply and purely, a socialist revolution. To this word you may add, according to the particular case, whatever adjective you like: "anti-imperialist," "agrarian," or "national revolutionary." Socialism supposes, precedes, encompasses all of these.

To a plutocratic, imperialist North America, we can effectively counterpose only a socialist Latin or Ibero-America. The era of free competition in the capitalist economy has finished in all areas and in all of its aspects. We live in the era of monopolies or, better yet, of empires. The Latin American countries came late to capitalist competition. The inside lanes had already been assigned. The destiny of these countries in the capitalist order is that of being simple colonies. Differences of language, race, and spirit have absolutely no decisive weight. It is ridiculous to still speak of the contrast between a materialist, Anglo-Saxon America and an idealist Latin America, between a blonde Rome and a pallid Greece. All these are unpardonably discredited topics. Rodo's myth no longer touches the soul in a useful or fundamental manner, nor has it ever. Let us inexorably put aside all these caricatures and semblances of ideologies and geographies, and let us seriously and honestly take account of reality.

Socialism is certainly not an Indo-American theory. But no theory, no contemporary system, is or could be. And socialism, although born in Europe as was capitalism, is neither specifically nor particularly European. It is a worldwide movement from which none of the countries that move in the orbit of Western civilization can escape. This civilization moves toward universality with a force and with means that no other civilization has ever possessed. Indo-America, in this world order, can and must have its own individuality and style, but not its own culture or particular destiny. A hundred years ago, we owed our independence as nations to the rhythm of Western history, which has inevitably imposed itself upon us since the era of colonization. Freedom, Democracy, Parliament, the Sovereignty of the People: all the great words pronounced by men of that era came from the European repertoire. History, nevertheless, does not measure the greatness of these men by the originality of their ideas, but by the effectiveness and genius with which they served them. And the peoples that have advanced furthest on our continent are those among whom these ideas took root the soonest and best. Interdependence and solidarity between peoples and between continents were nevertheless much less then than now. Socialism is ultimately in the American tradition. Incan civilization was the most advanced primitive communist organization that history has known.

We certainly do not wish socialism in America to be a copy and imitation. It must be a heroic creation. We must give life to an Indo-American socialism reflecting our own reality and in our own language. Here is a mission worthy of a new generation.

In Europe, the parliamentary and reformist degeneration of socialism has imposed a specific nomenclature since the war. Among those peoples where this phenomenon has not occurred, because socialism is just appearing in their historical process, the old and great word maintains its grandeur intact. They will also preserve it in the future, when the contingent and conventional need for demarcation that distinguishes today's practices and methods will have disappeared.

Capitalism or socialism: this is the problem of our epoch. We do not propose syntheses or compromises, which can only be speculated upon historically. Like Gobetti, we think and feel that history is one more reformism if revolutionaries act as such. Marx, Sorel, Lenin—here are the men who make history.

Many artists and intellectuals will possibly note that we fully respect the authority of teachers unexcusably compromised in the process of the *trahison des clercs*. We unhesitatingly confess that we consider ourselves in the domain of the temporal and the historical, and that we have no intention of abandoning them. We leave those spirits incapable of accepting and understanding their own epoch to their sterile afflictions and tearful metaphysics. Socialist materialism embraces all possibilities for spiritual, ethical, and philosophical ascent. And we never feel ourselves more fiercely, effectively, and religiously idealistic than when putting our ideas and our feet on the ground.

The Programmatic Principles of the Socialist Party[*]

The program should be a declaration of doctrine that affirms:

The international character of the modern economy, which does not allow any country to evade the currents of transformation that have arisen from the present conditions of production.

The international character of the proletarian revolutionary movement.

---

[*]Written in October 1928 and published in *Ideología y política*.

The Socialist Party adapts its practice to the country's concrete circumstances, but conforms to a broad class vision, and these very national circumstances are subordinated to the rhythm of world history. The independence revolution of more than a century ago was a joint movement of all the peoples subjugated by Spain; the socialist revolution is a common movement of all the peoples oppressed by capitalism. If the liberal revolution, nationalist in its principles, could not be carried out without the closest unity among the South American countries, it is easy to understand the historical law that, in an era of more accentuated interdependence and connection among nations, ordains that the social revolution, internationalist in its principles, must act with a much more disciplined and intensive coordination of the working-class parties. The *Manifesto* of Marx and Engels condensed the primary principle of the proletarian revolution in the historic phrase, "Workers of the world, unite!"

The sharpening of the contradictions of the capitalist economy. Capitalism is developing among a semi-feudal people such as ours at at a moment—with the arrival of the stage of monopolies and imperialism—when all liberal ideology, which corresponds to the stage of free competition, is no longer valid. Imperialism does not allow any of these semi-colonial peoples, whom it exploits as markets for its capital and commodities and as a store of raw materials, an economic program of nationalization and industrialization. It forces them into specialization and monoculture (oil, copper, sugar, and cotton in Peru). A crisis derives from this rigid determination of national production by the elements of the world capitalist market.

Capitalism finds itself in its imperialist stage. It is the capitalism of monopolies, finance capital, and imperialist wars to monopolize markets and sources of raw materials. The practice of Marxist socialism in this period is Marxism-Leninism. Marxism-Leninism is the revolutionary method of the stage of imperialism and monopolies. The Socialist Party of Peru adopts it as its method of struggle.

The capitalist economy of republican Peru, because of the absence of a strong bourgeois class and because national and international conditions have determined the slow advance of the country on the capitalist road, cannot liberate itself from the poisonous vestiges of colonial feudalism under a bourgeois regime in the thrall of imperialist interests and in collusion with *gamonalista* and clerical feudalism.

This process reinforces the country's colonial fate. The emancipation of the country's economy is only possible through the action of the proletarian masses in solidarity with the international anti-imperialist struggle. Only proletarian action can first stimulate and later realize the work of the bourgeois-democratic revolution, which the bourgeois regime is unable to develop and fulfill.

Socialism finds the elements of a socialist solution to the agrarian question both in the subsistence of the communities and the large-scale agricultural enterprises—a solution that will in part permit the exploitation of the land by small farmers where the sharecropping or smallholding system recommends the maintenance of individual management, while it advances toward the collective management of agriculture in the zones where this type of exploitation prevails. But this, just like the stimulus that it extends to the free resurgence of the indigenous people and the creative manifestation of their native power and spirit, in no way signifies a romantic and anti-historical tendency toward the reconstruction or resurrection of Incan socialism, which corresponded to historical conditions which have been completely superseded, and of which only those habits of cooperation and socialism among the indigenous peasants remain as a factor that can be used in the context of a fully scientific productive technique. Socialism presupposes a capitalist technique, science, and stage, and cannot signify the least regression in the acquisition of the conquests of modern civilization, but, on the contrary, the most methodical acceleration of the incorporation of these conquests into national life.

Only socialism can resolve the problem of an effectively democratic and egalitarian education, by virtue of which every member of society receives all the instruction to which their capacity gives them the right. The socialist educational regime is the only one that can fully and systematically apply the principles of the unified school, the school of labor, the school communities, and, more generally, all the ideas of modern revolutionary pedagogy, which are incompatible with the privileges of the capitalist school, which condemns the poor classes to cultural inferiority and makes higher education the monopoly of the rich.

Having fulfilled the bourgeois-democratic stage, the revolution becomes a proletarian revolution in its objectives and doctrine. The working-class party, qualified by its struggle for the exercise of power and the development of its own program, realizes the tasks of the organization and defense of the socialist order in this stage.

The Socialist Party of Peru is the vanguard of the working class, the political force that assumes the task of orientation and leadership in the struggle for the realization of its class ideals.

IMMEDIATE DEMANDS

- Full recognition of the workers' freedom of association, assembly, and the press.
- Recognition of the right to strike of all workers.
- Abolition of conscription into road gangs.
- Substituting the law on vagrancy with those articles in the proposed penal code put into force by the state that specifically considered the question of vagrancy, with the sole exception of those articles which are incompatible with the spirit and the penal criteria of the special law.
- Establishment by the state of social security and social assistance.
- Implementation of the laws on work accidents, children's and women's labor laws, and the eight-hour day in agricultural labor.
- Addition of malaria in the coastal valleys to the list of work illnesses, with the consequent landholders' responsibilities for assistance.
- Establishing a seven-hour day in the mines and other jobs that are unhealthy, dangerous, and harmful to workers' health.
- Forcing the mining and oil companies to permanently and fully recognize all the rights of their workers that are guaranteed by the country's laws.
- Increasing wages in industry, agriculture, mining, sea and land transport, and guano production in proportion to the cost of living and with the right of workers to a higher standard of living.
- Effective abolition of all forced or unpaid labor and the abolition or penalization of the semi-slave regime in the highlands.
- Endowment of the lands of the latifundia to the indigenous communities for distribution among their members in proportion sufficient to their needs.
- Expropriation without compensation, on behalf of the indigenous communities, of all property of the convents and religious congregations.
- The right of sharecroppers, tenants, etc., who work a plot for more than three consecutive years to obtain the definitive legal right to the use of their parcels, with annual rents no greater than 60 percent of the current standard.
- The lowering of this standard by at least 50 percent for all those who remain sharecroppers or tenants.
- Assigning lands gained for agriculture by irrigation works to cooperatives and poor peasants.
- Maintenance of all rights of employees recognized by relevant laws.
- Regulation of retirement rights by a parity commission in a form that does not imply the slightest reduction of those rights established by law.
- Establishment of a minimum wage and salary.
- Affirmation of the freedom of religion and religious education, at least in the terms of the constitutional article, and the consequent revocation of the last decree against non-Catholic schools.
- Free education at all levels.

These are the principal demands for which the Socialist Party will immediately struggle. They all correspond to the urgent requirements of the material and intellectual emancipation of the masses. They all should be actively supported by the working class and the conscious elements of the middle class. The freedom of the party to act publicly and legally, the constitutional protection and guarantees accorded citizens to create and distribute its press and to carry out its congresses and debates, are rights it demands by the very act of publicly founding itself as a group. Its closely associated groups that today address themselves to the people through this manifesto resolutely assume the mission of defending and propagating its principles and maintaining and promoting its organization at the cost of any sacrifice, with the consciousness of its duty and historical responsibility. And the working masses of the cities, fields, and mines and the indigenous peasantry, whose interests and aspirations we represent in the political struggle, will know to appropriate these demands and this theory, to persistently and vigorously fight for them, and in each struggle find the path that leads to the final victory of socialism.

The Indigenous Question*

I. A Consideration of the Problem

In Latin American bourgeois intellectual speculation, the race question serves, among other things, to disguise or evade the continent's real problems. Marxist criticism has the unavoidable obligation of establishing it in real terms, ridding it of all sophistic or pedantic equivocation. Economically, socially, and politically, the race question, like the land question, is fundamentally that of liquidating feudalism.

The indigenous races of Latin America find themselves in a blatant state of backwardness and ignorance because of the subjugation that has weighed upon them since the Spanish conquest. The interests of the exploiting class—first Spanish, then *criollo*—have inevitably tended, despite different facades, to explain the condition of the indigenous races on the basis of their inferiority or primitivism. This class has thereby done nothing more than reproduce in this internal, national question the reasoning of the white race in the question of the treatment and tutelage of the colonial peoples.

*Document sent to Constituent Congress of the Latin American Trade Union Confederation and published in *Amauta*, July–August 1929.

The sociologist Wilfredo Pareto, who reduces race to merely one of the various factors that determine the form of development of a society, has condemned the hypocrisy of the idea of race in the imperialist and slaving policies of the white peoples in the following terms:

> Aristotle's theory of natural slavery, *Politics*, I, 2, 3–23 (Rackham, pp. 15–31), is the theory put forward by modern civilized peoples to justify their conquests of peoples whom they call "inferior" and their domination over them. Aristotle said that some men are naturally slaves and others masters, and that it is proper for the ones to obey and the others to command, which is just and of benefit to all concerned. So say the modern peoples who decorate themselves with the title "civilized." They assert that there are people—themselves, of course—who were intended by nature to rule, and other peoples—those whom they wish to exploit—who were no less intended by nature to obey, and that it is just, proper, and to the advantage of everyone concerned that they do the ruling and the others the obeying. Whence it follows that if an Englishman, a German, a Frenchman, a Belgian, an Italian, fights and dies for his country, he is a hero; but if an African dares defend his homeland against any one of those nations, he is a contemptible rebel and traitor. So the Europeans are performing a sacrosanct duty in exterminating Africans in an effort to teach them to be civilized. And there are always plenty of people to admire such work "of peace, progress, and civilization," with mouths agape! With a hypocrisy truly admirable, these blessed civilized people claim to be acting for the good of their subject races in oppressing and exterminating them; indeed so dearly do they love them that they would have them "free" by force. So the English freed the Hindus from the "tyranny" of the rajahs. So the Germans freed the Africans from the tyranny of their Black kings. So the Italians freed the Arabs from the oppression of the Turks. So the French freed the Madagascans and—to make them freer still—killed not a few of them and reduced the rest to a condition that is slavery in all but the name. Such talk is uttered in all seriousness, and there are even people who believe it. The cat catches the mouse and eats it; but it does not pretend to be doing it for the good of the mouse. It does not proclaim any dogma that all animals are equal, nor lift its eyes hypocritically to heaven in worship of the Father of us all (*The Mind and Society*, v. 2, translated by Andrew Bongiorno and Arthur Livingston [New York: Harcourt, Brace, 1935], pp. 626–627).

The exploitation of the indigenous peoples in Latin America is also justified on the pretext that it serves the cultural and moral redemption of the oppressed races.

Meanwhile, the colonization of Latin America by the white race has had, as is easy to prove, only retarding and depressive effects in the life of the indigenous races. Their natural evolution has been interrupted by the debasing oppression of the white and the mestizo. Peoples like the Quechua and the

Aztec, who had achieved an advanced degree of social organization, retrogressed under the colonial regime to the condition of dispersed agricultural tribes. Those elements of civilization that subsist in the indigenous communities, are, mainly, those that survive from the old, autochthonous organization. With feudalized agriculture, white civilization has not created centers of urban life, nor even industrialization and mechanization; in the highlands latifundia, with the exception of certain cattle ranches, the rule of the white man does not represent any progress in respect to the aboriginal culture, even technologically.

What we call the indigenous problem is the feudal exploitation of the native peoples by the large agrarian landholders. The Indian, in 90 percent of cases, is not a proletarian, but a serf. Capitalism, as an economic and political system in Latin America, is showing itself unable to build an economy free of feudal encumbrances. The prejudice as to the inferiority of the indigenous race allows the maximum exploitation of the race's workers, and those who gain such benefits from it are not disposed to renounce such profit. In agriculture, the establishment of the wage system and the adoption of the machine do not remove the feudal character of large landholding. They simply perfect the system of exploitation of the land and of the peasant masses. A good part of our bourgeoisie and *gamonales* passionately maintain the theory of Indian inferiority; the indigenous question in their judgment is an ethnic problem whose solution depends on crossing the indigenous race with superior foreign races. The maintenance of a feudally based economy, however, stands in irreconcilable contradiction to an immigration sufficient to produce such a transformation through interbreeding. The wages paid in the coastal and highland haciendas (when the wage system is adopted in the latter) eliminate the possibility of employing European immigrants in agriculture. Peasant immigrants would never agree to work under Indian conditions; they can only be attracted by making them smallholders. The Indian has only been replaceable in the agricultural work of the coastal haciendas by the African slave or the Chinese coolie. At the moment, the Eastern wooded region known as the Montaña is the exclusive realm of plans for colonizing European immigrants. The thesis that the indigenous question is an ethnic problem is not even worthy of discussion, but it is worthwhile to note to what degree this proposed solution is in disaccord with the interests and potentialities of the bourgeoisie and *gamonalismo*, among whom one finds its adherents.

For Yankee or English imperialism, the economic value of our lands would be much less if, along with its natural riches, it did not have a backward and miserable indigenous population that it can exploit to the extreme with the assistance of the national bourgeoisies. The history of the Peruvian sugar industry, now in crisis, shows that its profits have primarily rested on cheap labor—that is, on the misery of its braceros. This industry has never been able to compete technologically with other countries in the world market. Its distance from the consumer market burdened its exports with high freight costs. But all these disadvantages were largely compensated for by the cheapness of its labor. The work of the enslaved peasant masses, housed in repugnant shanties, deprived of all freedom and rights, subjected to a backbreaking working day, placed the Peruvian sugar planters in a position to compete with those in other countries who better cultivated their land, or were protected by a protectionist tariff, or were better situated geographically. Foreign capitalism employs the feudal class to exploit these peasant masses to their benefit. But, at times, the inability of these *latifundistas* (heirs of medieval prejudices, haughtiness, and absolutism) to carry out their functions as directors of capitalist enterprises is such that they are obliged to take the administration of the latifundia and sugar mills into their own hands. This is what happens, especially in the sugar industry, which is almost completely monopolized in the Chicama valley by an English and a German firm.

Race has this primary importance in the problem of imperialism. But it also has another role, which keeps the question of the struggle for national independence in those American countries with a large percentage of indigenous people from paralleling the same problem in Asia or Africa. The feudal or bourgeois elements in our countries feel the same contempt for Indians, as well as for Blacks and mulattos, as do the white imperialists. This racist sentiment among the dominant class acts in a way absolutely favorable to imperialist penetration. There is nothing in common between the native señor or capitalist and his peons of color. The solidarity of racism and prejudice joins class solidarity in making the national bourgeoisies the docile instruments of Yankee or British imperialism. And this sensibility extends to the larger part of the middle classes, who imitate the aristocracy and the bourgeoisie in their disdain for the plebeian of color, even when it is quite obvious that they themselves are of mixed nationality.

The Black race, brought to Latin America by the colonizers to strengthen their power over the indigenous American race, passively fulfilled this colonialist function. Harshly exploited itself, it reinforced the oppression of the indigenous race by the Spanish conquistadors. A greater degree of mixture, familiarity, and proximity to the latter in the colonial cities converted it into the auxiliary of white rule, despite any outburst of their turbulent or restless spirit. The Blacks or mulattos, in their role as artisans or domestic servants, composed a plebeian caste of which the feudal class always disposed more or less unconditionally. The factory, workshop, and union free Blacks from this domesticity. Removing the frontier of race among proletarians, class consciousness morally and historically elevates the Blacks. Unionism signifies the definitive breaking of servile habits that one's condition as artisan or servant would otherwise maintain.

The Indian is in no way inferior to the mestizo in his abilities to assimilate progressive techniques of modern production. On the contrary, he is generally superior. The idea of his racial inferiority is too discredited now to merit the honor of a refutation. The prejudice of the white regarding the Indian, which has also been that of the mestizo, does not rest on any fact worthy of being taken into account in a scientific study of the question. The cocaine mania and alcoholism of the indigenous race, quite exaggerated by commentators, are no more than the consequence, the result, of white oppression. *Gamonalismo* foments and exploits these vices that from one point of view are nourished by the impulse to struggle against pain, which is particularly intense and active among a subjugated people. The Indians of antiquity drank only *chicha*, a fermented corn beverage, while, after the white man established the cultivation of sugar cane, they now drink alcohol. The production of alcohol from sugar cane is one of the most "secure" and stable businesses of the *latifundistas*, in whose hands also lies the production of coca leaf in the warm mountain valleys.

It has been some time since the Japanese experience demonstrated the ease with which peoples of races and cultures other than those of Europe could appropriate Western science and adapt themselves to the use of its productive technique. The Indian peasant in the mines and factories of the Peruvian sierra confirms this experience.

And Marxist sociology has already given a summary judgment against such racist ideas, all of them products of the imperialist spirit. Bukharin writes in *The Theory of Historical Materialism*:

> In the first place, the race theory is in contradiction with the facts. The "lowest" race, that which is said to be incapable, by nature, of any development, is the black race, the Negroes. Yet it has been shown that the ancient representatives of this black race, the so-called Kushites, created a very high civilization in India (before the days of the Hindus) and Egypt; the yellow race, which now also enjoys but slight favor, also created a high civilization in China, far superior in its day to the then existing civilizations of white men; the white men were then children as compared with the yellow men. We now know how much the ancient Greeks borrowed from the Assyro-Babylonians and the Egyptians. These few facts are sufficient to show that the "racial" explanation is no explanation at all. It may be replied: perhaps you were right, but will you go so far as to say that the average Negro stands at the same level, in his abilities, as the average European? There is no sense in answering such a question with benevolent subterfuges, as certain liberal professors sometimes do, to the effect that all men are of course equal, that according to Kant, the human personality is in itself a final consideration, or that Christ taught that there are no Hellenes, or Jews, etc. (cf. for example, Khvostov, *Theory of the Historical Process*, p. 247: "It is extremely probable that . . . the truth

is on the side of the advocates of race equality."). To aspire to equality between races is one thing; to admit the similarity of their qualities is another. We aspire to that which does not exist; otherwise we are attempting to force doors that are already open. We are now not concerned with the question: what must be our aim? We are considering the question of whether there is a difference between the level, cultural and otherwise, of white men and black men, on the whole. There *is* such a difference; the "white" men are at present on a higher level, but this only goes to show that at present these so-called races have changed places.

This is a complete refutation of the theory of race. At bottom, this theory always reduces itself to the peculiarities of races, to their immemorial "character." If such were the case, this "character" would have expressed itself in the same way in all the periods of history. The obvious inference is that the "nature" of the races is constantly changing with the conditions of their existence. But these conditions are determined by nothing more nor less than the relation between society and nature, i.e., the condition of the productive forces. In other words, the theory of race does not in the slightest manner explain the condition of social evolution. Here also it is evident that the analysis must begin with the movement of the productive forces (*Historical Materialism* [New York: International Publishers, 1925], pp. 127–128).

From prejudice as to the inferiority of the indigenous race, one begins to pass to the opposite extreme: that the creation of a new American culture will essentially be the work of autochthonous racial forces. To subscribe to this thesis is to fall into the most ingenuous and absurd mysticism. It would be foolish and dangerous to oppose the racism of those who deprecate the Indian because they believe in the absolute and permanent superiority of the white race with the racism of those who overestimate the Indian with a messianic faith in their mission as a race in the American renaissance.

The possibilities that the Indians will raise themselves materially and intellectually depend on a change in their socioeconomic conditions. They are not determined by race, but by economics and politics. By itself, the race has not risen, not will it rise, to an understanding of an emancipatory ideal. It will especially never acquire the power to impose and realize it. What ensures its emancipation is the dynamism of an economy and culture that carries the seed of socialism in its midst. The Indian race was not conquered by an ethnically or qualitatively superior race, but was conquered by its technology, which was far above the technology of the aboriginal peoples. Gunpowder, iron, and cavalry were not racial advantages; they were technological advantages. The Spaniards arrived in these distant regions because they possessed means of navigation that allowed them to cross the oceans. Navigation and commerce later permitted them to exploit some of the natural resources of its colonies. Spanish feudalism superimposed itself over indigenous agrarianism, in part respecting its communitarian forms. But this very adaptation created a static order, an economic system whose factors of stagnation were the best guarantee of indigenous servitude. Capitalist industry breaks this equilibrium, interrupts this stagnation, creating new productive forces and new relations of production. The working class grows gradually at the expense of artisanship and servitude. The nation's economic and social evolution enters into an era of activity and contradiction that, on the ideological plane, causes the appearance and development of socialist thought.

The influence of the racial factor in all of this is obviously insignificant in comparison to the economic factor—production, technique, science, etc. Without the material elements created by modern industry, or capitalism, if you will, would it be possible to even outline a plan for a socialist state based on the demands and the emancipation of the indigenous masses? The dynamism of this economy, this regime, which makes all relations unstable and which sets ideologies as well as classes in opposition, is undoubtedly what makes the indigenous resurrection feasible, a fact determined by the play of economic, political, cultural, and ideological forces, not racial ones. The greatest accusation against the republic's ruling class is that it has been able to formulate but not speed the process of transformation of the colonial economy into a capitalist economy with a more liberal, more bourgeois, more capitalist sense of its mission. To the emancipation and awakening of the indigenous peoples, feudalism opposes its stagnation and inertia; capitalism, with its conflicts and its own instruments of exploitation, pushes the masses on the road to their own demands, forcing them into a struggle in which they materially and mentally prepare themselves to preside over a new order.

The race question is not common to all the countries of Latin America, nor present to the same degree and with the same characteristics. In some Latin American countries it is regionalized and has little appreciable influence in the social and economic process. But in countries like Peru and Bolivia, and to a lesser degree in Ecuador, where the larger part of the population is indigenous, the demands of the Indian are the dominant popular and social demands.

In these countries, the racial factor is entangled with the class factor in a way that must be accounted for in any revolutionary politics. The Quechua or Aymara Indian sees the mestizo, the white, as his oppressor. And among the mestizo, only class consciousness can destroy the habitual disdain and repugnance for the Indian. It is not unusual to find prejudice as to the inferiority of the Indian among the very urban elements that proclaim themselves to be revolutionaries, and the refusal to recognize this prejudice as a simple inheritance or intellectual contagion of such an environment.

The language barrier imposes itself between the Indian peasant masses and the revolutionary workers' nuclei among the white or mestizo race.

But, because of the nature of its demands, socialist theory will soon root itself among the indigenous masses through Indian propagandists. What has been lacking to this point is the systematic preparation of these propagandists. The literate Indian, corrupted by the city, regularly becomes an accessory to the exploiters of his race. But in the city's revolutionary workers' milieu, the Indian is already beginning to assimilate revolutionary ideas, appropriate them, and understand their value as an instrument for the emancipation of their race, oppressed by the same class that exploits the worker in the factory, whom he is discovering to be a class brother.

The realism of a socialist politics that is certain and precise in its appreciation and use of the realities of these countries can and should convert the racial factor into a revolutionary factor. The present state in these countries rests on an alliance between the landowning feudal class and the mercantile bourgeoisie. Once *latifundista* feudalism is defeated, urban capitalism will lack the power to resist the rise of the workers. It is represented by a mediocre, weak bourgeoisie, created in privilege, without a combative and organized sensibility, which is daily losing its ascendancy over the fluctuating caste of intellectuals.

Socialist criticism in Peru has begun to establish a new basis for the indigenous question with the inexorable denunciation and repudiation of all bourgeois and philanthropic tendencies to consider it as a administrative, juridical, moral, religious, or educational problem (*Seven Interpretative Essays on Peruvian Reality*: "The Indigenous Question," by J. C. Mariátegui). The conclusions about the economic and political terms on which this question and the proletarian struggle to resolve it are based in Peru, and by analogy in the other Latin American countries with a large indigenous population, are the following in our opinion:

1. THE SOCIOECONOMIC SITUATION OF PERU'S INDIGENOUS POPULATION

There is no recent census that would let us know exactly the current size of the indigenous population. It is generally accepted that the indigenous people make up four-fifths of a total population calculated at a minimum of five million. This appraisal does not strictly take race into account, but rather the socioeconomic situation of the masses who constitute this four-fifths. There are provinces where the indigenous typology indicates an extensive intermixing. But in these regions, European blood has been completely assimilated by the indigenous medium, and the life of the *cholos* produced by this intermixing does not differ from the life of the Indians per se.

No less than 90 percent of this indigenous population works in agriculture. The development of the mining industry has recently brought, as a consequence, a growing employment of indigenous labor in the mines. But some of the mine workers remain farmers. There are Indians from the "communities" who spend most of the year in the mines, but who return to their small plots, which are inadequate for subsistence, during the agricultural seasons. A regime of feudal or semifeudal labor in agriculture remains to this day. In the sierra haciendas, wage labor, when it exists, is so incipient and deformed that the characteristics of the feudal regime are barely altered. Ordinarily, the Indians only obtain a minute portion of the fruits of their labor (see the chapter on "The Problem of Land" in *Seven Interpretive Essays on Peruvian Reality* for the different labor systems employed in the sierra). The soil is worked in a primitive form on almost all the land of the latifundia, and although the *latifundistas* always reserve the best, their yields, in many cases, are inferior to those of "community" lands. The indigenous "communities" maintain a part of their lands in some regions, but in too small proportions for their needs, so that their members are obliged to work for the *latifundistas*. The owners of the latifundia, masters of enormous tracts of land, largely uncultivated, have in many cases had no interest in depriving the "communities" of their traditional properties because the community tied to the hacienda allows them to count on their own secure labor force. When a hacienda does not have such a population, the owner, in accord with the authorities, appeals to the forced recruitment of *peones*, whom they remunerate miserably. Indians of both sexes, children included, are obliged to give free services to the landowners and their families, as well as to the authorities. Men, women, and children alternate in the service of the *gamonales* and authorities, not only in the hacienda houses, but also in the towns or cities in which they live. The grant of free services has been legally prohibited at various times, but in practice it still subsists, since no law can stand against the mechanics of the feudal order if its structure is maintained intact. The law on road service conscription has come to accentuate the feudal physiognomy of the sierra in the recent period. This law obligates all individuals to work six days every six months in opening or maintaining roads, or to pay a tax equal to such wages in each region. The Indians, in many cases, are forced to work at a great distance from their residence, which obliges them to sacrifice a greater number of days. They are the object of innumerable violations by the authorities under the pretext of road service, which for the indigenous masses has the character of the old colonial *mitas*.

Wage labor prevails in the mines. In the Junín and La Libertad mines, where the Cerro de Pasco and Northern Copper Corporations, the two great mining enterprises that exploit copper, have their headquarters, workers earn wages of 2.50 and 3.00 soles respectively. These wages are undoubtedly high in relation to the unbelievably abject wages (twenty or thirty cents) which are customary in the sierra haciendas. But the enterprises take advantage of the backward condition of the indigenous people in all its forms. Current social legislation is almost inoperative in the mines, where the laws on workers' compensation and the eight-hour day are not observed and the workers' right of association is not recognized. Any laborer accused of attempting to organize workers, even for only cultural or mutual purposes, is immediately fired by the company. For work in the galleries, companies generally employ "contractors," who, with the object of carrying out the work at the lowest cost, act as an instrument of exploitation of the braceros. The "contractors," nevertheless, ordinarily live in austere circumstances, crushed by the obligation to repay advances, which make them permanent debtors of the companies. When a work accident occurs, the companies use their lawyers to frustrate the rights of the indigenous peoples, abusing their misery and ignorance, indemnifying them arbitrarily and miserably. The Morococha catastrophe, which cost the lives of some dozens of workers, has recently led to the denunciation of the insecurity in which the miners work. Because of the poor state of some galleries and the execution of works that almost reached the bottom of a basin, a cave-in occurred which left many workers buried. The official number of victims was twenty-seven, but there were well-founded reports that the number was greater. The denunciations in some newspapers were influential in leading the company to appear more respectful than usual of the law in regard to indemnifying the relatives of the victims. Recently, the Cerro de Pasco Copper Company, with the goal of avoiding greater discontent, conceded its miners and white-collar employees a 10 percent wage increase as long as the current price of copper continues to hold. The situation of miners in remote provinces like Cotabambas is much more backward and distressing. The *gamonales* of the region are entrusted with the forced recruitment of Indians, and the wages are miserable.

Industry has barely penetrated the sierra. It is mainly represented by the textile factories of Cuzco, where the production of excellent qualities of wool is the greatest factor in their development. The personnel of these factories are indigenous, except for the administrators and foremen. The Indian has perfectly assimilated to mechanization. He is an attentive and sober worker, whom the capitalist skillfully exploits. The feudal environment in agriculture is extended to these factories, where a certain patriarchalism, using the protégés and wards of the owners as instruments for the subjugation of their comrades, opposes the formation of class consciousness.

In recent years, the stimulus of the price of Peruvian wool in foreign markets has initiated a process of industrialization of the southern farms and cattle ranches. Various *hacendados* have introduced modern technique, imported foreign studs that have increased the volume and quality of production, shaken off the yoke of intermediary merchants, and jointly established mills and other small industrial plants on their ranches. Apart from this, in the sierra, there are no other industrial improvements or plants other than those allocated for the production of sugar, syrup, and liquor for regional consumption.

For the exploitation of the coastal haciendas, where the population is insufficient, indigenous labor from the sierra is employed to a considerable extent. The large sugar and cotton plantations are supplied with the braceros necessary for agricultural labor by means of "*enganchadores*" (recruiters). These braceros earn daily wages that, while always abject, are much higher than those which are customary in the feudal sierra. But, in return, they suffer the consequences of backbreaking labor in a hot climate, nutrition insufficient for their work, and malaria, which is endemic in the coastal valleys. The *peón* from the sierra has difficulty avoiding malaria, which forces him to return to his region, many times tubercular and incurable. Although agriculture is industrialized on these haciendas (the land is worked with modern machines and methods, and the products benefit on well-equipped plantations and sugar mills), their atmosphere is not that of capitalism and wage labor in urban industry. The *hacendado* maintains his feudal spirit and feudal practices in the treatment of his workers. The rights established in labor legislation are not recognized. There is no law other than the owner's on the hacienda. Not even the faintest trace of a workers' association is tolerated. The supervisors deny entrance to any individual that the owner or administrator distrusts for any reason. During the colonial era, these haciendas were worked by Black slaves. With slavery abolished, Chinese coolies were brought in. And the *hacendado* has not lost the habits of the slave owner or feudal lord.

In the forest and jungle, agriculture is still quite incipient. The same "*enganche*" system is used as in the sierra, as to a certain degree are the services of the uncivilized tribes that are accustomed to white men. But the forest has a much more somber tradition regarding its labor system. The most barbarous and criminal slaving methods are applied in rubber exploitation when this product brings a high price. The crimes of Putumayo, sensationally denounced in the foreign press, are the darkest page in the history of the rubber workers. It is claimed that these crimes have been much exaggerated and fantasized abroad, and even that an attempt at blackmail is at the origin of these reports, but the truth is perfectly documented by the investigations and testimony of functionaries of the Peruvian judicial system, such as Judge Valcárcel and District Attorney Paredes, who proved the slaving and bloody methods of the overseers of the Casa Arana. And not even three years ago, an exemplary official, Dr. Chuquihuanca Ayulo, a great defender of the indigenous race—and an indigenous man himself—was dismissed from his position as attorney-general of the Department of Madre de Dios because of his denunciation of the slaving methods of the region's most powerful companies.

This summary description of the socioeconomic conditions of Peru's indigenous population establishes that, alongside a small number of wage-earning mine workers and a still-incipient agricultural working class, there exists a more or less attenuated regime of servitude on the latifundium, and that in the distant forest regions, the aboriginal peoples are frequently subjected to a system of slavery.

2. THE INDIGENOUS STRUGGLE AGAINST *GAMONALISMO*

When the attitude of the Indian to his exploiters is discussed, the impression is generally accepted that the Indian, degraded and oppressed, is incapable of any struggle, any resistance. The long history of indigenous insurrections and mutinies and the consequent massacres and repression are themselves enough to belie this impression. In the majority of cases, the Indian risings had at their origin a violent incident that forced them to revolt against an authority or a *hacendado*, but in other cases they have not had this character as a local mutiny. The rebellion followed a less incidental agitation and was propagated over a more or less extensive region. To repress it, considerable forces and truly mass murder had to be called upon. Thousands of rebel Indians have sown dread among the *gamonales* of one or more provinces. One of the risings that recently assumed extraordinary proportions was that led by Army Major Teodomiro Gutiérrez, a mestizo of mostly Indian blood from the sierra, who called himself Rumimaqui and presented himself as the redeemer of his race. Major Gutiérrez had been sent by the Billinghurst government to the department of Puno, where *gamonalismo* was carrying its exactions to an extreme, to carry out an investigation of indigenous denunciations and report to the government. Gutiérrez entered into intimate contact with the Indians. When the Billinghurst government was overthrown, he felt that any prospect for legal redress had disappeared and launched a revolt. Some thousands of Indians followed him, but, as always, disarmed and defenseless before the army, they were condemned to dispersion or death. The risings of La Mar and Huancané and other smaller ones followed in 1923, all bloodily repressed.

In 1921, an indigenous congress met under governmental auspices that was attended by delegations of various groups of communities. The object of these meetings was to formulate the demands of the indigenous race. The delegates articulated, in Quechua, energetic accusations against the *gamonales*, the authorities, and the priests. A committee defending the rights of the Tahuantinsuyo people was founded. Every year until 1924, a congress was held in which the government persecuted the revolutionary indigenous elements, intimidated their delegations, and detracted from the spirit and purpose of the assembly. The 1923 congress, which adopted conclusions disquieting to *gamonalismo* as well as those which demanded the separation of church and state and the abolition of the law on road service conscription, revealed the dangers of these conferences in which groups of indigenous communities from different regions entered into contact and coordinated their activity. That very year, the Regional Indigenous Workers Federation was founded, claiming to apply the principles and methods of anarcho-syndicalism to the organization of the Indians; though it was destined to be no more than an attempt, it at any rate represented an outspoken revolutionary orientation of the indigenous vanguard. With two Indian leaders of this movement exiled and others intimidated, the Regional Indigenous Workers Federation soon was reduced to a single person. And in 1927, the government declared its own committee for the rights of the Tahuantinsuyo people dissolved, under the pretext that its leaders were mere exploiters of the race whose defense they had arrogated. This committee had no more importance than that connected to its participation in the indigenous congresses and was composed of elements that lacked ideological and personal valor and that on not a few occasions had protested their adherence to government policies, considering them pro-indigenist; but for some *gamonales* it was still an instrument of agitation, a by-product of the indigenous congresses. The government, for its part, oriented its politics to associate itself with pro-indigenist declarations, promises to redistribute land, etc., a resolute act against the agitation of the Indians by revolutionary groups or groups susceptible to revolutionary influence.

The penetration of socialist ideas and the expression of revolutionary demands among the indigenous peoples has continued despite these vicissitudes. In 1927, a group for pro-indigenous activities, the Grupo Resurgimiento (Resurgence Group), was founded in Cuzco. It was composed of some intellectuals and artists, along with some Cuzco workers. This group published a manifesto that denounced the crimes of *gamonalismo* (see *Amauta*, no. 6). Shortly after its founding, one of its principal leaders, Luis E. Valcárcel, was jailed in Arequipa. His imprisonment lasted only a few days, but the Grupo Resurgimiento was nevertheless definitively dissolved by the authorities.

3. CONCLUSIONS ON THE INDIGENOUS QUESTION AND THE TASKS THEY IMPOSE

The indigenous question is identified with the land question. The ignorance, backwardness, and misery of the indigenous people are, we repeat, merely the result of their subservience. The feudal latifundium maintains the exploitation and absolute domination of the indigenous masses by the landowning class. The Indians' struggle has invariably centered on the defense of their lands against dispossession and absorption by the *gamonales*. Thus, there is an instinctive and profound indigenous demand: the demand for land. Giving an organized, systematic, and definite character to this demand is a task that we have the duty to actively realize.

The "communities," which have demonstrated a quite astounding level of resistance and persistence under conditions of extreme repression, represent a natural factor for the socialization of the land. The Indian has an established habit of cooperation. Even when communal property becomes individual property (and not only in the sierra, but also on the coast, where a greater degree of cultural amalgamation weighs against indigenous customs), cooperation is still maintained and heavy labor is carried out in common. The "community" can become a cooperative with minimal effort. Awarding the land of the latifundia to the "communities" is the necessary solution to the agrarian question in the sierra. On the coast, where large landholders are also all-powerful but communal property no longer exists, the solution inevitably tends toward the privatization of the land. The *yanaconas*, a group of harshly exploited sharecroppers, should be supported in their struggle against the landowner. The natural demand of these *yanaconas* is for the land that they work. On the haciendas that are directly exploited by their owners with the labor of *peones* who are recruited in part from the sierra and therefore lack a local connection to the land, the terms of the struggle are different. The demands for which they must struggle are the freedom to organize, suppression of the *enganche* (forced recruitment), wage increases, the eighthour day, and the enforcement of labor laws. Only when the *peón* has won these demands will he be on the road to his definitive emancipation.

It is very difficult for trade union or political propaganda to penetrate into the hacienda. Each hacienda on the coast is a fiefdom. No organization that does not accept the patronage and tutelage of owners and management is allowed, and only sports or recreational associations are found there. But the increase of automobile traffic, little by little, is opening a breach in the barriers that keep the haciendas closed to propaganda. This is the reason for the importance of the organization and active mobilization of transport workers in the development of the working-class movement in Peru. When the *peones* on the haciendas know that they can count on the fraternal solidarity of the unions and understand its value, the will to struggle that is missing today, but of which they have given proof more than once, will easily be awakened. The nuclei of adherents of trade unionism that are gradually formed on the haciendas will have the task of explaining to the masses their rights, defending their interests, practically representing their demands, and taking advantage of the first opportunity to form their own organizations to the degree that circumstances permit.

For the progressive ideological education of the indigenous masses, the workers' vanguard has at its disposal those militant elements of the Indian race that enter into contact with the union movement in the mines or urban centers (particularly the latter), assimilate its principles, and qualify themselves to play a role in the emancipation of their race. Workers coming from the indigenous milieu often return there temporarily or permanently. Their idiom allows them to effectively fulfill a mission as instructors of their racial and class brothers. The Indian peasants will only truly understand people from their midst, who speak their own language. They will always distrust the white, the mestizo; in turn, the white and mestizo can only with the greatest difficulty take on this hard work of coming to the indigenous milieu and bringing class propaganda.

The methods of self-education, the regular reading of the organs and tracts of the Latin American trade union and revolutionary movement, and correspondence with comrades in the urban centers will be the means by which these elements successfully fulfill their educational mission.

The regional coordination of the indigenous communities, aid for those who suffer persecution by the courts or the police (the *gamonales* prosecute for common crimes those indigenous people who resist them or whom they wish to dispossess), the defense of communal property, the organization of small libraries and study centers: these are activities in which the indigenous adherents of our movement must always play a principal and leading role, with the dual purpose of giving serious direction to the class orientation and education of the indigenous people and sparing the influence of disorienting elements (anarchists, reformist demagogues, etc.)

In Peru, the organization and education of the mining proletariat is, along with that of the agricultural proletariat, one of the questions that we immediately face. The mining centers, the foremost of which (La Oroya) is becoming the most important source of profits in South America, are places where class propaganda can work to advantage. Besides in themselves representing important proletarian concentrations in conditions similar to other wage earners, indigenous day laborers work alongside industrial workers from the cities, who bring their class spirit and principles to these centers. The indigenous people in the mines continue being peasants to a great degree, so that adherents won among them are also elements won among the peasant class.

This labor will be difficult in all regards, but its progress will fundamentally depend on the ability of those elements that carry it out and on their precise and concrete appreciation of the objective conditions of the indigenous question. The problem is not racial, but social and economic; but race has a role in it and in the methods of confronting it. For example, for reasons of mentality and language, only militants coming from the indigenous milieu can gain an effective and immediate influence over their comrades.

Perhaps an indigenous revolutionary consciousness will form slowly, but once the Indians have made the socialist ideal their own, they will serve it with a discipline, tenacity, and strength that few proletarians from other milieus will be able to surpass.

The realism of a revolutionary, sure, and precise politics, in which the appreciation and utilization of the circumstances upon which one must act in these countries in which the indigenous or Black population has an important size and role, can and must convert the racial factor into a revolutionary factor. It is indispensable to give the movement of the indigenous or Black proletariat, both agricultural and industrial, a clear, class-struggle character. A Brazilian comrade has written:

> One must give the indigenous and enslaved Black populations the certitude that only a government of workers and peasants of all races that inhabit the territory will truly emancipate them, that only such a government can end the *latifundista* and industrial capitalist regime and definitively free them from imperialist oppression.

PART IV
Latin America

Mariátegui considered the Peruvian nationalist movement to be part of a broader regrouping of anti-imperialist forces throughout Latin America. Although their nations were destined to division and competition while still subordinate to foreign capital, the Bolivarian ideal of Latin American unity connected the continent's intellectual and social vanguards. Mariátegui himself was to join figures like José Martí, Rubén Darío, José Vasconcelos and José Ingenieros as a major cultural influence outside his own country. The first essays in this section are related to his efforts to help the process of ideological clarification among Latin America's progressive intellectuals; the three essays on Mexico reflect his close study of political developments there as a testing ground for revolutionary strategy in the continent's other countries; the final document, "Anti-Imperialist Viewpoint," was presented to the first Latin American Communist Conference and is his most sophisticated analysis of class relations in Indo-America.

The Unity of Indo-Hispanic America*

The peoples of Spanish-speaking America are moving in a similar direction. The solidarity of their historical destinies is not the illusion of Americanist literature. These peoples are, in fact, not only brothers rhetorically, but historically. They issue from a single womb. The Spanish conquest, destroying the autochthonous cultures and groups, standardized the ethnic, political, and moral physiognomy of Hispanic America. The Spaniards' methods of colonization solidarized the fate of its colonies. The conquistadors imposed their religion and feudalism on the indigenous populations. Spanish blood mixed with Indian blood. They thereby created nuclei of creole populations, the germ of future nationalities. Soon, identical ideas and emotions stirred the colonies against Spain. The process of formation of the Indo-Hispanic peoples had, in short, a uniform trajectory.

The generation of the liberators felt this South American unity intensely. A united continental front opposed Spain. Its caudillos did not obey a nationalist ideal, but an Americanist one. This attitude corresponded to a historical necessity. Moreover, there could be no nationalism where there were not yet nationalities. The revolution was not a movement of the indigenous populations. It was a movement of the *criollo* populations, among whom the echoes of the French revolution had generated a revolutionary spirit.

But the succeeding generations did not follow along the same path. Emancipated from Spain, the former colonies remained pressed by the necessities of the task of national formation. The Americanist ideal, superior to the contingent reality, was abandoned. The revolution of independence had been a great romantic act, its leaders and inspirers exceptional men. The idealism of this act and these men had allowed them to raise themselves to a height unattainable by less romantic actions and men. Absurd disputes and criminal wars rent the unity of Indo-Hispanic America. At the same time, some peoples developed more certainly and quickly than others. Those nearest to Europe were fertilized by immigration. These benefited from greater contact with Western civilization. The Hispanic-American countries thereby began to differentiate.

---

* *Variedades*, December 6, 1924.

At the moment, while some nations have liquidated their fundamental problems, others have not progressed far toward their solution. While some nations have come to have a normal democratic system, deep residues of feudalism still remain in others. The process of development in all these nations follows the same course, but is fulfilled in some more rapidly than in others.

But what separates and isolates the Hispanic-American countries is not the diversity of their political timetables. It is the impossibility that incompletely formed nations, nations that in their majority have scarcely been sketched out, can agree to and articulate an international system or conglomeration. Historically, the commune precedes the nation. The nation precedes any league of nations.

The insignificance of Hispanic-American economic links appears as a specific cause of this dispersion. Barely any commerce or exchange exists between these nations. All of them are, more or less, producers of raw materials and foodstuffs that they send to Europe and the United States, from which they in exchange receive machinery, manufactured goods, etc. They all have a similar economy and analogous trade. They are agricultural countries. They trade, therefore, with industrial countries. There is no cooperation among the Hispanic-American peoples; on the contrary, at times there is competition. They do not need, do not complement, and do not seek after each other. They function economically as colonies of European and North American industry and finance.

Despite the lack of credit conceded to the materialist conception of history, it cannot be ignored that economic relations are the main agent of communication and articulation between peoples. Perhaps the economic deed is neither anterior nor superior to the political deed. But they are at least consubstantial and in solidarity. Modern history teaches this at every step. (German unity came through the *Zollverein*. This tariff system, which annulled the borders between German states, was the motor force of this unity, which their defeat, the post-war period, and the maneuvers of the Poincarists have been unable to break. Austria-Hungary, despite the heterogeneity of its ethnic makeup, has also constituted one economic organism in recent years. The nations that the peace treaty has separated from Austria-Hungary are thus somewhat artificial, despite the obvious autonomy of their ethnic and historical roots. Cohabitation in the Austro-Hungarian Empire had finally welded them economically. The peace treaty has given them political autonomy, but has not been able to give them economic autonomy. These nations have had to seek a partial restoration of their joint functioning through tariff agreements. Lastly, the politics of international cooperation and assistance that are being attempted in Europe develop from the reality of the economic interdependence of the European nations. These policies are not driven by abstract pacifist ideals, but by concrete economic interest. The problems of the peace have shown the economic unity of Europe. The moral and cultural unity of Europe is no less evident, but is less valid in inducing Europe to pacify itself.)

It is true that these young national formations find themselves scattered in an immense continent. But, in our era, economics is more powerful than space. Its fibers, its nervous system, suppress or abolish distances. The exigencies of communication and transportation in Indo-Hispanic America are a consequence of the exigencies of economic relations. A railroad is not built to satisfy a spiritual or cultural need.

Spanish-speaking America finds itself divided, split, and Balkanized in practice. Nevertheless, its unity is not a utopia or an abstraction. The people who make Hispanic-American history are not dissimilar. There is no appreciable difference between the Peruvian *criollo* and the Argentine. The Argentine is more optimistic, more affirmative than the Peruvian, but both are irreligious and sensual. Between them, there are more differences of shade than of color.

Landscapes differ, objects differ from one region of Spanish America to another, but the people differ barely at all. And the subject of history is, above all, humanity. Economics, politics, religion are forms of human reality. Their history is, in its essence, the history of humanity.

The identity of Hispanic-Americans finds one of its expressions in intellectual life. The same ideas, the same emotions travel through all of Indo-Hispanic America. All powerful intellectual personalities have an influence on the continental culture. Sarmiento, Martí, and Montalvo do not belong exclusively to their respective countries; they belong to Hispanic America. The same can be said of Darío, Lugones, Silva, Nervo, Chocano, and other poets. Rubén Darío is present throughout Hispanic-American literature. At the moment, the ideas of Vasconcelos and Ingenieros are having continental repercussions. Vasconcelos and Ingenieros are the teachers of an entire generation of our America. They are the directors of its mentality.

It is absurd and presumptuous to speak of a properly and genuinely American culture in birth and development. The only evident fact is that there is a vigorous literature that already reflects the Hispanic-American mentality and spirit. This literature—poetry, fiction, criticism, sociology, history, philosophy—is not yet connected to the peoples; but it is connected, if only partially and weakly, to the intellectual castes.

Our era has finally created a more living and extensive discourse, which has established a revolutionary sentiment among Hispanic-American youth. More spiritual than intellectual, this discourse recalls the one that united the generation of independence. Now as then, a revolutionary spirit unites Indo-Hispanic America. Bourgeois interests are competitive or antagonistic; the interests of the masses are not. All of America's new humanity feels itself in solidarity with the Mexican revolution, its fate, its ideals, and its people. The tranquil toasts of diplomats will not unite these peoples. The historical choices of the multitudes will unite them in the future.

Is There Such a Thing as Hispanic-American Thought?*

I

I asked this question four months ago in an article on the idea of a congress of Ibero-American intellectuals. The idea of a congress has made much progress in these four months. It now seems to be an idea that has had a hesitating but simultaneous impact among various intellectual nuclei of Indo-Iberian America, an idea that has sprouted concurrently in the different nerve centers of the continent. Still schematic and embryonic, it is beginning to evolve and gain corporeity.

In Argentina, an energetic and willing group is proposing to take on the task of encouraging and realizing it. The work of this group is tending to connect with other similar Ibero-American groups. Some questionnaires are circulating among these groups to outline or suggest the subjects that the congress should discuss. The Argentine group has sketched out the program of a "Latin-American Union." In short, the preliminary elements exist for a debate, in the course of which the goals and bases of this movement of Hispanic-American coordination or organization will be elaborated and set forth as its initiators are wont to define them, though still a bit abstractly.

II

It therefore seems to me time to consider and clarify the question posed in the article I mentioned previously. Is there already a characteristically Hispanic-American thought? I feel that the statements of the supporters of such an organization go too far in this respect. Certain concepts in the message

---

* *Mundial*, May 1, 1925.

of Alfredo Palacios to the university youth of Ibero-America have led some immoderate and tropical temperaments to an exorbitant estimation of the value and power of Hispanic-American thought. Palacios's message, enthusiastic and optimistic in its assertions and phraseology as was proper in its character as polemic or proclamation, has engendered a series of exaggerations. It is therefore indispensable to rectify these excessively categorical concepts.

"Our America," writes Palacios, "has, until now, had Europe as its guide. Its culture has been nurtured and oriented there. But the last war has made evident what had already been prophesied—that at the heart of this culture were the seeds of its own dissolution." It is impossible to be surprised that these sentences have stimulated an erroneous interpretation of the theory of the decline of the West. Palacios seems to announce a radical liberation of our America from European culture. The tense of the verb lends itself to misinterpretation. The simplistic reader might deduce from Palacios's phrase that "until now, European culture has nurtured and oriented" America, but that it no longer nurtures or orients it. He concludes, at the least, that Europe has now lost the right and ability to spiritually and intellectually influence our young America. And this conclusion is inevitably accentuated and sharpened when Palacios adds a few lines later that "neither the European path nor its old culture serves us" and wants us to emancipate ourselves from the past and from European examples.

Our America, according to Palacios, feels itself on the verge of giving birth to a new culture. Taking this opinion or prophecy to an extreme, the journal *Valoraciones* says that "we are closing the book on these old topics, agonized expressions of the decrepit soul of Europe."

Should we see this optimism as a sign and testimony to the affirmative spirit and creative will of the new Hispanic-American generation? I believe it should first be recognized as characteristic of our America's old and incurable verbal self-aggrandizement. America's faith in its future has no need to subsist on an artificial and rhetorical exaggeration of its present. It is fine that America believes itself the home of a future civilization. It is fine to say that "the spirit will speak for my race." It is fine to consider oneself chosen to teach the world a new truth, but not to imagine oneself on the eve of replacing Europe or to declare the intellectual hegemony of the European peoples already finished and transcended.

Western civilization finds itself in crisis, but there is no indication that it is about to definitively collapse. Europe is not exhausted and paralyzed, as it is absurdly claimed. It has maintained its creative power despite the war and post-war. Our America continues importing ideas, books, machines, and fashions from Europe. What is ending, what is declining, is the cycle of capitalist civilization. A new social form, a new political order, is being formed in the heart of Europe. The theory of the West's decline, the product of the Western laboratory, did not envision the death of Europe, but of the culture whose seat is there. This European culture, which Spengler judges to be in decline without prophesying its immediate demise, succeeded Greco-Roman culture, which was also European. No one dismisses, no one excludes the possibility that Europe will renew and transform itself again. In the historical panorama which our viewpoint commands, Europe presents itself as the continent of the greatest rebirths. Aren't the greatest contemporary artists, the greatest contemporary thinkers, still European? Europe feeds on the world's vital fluids. European thought is immersed in the most distant mysteries, in the oldest civilizations. But this also shows its possibilities for convalescence and rebirth.

III

Let us return to our question. Is there a characteristically Hispanic-American thought? The existence in Western culture of French thought, of German thought, seems evident to me. The existence of Hispanic-American thought in the same sense does not seem equally evident. All the thinkers of our America have been educated in European schools. The spirit of the race is not felt in their work. The continent's intellectual production lacks its own characteristics. It does not have an original profile. Hispanic-American thought is generally only a rhapsody composed from the motifs and elements of European thought. To prove this, one can merely review the work of the highest representatives of the Indo-Iberian intellect.

The Hispanic-American spirit is being elaborated. The continent, the race, is also in formation. The Western sediments in which the seeds of Hispanic-American or Latin American thought are developing—in Argentina and Uruguay, one can speak of Latin ones—have not succeeded in uniting or combining with the soil on which it has been deposited by the colonization of America.

In the greater part of our America, they constitute a shallow and independent stratum through which the indigenous soul—humiliated and diffident because of the brutality of a conquest whose methods have not yet changed among some Hispanic-American peoples—cannot be seen. Palacios says:

> We are nascent peoples, free of ties and atavisms, with immense possibilities and vast horizons before us. The intermingling of races has given us a new soul. Humanity is encamped inside our borders. We and our children are the synthesis of races.

In Argentina, it is possible to believe this; not in Peru and among other peoples of Hispanic America. Here, this synthesis does not yet exist. The elements of our nationality in formation have not yet been fused or welded. The profuse indigenous layer is kept almost totally foreign to the process of formation of this *Peruanidad* that our self-styled nationalists are wont to exalt and inflate—these preachers of a nationalism without roots in the Peruvian soil, learned from Europe's imperialist gospels, and which is, as I have already had the opportunity to point out, the most foreign and artificial sentiment that exists in Peru.

IV

The debate that is beginning should precisely clarify all these questions. We should not prefer the easy fiction of declaring them resolved. The idea of a congress of Ibero-American intellectuals will be credible and productive to the extent that they can be outlined. The value of the idea lies almost completely in the debate that it inspires.

The program of the Argentine section of the projected Latin-American Union, the questionnaire of the Costa Rican journal *Repertorio Americano*, and the questionnaire of the group working here for this congress invite the intellectuals of our America to meditate on and discuss many fundamental problems of our continent in formation. The program of the Argentine section has the tone of a declaration of principles. This is undoubtedly premature. For the moment, it is only a question of outlining a plan of work and discussion. But a modern spirit and a will for renovation inspire the work of the Argentine section. This spirit, this will, gives it the right to lead the movement. Because the congress will represent or organize absolutely nothing if it does not represent and organize the new Hispanic-American generation.

Ibero-Americanism and Pan-Americanism*

I

Ibero-Americanism reappears sporadically in Spanish and Spanish-American debates. It is an idea or theme that from time to time engages discussions among our language's intellectuals (it seems to me that we cannot truly call them the intellectuals of *la raza*).

* *Mundial*, May 8, 1925.

But the discussion is now broader and more intensive. Ibero-American topics are now becoming of conspicuous interest in the Madrid press. A convergence or coordination of Ibero-American intellectual forces, proposed and led by some writers' circles of our America, lends a concrete meaning and new profile to these topics at the moment.

This time, the discussion repudiates official Ibero-Americanism in many cases and ignores it in others (Don Alfonso's official Ibero-Americanism is incarnated in the Bourbonic and decorative stupidity of a royal child, in the courtly mediocrity of a Francos Rodríguez). Ibero-Americanism is being stripped of all its diplomatic ornamentation in this dialogue of free intellectuals. It thus reveals to us its reality as the ideal of the majority of the representatives of intelligence and culture in Spain and Indo-Iberian America.

Pan-Americanism, though, does not enjoy the favor of intellectuals. It has no enumerable, tangible supporters among this abstract and inorganic group. It has merely some incipient sympathies. Its existence is exclusively diplomatic. The most obtuse minds can easily see that it is a cover for North American imperialism. Pan-Americanism is not manifest as a continental ideal, but rather, unequivocally, as a natural ideal of the Yankee empire (rather than a great democracy, as its apologists in these latitudes would like to classify it, the United States is a great empire). But despite all this or, rather, because of it, Pan-Americanism exercises a powerful influence in Indo-Iberian America. North American policy is not too concerned with having the ideals of its empire pass as the ideals of the continent, nor bothered by the lack of an intellectual consensus. Pan-Americanism embroiders its propaganda on a solid framework of interests. Yankee capital is invading Indo-Iberian America. The circuits of Pan-American commercial traffic are the routes of this expansion. North American money, technology, machinery, and merchandise increasingly predominate in the economies of these Central and Southern nations. It might very well be that the Empire of the North looks happily on a theoretical independence of the intellect and spirit of Indo-Hispanic America. Little by little, economic and political interests are ensuring the adherence or, at least, the submission of most intellectuals. In the meantime, the professors and functionaries that Mr. Rowe's Pan-American Union are able to mobilize suffice for Pan-American expositions.

II

Nothing is therefore more useless than amusing oneself with platonic confrontations between Ibero-American and Pan-American ideals. The number and quality of its intellectual adherents little serve Ibero-Americanism. The eloquence of its literati serves even less. While Ibero-Americanism finds support in emotions and traditions, Pan-Americanism finds support in interests and commerce. The Ibero-American bourgeoisie has much more to learn in the school of the new Yankee imperialism than that of the old Spanish nation. The Yankee model, the Yankee style, is being propagated throughout Indo-Iberian American, while the Spanish heritage is being destroyed and lost. The *hacendado*, the banker, and the rentier of Spanish America look much more attentively toward New York than Madrid. The dollar's rate of exchange interests them a thousand times more than the thoughts of Unamuno or Ortega y Gasset's *Review of the West*. To these people who govern the economy, and therefore the politics, of Central and South America, the Ibero-American ideal has little import. In the best of cases, they feel disposed to marry it to the Pan-American ideal. The travel agents of Pan-Americanism, on the other hand, seem more effective, though less picturesque, than the travel agents—those academic choristers—of official Ibero-Americanism, which is the only thing that a prudent bourgeois can take seriously.

III

The new Hispanic-American generation should clearly and precisely define the nature of its opposition to the United States. It should declare itself the adversary of the empire of Dawes and Morgan, not of the peoples or the individuals of North America. The history of North American culture offers many noble examples of intellectual and spiritual independence. Roosevelt is the trustee of the spirit of the empire, but Thoreau is the trustee of the spirit of humanity. Henry Thoreau, who now receives the homage of Europe's revolutionaries, also has the right to the devotion of the revolutionaries of our America. Is it the fault of the United States if we Ibero-Americans know more of the thoughts of Roosevelt than those of Henry Thoreau? The United States is certainly the homeland of Pierpont Morgan and Henry Ford, but also of Ralph Waldo Emerson, William James, and Walt Whitman. The nation that has produced the greatest captains of industry has also produced the greatest masters of continental idealism. And today, the same disquiet that is stirring the vanguard of Spanish America is moving the vanguard of North America. The problems of the new Hispanic-American generation are the same as those of the new North American generation, with differences of locale and degree. Waldo Frank, one of the new men of the North, says things in his studies of our America that are valid for the people of his America and of ours.

The new men of Indo-Iberian America can and should come to an understanding with the new men of Waldo Frank's America. The work of the new Ibero-American generation can and should be articulated in solidarity with the work of the new Yankee generation. Both generations coincide. Their language and ethnicity differ, but they announce and unite the same historical sensibility. Waldo Frank's America, like ours, is the adversary of the empire of Pierpont Morgan and oil.

On the other hand, the same historical sensibility that places us close to this revolutionary America separates us from the reactionary Spain of the Bourbons and Primo de Rivera. What can the Spain of Vásquez de Maella and Maura, of Pradera and Francos Rodríguez, teach us? Nothing, not even the methods of a great industrial and capitalist state. The civilization of Power does not have its capital in Madrid or Barcelona, but in New York, in London, in Berlin. The Spain of the Catholic kings holds absolutely no interest for us. Let Señor Pradera and Señor Francos Rodríguez stand by her fully.

IV

Ibero-Americanism has need of a bit more idealism and a bit more realism. It has yet to be joined to the new ideals of Indo-Iberian America. It has yet to insert itself into the new historical reality of these peoples. Pan-Americanism finds support in the interests of the bourgeois order; Ibero-Americanism should find its support in the multitudes who are working to create a new order. Official Ibero-Americanism will always be an academic, bureaucratic, impotent ideal, with no roots in reality. As the ideal of the nuclei of renovators, it will become instead a fighting, active, mass ideal.

Mexico and the Revolution*

The dictatorship of Porfirio Díaz produced a situation of superficial economic well-being but deep social distress in Mexico. In power, Porfirio Díaz was an instrument, proxy, and prisoner of the Mexican plutocracy. During the Reformist revolution and the revolution against Maximilian, the Mexican people attacked the feudal privileges of the plutocracy. With Maximilian defeated, the landlords took control of one of the generals of this liberal and nationalist revolution, Porfirio Díaz. They made him the leader of a bureaucratic military dictatorship designated to suffocate and repress these revolutionary demands. Diaz's policies were essentially plutocratic ones. Cunning and deceitful laws dispossessed the Mexican Indian of his land to the benefit of national

---

* *Variedades*, January 5, 1924.

and foreign capitalists. The *ejidos*, the traditional lands of the indigenous communities, were absorbed by the latifundia. The peasant class was totally proletarianized as a result. The plutocrats, the *latifundistas*, and their entourage of lawyers and intellectuals constituted a faction, structurally analogous to *civilismo* in Peru, that dominated a feudalized country with the support of foreign capital. Porfirio Díaz was its ideal gendarme. This so-called "scientific" oligarchy feudalized Mexico. It militarily maintained a large praetorian guard. It protected foreign capitalists, who were treated with special favor. It encouraged lethargy and desensitization among the masses, momentarily deprived of a motivator, a leader. But a people that had so stubbornly fought for its right to the land could not renounce its demands and resign itself to the existence of this feudal regime. Moreover, the growth of factories was creating an industrial proletariat that foreign immigration was pollinating with new social ideas. Small socialist and syndicalist nuclei appeared. Flores Magón, from Los Angeles, injected a dose of socialist ideology into Mexico. And most important, a bitter revolutionary temperament was seething in the countryside. Any leader, any incident could kindle it and inflame the country.

As the end of Porfirio Díaz's seventh term neared, the leader appeared: Francisco Madero. Madero, who until that time was a farmer of no political import, published a book against his re-election. This book, which was an indictment of the Díaz government, found an immense popular response. At first, Porfirio Díaz, with the vain confidence in one's own power that blinds waning despots, was not worried over the commotion aroused by Madero and his book. He judged Madero's person to be inferior and powerless. Madero, acclaimed and followed like an apostle, nevertheless roused a powerful current against re-election. And finally, the dictatorship, alarmed and upset, felt the need to combat it forcibly. Madero was jailed. The reactionary offensive dispersed the anti-re-electionist party, the *"científicos"* re-established their authority and power, Porfirio Díaz won for the eighth time, and the celebration of Mexico's centenary was the pompous apotheosis of his dictatorship. These successes filled Díaz and his band with optimism and confidence. The end of his government was nevertheless near. Madero, released conditionally, fled to the United States, where he devoted himself to organizing the revolutionary movement. Orozco joined the first revolutionary army shortly thereafter. And the rebellion spread quickly. The *"científicos"* tried to attack it with political weapons. They declared themselves ready to satisfy revolutionary aspirations. They passed a law blocking another re-election. But this maneuver could not contain a movement on the march. The anti-re-election banner was a contingent one. Around it had gathered all the discontented, all the exploited, all the idealists. The revolution did not yet have a program, but it was beginning to be sketched out. Its first concrete demand was for the land usurped by the *latifundistas*.

The Mexican plutocracy, with the sharp instinct for self-preservation of all plutocracies, rushed to negotiate with the revolutionaries. It thereby kept the revolution from defeating the dictatorship by force. Porfirio Díaz handed over the government in 1912 to De la Barra, who presided over an election. Madero came to power through a compromise with the *"científicos."* He consequently accepted their collaboration. He maintained the old parliament. These transactions, these deals, weakened and undermined him. The *"científicos"* sabotaged the revolutionary program and isolated Madero from the social strata from which he had recruited his converts, and at the same time prepared their own reconquest of power. They lay in wait for the moment to remove a weakened and ruined Madero from the presidency of the republic. Madero rapidly lost his popular base. Now came the insurrection of Félix Díaz, and then the betrayal of Victoriano Huerta, who stormed the government over the bodies of Madero and Pino Suárez. The "scientific" reaction appeared victorious. But the pronunciamento of a military chief could not stop the march of the Mexican revolution. All the roots of this revolution were still alive. General Venustiano Carranza took up the banner of Madero, and, after a period of struggle, expelled Victoriano Huerta from power. The demands of the revolution were sharpened and better defined, and Mexico revised and reformed its constitution in accordance with these demands. Article 27 of the constitutional reform of Querétaro declares that the land belongs originally to the nation and orders the breakup of the latifundia. Article 123 incorporates various aspirations of the workers into the constitution: a maximum length for the working day, a minimum wage, health and retirement insurance, compensation for accidents on the job, and profit-sharing.

But the conditions did not exist to realize the revolution's program once Carranza was elected president. His position as a landlord and his commitments to the *latifundista* class kept him from carrying out the agrarian reform. The division of the land promised by the revolution and ordered by the constitutional reform did not occur. The Carranza regime gradually petrified and bureaucratized. Carranza finally claimed the right to designate his successor. The country, constantly aroused by the revolutionary parties, rose up against this idea. Carranza, virtually abandoned, died at the hands of an irregular band. And under the provisional presidency of De la Huerta, elections were carried out which brought General Obregón to the presidency.

The Obregón government has taken a resolute step toward satisfying one of the deepest desires of the revolution: it has given land to the poor peasants. A collectivist regime has flourished under its protection in the state of Yucatán. Its prudent and well-organized policies have normalized Mexican life, and it has persuaded the United States to recognize the Mexican regime. But the most revolutionary and transcendent activity of the Obregón government has been its work in education. José Vasconcelos, whose image is among the greatest in modern America, has led an extensive and radical reform of public education. He has used the most original methods to decrease illiteracy; he has opened the universities to the poorer classes; he has spread the works of Tolstoy and Romain Rolland to all the schools and libraries like a modern evangelist; he has incorporated into law the state's obligation to support and educate orphans and the children of the disabled; and he has sown the immense and fertile lands of Mexico with schools, books, and ideas.

Portes Gil versus the CROM*

There is no longer any possible doubt about the reactionary tendency of the policies of the provisional president of Mexico. The offensive against the CROM (Mexican Regional Workers Confederation), while its real motives are concealed with demagogic language, proposes nothing else than demolishing or diminishing the political power of the working masses, an unequivocally counterrevolutionary objective that no rhetoric can hide or disguise.

The responsibility and initiative for these policies do not belong to Portes Gil, who in his leadership obeys factors greater than his personal judgment. Here is another factor that is no less certain. Portes Gil has not changed the government's attitude toward the CROM because of a sudden inspiration. His selection as provisional president was decided by the forces opposed to the CROM that have grown in recent years in the governmental bloc. The incubation process of this government began when the boldest enemies of the CROM accused its leader Morones of being the Machiavellian instigator of the assassination of General Obregón. From that moment, the popular front that governed Mexico in the name of the principles of the revolution was definitively broken. The rise to power of the so-called Obregonistas had to lead to the revolution, the crisis, that we are currently witnessing.

During the governments of Obregón and Calles, the stabilization of the revolutionary regime had been obtained by virtue of a tacit pact between the insurgent petty bourgeoisie and the workers' and peasants' organizations to collaborate on a strictly reformist basis. This could be pursued using radical

---

* *Variedades*, January 19, 1929.

phraseology against reactionary attacks, aiming to keep alive the masses' enthusiasm. But all radicalism in reality had to be sacrificed to a politics of normalization and reconstruction. The conquests of the revolution could only be consolidated at this price. The CROM, which arose and grew under revolution's leadership—its baptism was at the workers' convention of Saltillo in 1918—lacked the capacity and ambition to materially and intellectually dominate in the government, both at the time of the first election of Obregón and the time of Calles's election. By 1926, its adherents, which at the Saltillo convention only numbered seven thousand, had grown only by five thousand. The whole process of development of the CROM had occurred under the governments of Obregón and Calles, which they supported, while receiving the indispensable guarantees for its work of organizing the worker and peasant masses in its ranks. At the moment of its greatest mobilization, the CROM calculated its membership at two million. Its political role—despite its representation in the government—was not related to its social power. But it would not have been able to build and increase it in so little time without the conjuncture of an exceptional situation, like that of Mexico and its government after long years of victorious revolutionary agitation.

Under this regime, not only have the workers' forces developed, channeled in a reformist direction, but also the forces of capital and the bourgeoisie. The most unskilled energies of the reaction had been consumed in the attempt to attack the revolution from the outside. The wisest operated inside the revolution, waiting for the hour of Thermidorian reaction to sound.

The Mexican state was not a socialist state, either in theory or in practice. The revolution had respected the principles and forms of capitalism. What was socialist about this state consisted of its working-class political base. However moderate its politics, the CROM, as a class organization, had to increasingly accentuate its program of socialization of wealth. But the capitalist class solidified in the context of the regime created by the revolution at the same time as the working class. And they had in their favor a greater political maturity. The petty bourgeois elements, the military caudillos of the revolution, placed between these two influences, had to regularly give way to capitalist influence.

The conflict that has exploded was thereby prepared, somewhat precipitously with the assassination of the president-elect, General Obregón, the only caudillo who, after Calles, had been able to prolong the compromise between the two rival forces.

The CROM joined combat under unfavorable conditions and at an unfavorable moment. Its reformist general staff—Morones and his lieutenants—could not transcend a pacifist, legal, evolutionist practice in the struggle against authority. Morones pronounced ardent and polemical speeches at the last convention of the CROM, but did not affirm the right and will of the working class to take the government into its hands as soon as its situation and strength would allow. It can be clearly seen that Morones is not renouncing his opportunism, and that he trusts more in the possibility of exploiting the divisions and rivalries among the caudillos than in the possibility of leading the working masses to a genuinely revolutionary politics. The recourse of bringing Calles to the convention was a maneuver of this strategic type.

For this reason, the efforts of various workers' organizations independent of the CROM to establish a united proletarian front, which includes all the active sectors, through a national peasant assembly have great consequence and significance. The slogan of the Communist Party and the worker and peasant groupings that follow it is the following: "Long live the CROM! Down with its Central Committee!" All the power of the workers is called to the aid of the CROM in its struggle against the reactionary offensive. They condemn any intransigent inclination to give birth to a new confederation. They understand that the CROM constitutes a starting point that the proletariat should not squander.

The revolution faces its gravest test. And Mexico is today, more than ever, the site of a revolutionary experiment. Class politics in this country is entering its most interesting phase.

Notes on the New Course of Mexican Politics*

The careful observation of Mexican events will allow us to illuminate for the theoreticians and practitioners of Latin American socialism some questions that frequently embroil and confuse the dilettantish interpretations of tropical super-Americanists. Both in times of revolutionary flow and revolutionary ebb, and perhaps more precisely and clearly in the latter, the historical experiment begun in Mexico with Madero's insurrection and the overthrow of Porfirio Díaz provides an observer with a valuable and unique collection of proofs of the inevitable attraction toward capitalism and the bourgeoisie

* *Variedades*, March 19, 1930.

of all political movements led by the petty bourgeoisie, with all its particular ideological confusionism.

Mexico allowed these hasty and immoderate apologists the tacit hope that its revolution would provide Latin America with a patron and method for a socialist revolution governed by essentially Latin American factors, with the most sparing use of European theorizing. The facts have put the stop to this tropical, messianic hope. And no circumspect critic would today risk subscribing to the hypothesis that the leaders and projects of the Mexican revolution are leading the Aztec people toward socialism.

Luis Araquistain, in a book written with obvious sympathy for the work of the political regime that he studied in Mexico two years ago, feels himself obliged, for no other reason than the elemental duty of objectivity, to undo the legend of "socialist revolution." This is also the more specific and systematic object of a series of articles by the young Peruvian writer Esteban Pavletich, who has been in direct contact with the people and events of Mexico since 1926. The very writers who are followers or allies of the regime admit that, for the moment, the policies of the regime are not tending to create a socialist state. Froylán C. Manjarrez, in a study appearing in the journal *Crisol*, claims that, for the stage of gradual transition from capitalism to socialism, life

> now offers us this solution: between the capitalist state and the socialist state, there is an intermediate state—the state as regulator of the national economy, whose mission corresponds to the Christian idea of property, today triumphant, which assigns it social functions.

Without being teleological or deterministic, the Italian fascists arrogate to themselves the role of creating precisely this type of national and unitary state. The class state is condemned in the name of a state above class interests, a state that conciliates and arbitrates these interests, depending on the case. It is not strange that this eminently petty-bourgeois idea, particularly supported by fascism in the context of its unequivocally and unmistakably counterrevolutionary activities, now appears in the theory of a political regime that is the consequence of a revolutionary upsurge. The world's petty bourgeoisies take after each other, though some imagine themselves successively as Machiavelli, the Middle Ages, and the Roman Empire, and others piously dream of an idea of property that assigns it social functions. The regulatory state of Froylán C. Manjarrez is none other than the fascist state. It little matters that Manjarrez prefers to see it in the German state as it appears in the Weimar constitution.

Neither the Weimar constitution nor the presence of the Socialist Party in the government has freed the German state of its character as a class state, a bourgeois-democratic state. The German Socialists, who drew back from the revolution in 1918—an attitude that has its formal expression precisely in the Weimar constitution—propose nothing more than the slow, prudent transformation of this state, which they know to be dominated by capitalist interests. As reformist leaders like the Belgian Vandervelde explain, ministerial collaboration is necessary because of the need to defend the interests of the working class from inside the government against the predominance of capitalism and because of the importance and responsibilities of the Socialist parliamentary faction. On the other hand, incidents like the removal from the government of the Social Democrat Hilferding, the finance minister, because of his conflict with Schacht, the dictator of the Reichbank and the trustee of the big financial bourgeoisie, should be enough to make the German socialists remember the real power of capitalist interests in the government and the practical circumstances of Social Democratic collaboration.

What does categorize and classify the German state is the degree to which it realizes bourgeois democracy. Germany's political evolution is not measured by the vague designs for the nationalization of industry in the Weimar constitution, but by the effectiveness of its bourgeois-democratic institutions: universal suffrage, parliamentarism, the right of all parties to exist legally and propagate their ideas, etc.

The retrogression in Mexico in the period after Obregón's death, the rightward march of the Portes Gil and Ortiz Rubio regimes, can similarly be measured by the suspension of the democratic rights of the previously accepted extreme left forces. Persecuting the militants of the United Mexican Union Confederation (CSUM), the Communist Party, Workers Aid, and the Anti-Imperialist League for their criticism of its surrender to imperialism and for their propagation of a proletarian program, the Mexican government disowns the true mission of the Mexican revolution: replacing the despotic and semi-feudal Porfirista regime with a bourgeois-democratic regime.

The regulatory state, the intermediary state, defined as an organ of the transition from capitalism to socialism, appears concretely as a regression. Not only is it incapable of ensuring the proletarian political and economic organizations the guarantees of bourgeois-democratic legality, but it assumes the task of attacking and destroying them when it feels itself the least bit irritated by their most elementary manifestations. It proclaims itself the absolute and infallible repository of the revolution's ideals. It is a state with a paternalist sensibility that, without professing socialism, opposes the proletariat—the class that is historically charged with fulfilling this duty—when it affirms and exercises its right to struggle for it, independent of all bourgeois and petty bourgeois influences.

None of these arguments put in dispute the social depth of the Mexican revolution or its historical significance. The political movement that defeated *Porfirismo* in Mexico, in all that it has meant as an advance and victory over feudalism and its oligarchies, has nourished mass sentiment, found support in its strength, and has been driven by an indisputably revolutionary spirit. It is an extraordinary and instructive experience in all these aspects. But the character and objectives of this revolution, considering the men who have led it, the economic situation from which it arises, and the nature of its development, are those of a bourgeois-democratic revolution. Socialism cannot be brought on without a class party. It can only be the result of socialist theory and practice. The intellectual supporters of the regime grouped around the journal *Crisol* have taken upon themselves the task of "defining and illuminating the ideology of the revolution." They thereby recognize that it is neither defined nor illuminated. The latest repressive acts, directed in the first place against foreign political refugees—Cubans, Venezuelans, etc.— indicate that this illumination is coming slowly. The Mexican revolution's politicians, while otherwise quite different from each other, show themselves less and less disposed to conduct it as a bourgeois-democratic revolution. They have already put it into reverse gear. And its theoreticians in the meantime are serving up with Latin American eloquence the theory of the regulatory state, the intermediary state, which seems piece for piece like the fascist theory of the state.

Anti-Imperialist Viewpoint*

To what degree is the situation of the Latin American republics similar to that of the semi-colonial countries? The economic condition of these republics is undoubtedly semi-colonial, and this characteristic of their economies tends to be accentuated as capitalism, and therefore imperialist penetration, develops. But the national bourgeoisies, who see cooperation with imperialism as their best source of profits, feel themselves secure enough as mistresses of power not to be too greatly preoccupied with national sovereignty. The South American bourgeoisies, not yet facing Yankee military occupation (with the exception of Panama), are not disposed to admit the necessity of struggling for their second independence, as Aprista propaganda naively supposes. The state, or better yet the ruling class, does not seem to feel the

---

* Thesis presented to the First Latin American Communist Conference (June 1929). Included in *Ideología y política*.

need for a greater or more secure degree of national autonomy. The revolution for independence is relatively too near, its myths and symbols too alive in the consciousness of the bourgeoisie and petty bourgeoisie. The illusion of national sovereignty still lives on. It would be a serious mistake to claim that this social layer still has a sense of revolutionary nationalism, as in those places where it does represent a factor for anti-imperialist struggle in semi-colonial countries enslaved by imperialism, for example, in Asia in recent decades.

Over a year ago, in our discussion with Aprista leaders in which we rejected their desire to propose the creation of a Latin American Kuomintang, we put forward the following thesis as a way to avoid Eurocentric plagiarism and to accommodate our revolutionary activity to a precise appreciation of our own reality:

> Collaboration with the bourgeoisie and even many feudal elements in the anti-imperialist struggle in China are explicable in terms of race and national culture that are not relevant for us. A Chinese nobleman or bourgeois feels himself Chinese to the core. He matches the white man's contempt for his stratified and decrepit culture with his own contempt and pride in his millennia-long tradition. Anti-imperialism can therefore find support in such sentiments and in a sense of Chinese nationalism. Circumstances are not the same in Indo-America. The native aristocracy and bourgeoisie feel no solidarity with the people in possessing a common history and culture. In Peru, the white aristocrat and bourgeois scorn the popular and the national. They consider themselves white above all else. The petty bourgeois mestizo imitates their example. The Lima bourgeoisie fraternizes with the Yankee capitalists, even with their mere employees, at the Country Club, the Tennis Club, and in the streets. The Yankee can marry the native señorita without the inconvenience of differences in race or religion, and she feels no national or cultural misgivings in preferring marriage with a member of the invading race. The middle-class girl has no qualms in this regard, either. The girl who can trap a Yankee employed by the Grace Company or the Foundation does it with the satisfaction of thereby raising her social position. The nationalist factor, for these inescapable objective reasons, is neither decisive nor basic to the anti-imperialist struggle in our environment. Only in countries such as Argentina, where there is a large and rich bourgeoisie proud of their country's wealth and power and where the national character for this reason has clearer contours than in more backward countries, could anti-imperialism (perhaps) penetrate more easily among bourgeois elements. But this is for reasons related to capitalist expansion and development, rather than for reasons of social justice and socialist theory as in our case.

The betrayal by the Chinese bourgeoisie and the failure of the Kuomintang have not yet been understood in their full magnitude. Their capitalist style of nationalism (one not related to social justice or theory) demonstrates how little we can trust the revolutionary nationalist sentiments of the bourgeoisie, even in countries like China.

As long as the imperialists are able to "manage" the sentiments and formalities of these states' national sovereignty and are not forced to resort to armed intervention or military occupation, they can definitively count on the collaboration of their bourgeoisies. While they may depend upon the imperialist economy, these countries, or rather their bourgeoisies, consider themselves as much the masters of their own fate as Romania, Bulgaria, Poland, and the other "dependent states" of Europe.

This factor of political psychology should not be discounted in the precise estimation of the possibilities of anti-imperialist action in Latin America. Neglect of this matter has been one of the characteristics of Aprista theory.

The fundamental difference between us in Peru who originally accepted the APRA (as a project for a united front, never as a party or even as an effective organizer of struggle), and those outside Peru who later defined it as a Latin American Kuomintang, is that the former remain faithful to the revolutionary, socioeconomic conception of anti-imperialism; the latter, meanwhile, explain their position by saying: "We are leftists (or socialists) because we are anti-imperialists." Anti-imperialism thereby is raised to the level of a program, a political attitude, a movement that is valid in and of itself and that leads spontaneously to socialism, to the social revolution (how, we have no idea). This idea inordinately overestimates the anti-imperialist movement, exaggerates the myth of the struggle for a "second independence," and romanticizes that we are already living in the era of a new emancipation. This leads to the idea of replacing the anti-imperialist leagues with political parties. From an APRA initially conceived as a united front, a popular alliance, a bloc of oppressed classes, we pass to an APRA defined as the Latin American Kuomintang.

For us, anti-imperialism does not and cannot constitute, by itself, a political program for a mass movement capable of conquering state power. Anti-imperialism, even if it could mobilize the nationalist bourgeoisie and petty bourgeoisie on the side of the worker and peasant masses (and we have already definitively denied this possibility), does not annul class antagonisms nor suppress different class interests.

Neither the bourgeoisie nor the petty bourgeoisie in power can carry out anti-imperialist politics. To demonstrate this we have the experience of Mexico, where the petty bourgeoisie has just allied with Yankee imperialism. In its relations with the United States, a "nationalist" government might use different language than the Leguía government of Peru. This government is clearly, unabashedly Pan-Americanist and Monroeist. But any other bourgeois government would carry out the same practical policies on loans and concessions. Foreign capital investment in Peru grows in direct and close relation to the country's economic development, the exploitation of its natural riches, its population, and the improvement of its routes of communication. How can the most demagogic petty bourgeois oppose this capitalist penetration? With nothing but words; with nothing but a quick, nationalist fix. The taking of power by anti-imperialism, if it were possible, would not represent the taking of power by the proletarian masses, by socialism. The socialist revolution will find its most bloody and dangerous enemy (dangerous because of their confusionism and demagogy) in those petty bourgeois placed in power by the voices of order.

Without ruling out the use of any type of anti-imperialist agitation or any action to mobilize those social sectors that might eventually join the struggle, our mission is to explain to and show the masses that only the socialist revolution can stand as a definitive and real barrier to the advance of imperialism.

These factors differentiate the situation of the South American countries from that of the Central American nations. There, Yankee imperialism, by resorting to armed intervention without the slightest hesitation, does provoke a patriotic reaction that could easily win a part of the bourgeoisie and petty bourgeoisie to an anti-imperialist perspective. Aprista propaganda, conducted personally by Haya de la Torre, has obtained better results here than in any other part of America. His confusionist and messianic perorations, which claim to be related to the economic struggle, actually appeal to racial and emotional factors, thereby meeting the necessary conditions for impressing the petty bourgeois intellectual. Class parties and powerful, clearly class-conscious union organizations are not destined for the same quick growth here as in South America. In our countries, the class factor is more decisive and more developed. There is no reason to resort to vague populist formulas behind which reactionary tendencies can only prosper. At the moment, *Aprismo*, as propaganda, is limited to Central America; in South America, it is being totally liquidated, a consequence of the populist, "bossist," and petty bourgeois deviation that sees it as a Latin American Kuomintang. The next Anti-Imperialist Congress in Paris, which will have to unify the anti-imperialist organizations and distinguish between anti-imperialist programs and agitation and the tasks of class parties and trade unions, will put an absolute end to this question.

Do the interests of imperialist capitalism necessarily and inevitably coincide with the feudal and semi-feudal interests of our countries' landowning classes? Is the struggle against feudalism unavoidably and completely identical with the anti-imperialist struggle? Certainly, imperialist capitalism uses the power of the feudal class to the degree that it considers it the politically dominant class. But their economic interests are not the same. The petty bourgeoisie, even the most demagogic, can end up in the same intimate alliance with imperialist capitalism if it, in practice, dilutes its most conspicuous nationalist impulses. Finance capital would feel more secure if power were in the hands of a larger social class that is in a better position than the old, hated feudal class to defend the interests of capitalism and serve as its guard and water boy by satisfying certain overdue demands and distorting the masses' class orientation. The creation of a class of smallholders, the expropriation of the latifundia, and the liquidation of feudal privileges are not in opposition to the interests of imperialism in an immediate sense. On the contrary, to the degree that feudal vestiges still remain despite the growth of the capitalist economy, the movement for the liquidation of feudal privileges coincides with the interests of capitalist development as promoted by imperialist experts and investments. The disappearance of the large latifundia, the creation of an agrarian economy through what bourgeois demagoguery calls the "democratization" of the land, the displacement of the old aristocracies by a more powerful bourgeoisie and petty bourgeoisie better able to guarantee social peace: none of this is contrary to imperialist interests. The Leguía regime in Peru, as timid as it has been in regard to the interests of the *latifundistas* and *gamonales* (who support it to a great degree), has no problem resorting to demagogy, declaiming against feudalism and feudal privilege, thundering against the old oligarchies, and promoting a program of land distribution to make every field worker a small landowner. *Leguiísmo* draws its greatest strength from precisely this type of demagogy. *Leguísmo* does not dare lay a hand on the large landowners. But the natural direction of capitalist development—irrigation works, the exploitation of new mines, etc.— is in contradiction to the interests and privileges of feudalism. To the degree that the amount of cultivated land increases and new centers of employment appear, the *latifundistas* lose their principal power: the absolute and unconditional control of labor. In Lambayeque, where a water diversion project has been started by the American engineer Sutton, the technical commission has already run up against the interests of the large feudal landowners. These landowners grow mainly sugar. The threat that they will lose their monopoly of land and water, and thereby their means of controlling the work force, infuriates these people and pushes them toward attitudes that the government considers subversive, no matter how closely it is connected to these elements. Sutton has all the characteristics of the North American capitalist businessman. His outlook and his work clash with the feudal spirit of the *latifundistas*. For example, Sutton has established a system of water distribution that is based on the principle that these resources belong to the state; the *latifundistas* believe that water rights are part of their right to the land. By this theory, the water was theirs; it was and is the absolute property of their estates.

And is the petty bourgeoisie, whose role in the struggle against imperialism is so often overestimated, necessarily opposed to imperialist penetration because of economic exploitation? The petty bourgeoisie is undoubtedly the social class most sensitive to the fascination of nationalist mythology. But the economic factor which predominates is the following: in countries afflicted with Spanish-style poverty, where the petty bourgeoisie, locked in decades-old prejudice, resists proletarianization; where, because of their miserable wages, they do not have the economic power to partially transform themselves into a working class; where the desperate search for office employment, a petty government job, and the hunt for a "decent" salary and a "decent" job dominate, the creation of large enterprises that represent better-paid jobs, even if they enormously exploit their local employees, is favorably received by the middle classes. A Yankee business represents a better salary, possibilities for advancement, and liberation from dependence on the state, which can only offer a future to speculators. This reality weighs decisively on the consciousness of the petty bourgeois looking for or in possession of a position. In these countries with Spanish-style poverty, we repeat, the situation of the middle classes is not the same as in those countries where these classes have gone through a period of free competition and of capitalist development favorable to individual initiative and success and to oppression by the giant monopolies.

In conclusion, we are anti-imperialists because we are Marxists, because we are revolutionaries, because we oppose capitalism with socialism, an antagonistic system called upon to transcend it, and because in our struggle against foreign imperialism we are fulfilling our duty of solidarity with the revolutionary masses of Europe.

PART V
Marxism and Philosophy

It is a central paradox of Marxism that a social revolution, while prepared by objective developments, must be carried out by conscious historical subjects. Won to Marxist ideas in the international crisis after World War I, Mariátegui, like many young intellectuals, was attracted to their active and creative side as exemplified by Lenin and the Bolshevik Party. And throughout his career, Mariátegui felt compelled to polemicize with the timid positivism and evolutionism of the Second International, not only for its reformist politics, but also for its lack of heroism and spirit. Readers will decide for themselves whether his controversial appeal to the authority of various idealist philosophies and concepts like Georges Sorel's "revolutionary myth" compromises the materialism of his social and political analysis (but let them refer to the critique of mechanical materialism in the first of Marx's "Theses on Feuerbach," the echoes of Gramsci's use of Romain Rolland's epigram, "Pessimism of the intelligence, optimism of the will," and the closing phrase of "Anniversary and Balance Sheet" in a previous section: ". . . we never feel ourselves more fiercely, effectively, and religiously idealistic than when putting our ideas and our feet on the ground"). The first three essays in this section were written in 1925 for the liberal weekly *Mundial*, and later edited by Mariátegui for inclusion in a book, *El alma matinal* (The Dawning Spirit), which was published only after his death. Similarly, the last four were published in *Amauta* from 1927 to 1929, then edited for a posthumously published critique of Belgian Social Democrat Henri de Man, *Defensa del Marxismo* (Defense of Marxism). Mariátegui himself recognized the unorthodoxy of his philosophical ideas, commenting that the Argentine Communist journal *Vanguardia* would probably have rejected the latter manuscript.

Two Conceptions of Life*

I

The world war has not merely changed or shattered the economy and politics of the West. It has also changed or shattered its outlook and spirit. Its economic consequences, set forth and interpreted by John Maynard Keynes, are no more evident or observable than its spiritual and psychological consequences. Through a series of experiments, politicians and statesmen will perhaps hit upon a formula and method to resolve the former. But they will certainly find no theory and practice adequate to negate the latter. It seems to me more probable that they will have to adapt their programs to the pressure of the spiritual atmosphere, whose influence their work cannot evade. What differentiates the people of this era is not only ideology, but, above all, emotion. Two opposing conceptions of life, one pre-war, the other post-war, obstruct the mutual intelligibility of people who seemingly serve the same historical interest. Here is the central conflict of the contemporary crisis.

Evolutionist, historicist, and rationalist philosophy united the two antagonistic classes in the pre-war period, above and beyond political and social boundaries. Material well-being and the physical power of the modern city had produced a superstitious respect for the idea of Progress. Humanity seemed to have found a definite path. Conservatives and revolutionaries in practice accepted the consequences of the evolutionist thesis. Both concurred in a similar adherence to the idea of progress and a similar aversion to violence.

There was no lack of people whom this foolish and convenient philosophy could not seduce or captivate. Georges Sorel, for example, one of the keenest writers of pre-war France, denounced the illusion of progress. Don Miguel de Unamuno preached quixotism. But the majority of Europeans had lost the taste for adventure and heroic myths. Democracy won the favor of the socialist and trade union masses, pleased by their easy, gradual gains, proud of their cooperatives, their organization, their "peoples' centers," and their bureaucracy. The captains and orators of the class struggle enjoyed a safe popularity, which calmed all their souls' revolutionary fancy. The bourgeoisie let themselves be led by intelligent and progressive leaders who, convinced of the stupidity and imprudence of a policy of persecuting the

---

* *Mundial*, January 9, 1925.

ideas and members of the proletariat, preferred a policy intended to domesticate and mollify them with shrewd agreements.

A decadent and effete mood subtly spread through the upper strata of society. The Italian critic Adriano Tilgher, in one of his remarkable essays, defines the last generation of the Parisian bourgeoisie in the following manner:

> Product of a mostly secular civilization, sated with experience and reflection, analytical and introspective, artificial and bookish, it was the lot of the generation that grew up before the war to live in a world that seemed forever consolidated and secured against all possibility of change. And it adapted effortlessly to this world. As a generation, it was all nerves and brain, spent and exhausted by the great strain of its predecessors. It could not bear tenacious effort, prolonged tension, abrupt convulsions, loud voices, bright lights, open and stormy air; it loved shadow and twilight, dulcet and discreet light, muffled and distant sounds, measured and regular movement.

The ideal of this generation was to live gently.

II

When the European atmosphere became electrically supercharged as the war neared, the nervous system of this sensuous, elegant, and hyperesthetic generation suffered an unusual malaise and a strange nostalgia. Somewhat bored with "living gently," they trembled with morbid appetite and unhealthy desire. Almost anxiously, almost impatiently, they demanded war. War did not seem a tragedy, a cataclysm, but a sport, a stimulant, a spectacle. Well, war—like in a novel by Jean Bernier, who foresaw and foretold it—"War would be quite chic."

But the war did not correspond to this frivolous and stupid prediction. War did not wish to be so mediocre. Paris felt the claw of this martial drama in its gut. Europe, burned and lacerated, shed its mentality and psychology.

All the romantic energy of Western man, anesthetized by the long decades of easy and unctuous peace, was reborn, tempestuous and powerful. The cult of violence revived. The Russian Revolution filled socialist theory with a warlike and mythic spirit. And the fascist phenomenon followed on the Bolshevik phenomenon. Bolsheviks and fascists did not seem like the pre-war revolutionaries and conservatives. They lacked the old superstition of progress. They were witness, conscious or unconscious, that the war had shown humanity that events beyond the prescience of Science and contrary to the interests of Civilization could still occur.

The bourgeoisie, frightened by Bolshevik violence, called upon fascist violence. It had little faith that legal efforts were enough to defend it from the assaults of the revolution. But, little by little, nostalgia for the crass pre-war tranquility soon appeared in its psyche. This high-tension life disgusts and tires it. The old socialist and trade union bureaucracy shares this nostalgia. Why not, they ask, go back to the good old days before the war? A similar sentiment toward life spiritually connects and harmonizes these sectors of the bourgeoisie and the proletariat, who work as silent partners to disempower both Bolshevik and fascist methods. This episode of the contemporary crisis has its most clear and precise contours in Italy. Here, the old bourgeois guard has abandoned fascism and has joined the old socialist guard on the field of democracy. The program of all these people is condensed into a single word: normalization. Normalization would mean the return to the tranquil life, the dismissal or burial of all the romanticism, heroism, and quixotism of the right and the left: no regression, with the fascists, to the Middle Ages; no advance, with the Bolsheviks, toward Utopia.

Fascism speaks a belligerent and violent language that alarms those whose only ambition is normalization. Mussolini has said in a speech:

> It is not worth the trouble to live like men and as a party, and especially not to call oneself fascist, if we don't realize that we are in the middle of a storm. Anyone can sail in fair weather, when the wind fills the sails, when there are no waves or hurricanes. The beautiful, the great, and, I would say, the heroic is to sail when the tempest grows stronger. A German philosopher said, "Live dangerously." I would like this to be the slogan of young Italian fascism: Live dangerously. This means being ready for any sacrifice, any danger, any action to defend the fatherland and fascism.

Fascism does not imagine the counterrevolution as a vulgar police affair, but as an epic and heroic enterprise. This is an excessive, incandescent, exorbitant idea to the old bourgeoisie, which absolutely does not want to go so far. Let it stop and frustrate the revolution, certainly, but with good manners, if possible. The club should be used only in extreme cases. And in any case, one shouldn't touch the constitution or the parliament. One should leave things as they were. The old bourgeoisie wants to live gently and legally—"freely and peacefully," as the *Corriere della Serra* of Milan wrote, polemicizing with Mussolini. But both terms signify the same desire.

The revolutionaries, on their part, like the fascists, propose to live dangerously. An analogous romantic impulse, a similar quixotic spirit, can be seen and observed among the revolutionaries as among the fascists.

The new humanity, in both its antithetical expressions, claims a new insight into life. This insight does not appear solely in the belligerent prose of politicians. We find this phrase in some of the digressions of Luis Bello: "I think it appropriate to correct Descartes. I fight, therefore I am." This correction is opportune. The philosophical formula of a rationalist age had to be "I think, therefore I am." But the same formula does not serve this romantic, revolutionary, and quixotic age. Life, more than thought, now wishes to be action, that is, struggle. Modern humanity has need of faith.

And the only faith that can fill its deepest self is a combative faith. Who knows when the time of living gently will return. The gentle, pre-war life generated only skepticism and nihilism. And from the crisis of this skepticism and nihilism is born the rude, powerful, peremptory necessity of a faith and a myth that moves humanity to live dangerously.

Man and Myth*

I

All the modern intellect's investigations into the world crisis arrive at a unanimous conclusion: bourgeois civilization suffers from the lack of myth, of faith, of hope. This lack is the expression of its material bankruptcy. The experience of rationalism has had the paradoxical effect of leading humanity to the disconsolate conviction that reason can offer no way forward. Rationalism has only served to discredit reason. Mussolini has said that demagogues have murdered the idea of liberty. It is undoubtedly truer to say that the rationalists have murdered the idea of reason. Reason has eradicated the remains of the ancient myths from the soul of bourgeois civilization. For some time now, Western man has raised reason and science to the place of the old gods. But neither reason nor science can be myth. Neither reason nor science can satisfy all the need of the infinite that exists in man. Reason itself has been charged with demonstrating to humanity that it is not enough, that only myth possesses the precious virtue of satisfying its deepest self.

Reason and science have corroded and dissolved the prestige of the ancient religions. Eucken, in his book on the meaning and value of life, clearly and skillfully explains the mechanism of this dissolution. The creations of science have given humanity a new sense of its power. Man, formerly overwhelmed by the supernatural, has suddenly discovered an enormous ability to correct and rectify nature. This sensation has removed the roots of the old metaphysics from his spirit.

But man, as philosophy defines him, is a metaphysical animal. He does not live productively without a metaphysical conception of life. Without

---

* *Mundial*, January 16, 1925.

myth, man's existence has no historical meaning. History is made by people possessed and enlightened by a higher belief and a superhuman hope; others are the anonymous chorus of the drama. The crisis of bourgeois civilization became evident the moment that this civilization displayed its lack of myth. In an era of haughty positivism, Renan melancholically pointed out the decline of religion and was disquieted for the future of European civilization. "Religious people," he wrote, "live by the spirit. By what will people live after us?" This despairing question still awaits a response.

Bourgeois civilization has fallen into skepticism. The war seemed to reanimate the myths of the liberal revolution: liberty, democracy, peace. But the bourgeois Allies soon sacrificed them to their interests and grudges at the Versailles Conference. The rejuvenation of these myths nevertheless served to allow the liberal revolution to be fulfilled in Europe. Their invocation condemned the surviving remnants of feudalism and absolutism in Eastern Europe, Russia, and Turkey. And, most of all, the war authentically and tragically proved the value of myth once more. The peoples capable of victory were those capable of a mass myth.

II

Modern man feels the peremptory need of myth. Skepticism is sterile, and humanity does not submit to sterility. An exasperating and at times impotent "will to create," so acute in post-war humanity, was already intense and categorical in pre-war humanity. A poem by Henri Frank, *The Dance behind the Ark*, is the document I have closest at hand regarding the condition of literature's spirit during the last years before the war. In this poem beats a great and profound emotion. This is why I especially wish to quote from it. Henri Frank speaks to us of his profound "will to create." As an Israelite, he first tries to illuminate his soul with faith in the god of Israel. This attempt is in vain. The words of his fathers' god sound foreign to our era. The poet does not understand them. He declares himself deaf to their meaning. As a modern man, the word from Sinai cannot captivate him. A dead faith cannot be revived. Their twenty centuries weigh upon them. "Israel has died from having given a God to the world." The voice of the modern world proposes its false and precarious myth: reason. But Henri Frank cannot accept it. "Reason," he says, "is not the universe."

"Reason without God is a room without a lamp."

The poet leaves in search of God. He has need to satisfy his thirst for the infinite, for eternity. But this pilgrimage is fruitless. The pilgrim should content himself with the illusion of daily life. "Ah, to know to boldly seize each moment—the fleeting hope and the ephemeral essence." He finally thinks that "truth is enthusiasm without hope." Man carries his truth within himself.

"If the ark is empty where you hoped to find the law, nothing is real but your dance."

III

Philosophers bring us a truth analogous to that of the poets. Modern philosophy has swept away the mediocre positivist edifice. It has illuminated and demarcated the modest confines of reason and has formulated the current ideas of myth and action. According to these theories, it is useless to seek an absolute truth. Today's truth will not be the truth of tomorrow. A truth is valid only for an era. We should content ourselves with a relative truth.

But this relativist language is not accessible or intelligible to the multitude. The multitude is not so subtle. Humanity resists following a truth that it does not believe absolute and supreme. It is futile to recommend the superiority of faith, of myth, of action. One must propose a faith, a myth, an action. Where are we to find a myth capable of spiritually reanimating this declining order?

This question exasperates the intellectual and spiritual anarchy of bourgeois civilization. Some souls struggle to restore the Middle Ages and the Catholic ideal. Others work for a return to the Renaissance and the classical ideal. Fascism, in its theoreticians' own words, assumes a medieval and Catholic sensibility; they imagine themselves representing the spirit of the Counter-reformation, but on the other hand claim to incarnate the idea of the nation, a typically liberal concept. Such theorizing seems to delight in the invention of the most affected sophisms. But all attempts to revive olden myths are destined to immediate failure. Every era wishes its own sense of the world. Nothing is more sterile than to try to revive an extinct myth. Jean Bloch, in an article published in the review *Europe*, writes some words of profound truth in this regard. In the Chartes cathedral, Bloch felt the wondrously believing voice of the far-off Middle Ages. But he warns how and how much this voice is foreign to the preoccupations of this epoch. "It would be mad," he writes, "to think that the same faith would repeat the same miracle. Seek around you, somewhere, for a new, active myth, capable of miracles, fit to fill the miserable with hope, rouse martyrs, and transform the world with promises of goodness and virtue. When you have found it, designated it, named it, you will absolutely not be the same person."

Ortega y Gasset speaks of the "disenchanted soul." Romain Rolland speaks of the "enchanted soul." Which of the two is right? Both souls coexist. The "disenchanted soul" of Ortega y Gasset is the soul of decadent bourgeois civilization. The "enchanted soul" of Romain Rolland is the soul of the forgers of a new civilization. Ortega y Gasset sees only the sunset, the twilight, *der Untergang*. Romain Rolland sees the sunrise, the dawn, *der Aufgang*. What most clearly and obviously differentiates the bourgeoisie and the proletariat in this era is myth. The bourgeoisie finally has no myth. It has become incredulous, skeptical, nihilist. The reborn liberal myth has already aged. The proletariat has a myth: the social revolution. It moves toward this myth with a vehement and active faith. The bourgeoisie denies; the proletariat affirms. The bourgeois mind amuses itself with a rationalist critique of the methods, the theories, the technique of the revolutionaries. What incomprehension! The revolutionaries' power is not in their science; it is in their faith, their passion, their will. It is a religious, mystical, spiritual power. It is the power of myth. Revolutionary emotion, as I wrote in an article on Gandhi, is a religious emotion. Religious motives have been displaced from the heavens to earth. They are not divine; they are human, social.

The religious, mystical, metaphysical character of socialism has been established for some time now. Georges Sorel, one of the greatest representatives of twentieth-century French thought, said in his *Reflections on Violence*:

> An analogy has been found between religion and revolutionary socialism, both of which propose the preparation and even the reconstruction of the individual for a gigantic task. But Bergson has taught us that not only religion can fill the region of the deepest self. Revolutionary myths can also fulfill the same purpose.

Renan, as Sorel himself recalls, notes the religious faith of the socialists, showing their resistance to all discouragement: "After each frustrated experiment, they begin again. They have not found the solution; they will find it. The thought that a solution does not exist has never arisen. Here is their power."

The same philosophy that teaches us the need for myth and faith is generally unable to understand the faith and myth of the new era: "the poverty of philosophy," as Marx put it. The professional intellects will not find the road of faith; the masses will find it. It will later fall to the philosophers to codify the thought that emerges from this great mass achievement. Were the philosophers of Roman decadence able to understand the language of Christianity? The philosophy of bourgeois decadence can have no better fate.

Pessimism of the Real and Optimism of the Ideal*

I

It seems to me that José Vasconcelos has found a formula concerning pessimism and optimism that not only defines the sentiment of the new Ibero-American generation in regard to the contemporary crisis, but also fully corresponds to the mentality and sensibility of a era in which, despite the theory of Don José Ortega y Gasset on the "disenchanted soul" and the "decline of revolutions," millions of people are working with a mystical courage and a religious passion to create a new world. "Pessimism of the real, optimism of the ideal" is Vasconcelos's formula.

"Never to resign ourselves, but to always be beyond and superior to the moment," writes Vasconcelos. "Repudiate reality and struggle to destroy it, not for a lack of faith, but for an excess of faith in human capacities and the firm conviction that evil is never permanent or justifiable, and that it is always possible and practical to redeem, purify, and improve the collective condition and the individual conscience."

The attitude of the person who proposes to rectify reality is, certainly, more optimistic than pessimistic. He is a pessimist in his protest and his condemnation of the present; but he is an optimist regarding his hope in the future. All the great human ideals have started with a negation, but all have also been an affirmation. Historically, religions have perennially represented this pessimism of reality and optimism of the ideal that this Mexican writer preaches in our time.

We who do not content ourselves with mediocrity, who resign ourselves even less to injustice, are frequently designated as pessimists. But, in fact, pessimism rules our spirit much less than optimism. We do not think that the world should be unalterably and eternally as it is. We think that it can and should be better. The optimism we reject is the facile and lazy panglossian optimism of those who think that we live in the best of all possible worlds.

---

* *Mundial*, August 21, 1925.

II

There are two types of pessimists, just as there are two types of optimists. The exclusively negative pessimist limits himself to establishing, with a gesture of impotence and desperation, the wretchedness of things and the uselessness of effort. He is a nihilist, melancholically awaiting his final disillusion. As Artzibachev said, the extreme case limits. But this type is fortunately uncommon. He belongs to a rare rank of disenchanted intellectuals. Moreover, he is a product of a decadent epoch or a people in ruin.

Among intellectuals, it is not unusual to find a feigned nihilism that serves as a philosophical pretext for their refusal to cooperate with any great effort of renovation or to explain their disdain for all mass work. But the fictitious nihilism of this class of intellectuals is not even a philosophical attitude. It reduces itself to a secret and artificial disdain for great human myths. It is an unconfessed nihilism that dares not rise to the surface of the work or life of the negative intellectual who gives himself up to this theoretical exercise as to a solitary vice. The intellectual, a nihilist in private, is likely to be a public member of a pro-temperance organization or a society for the prevention of cruelty to animals. The only purpose of his nihilism is to defend himself from or guard against grand passions. Before petty ideals, the false nihilist comports himself with the most vulgar idealism.

III

It is with pessimistic and negative spirits of this stripe that our optimist of the ideal refuses to allow himself to be confused. Absolutely negative attitudes are sterile. Action arises from negations and affirmations. The new generation of our America, as throughout the world, is above all a generation that shouts out its faith, that sings its hope.

IV

A skeptical disposition prevails in contemporary Western philosophy. This philosophical attitude, as its penetrating critics note, is an appropriate aspect of a civilization in decline. A disenchanted attitude toward life only flourishes in a decadent world. But not even this modern skepticism or relativism has any relationship or affinity with the cheap and false nihilism of the impotent, or with the absolute and morbid nihilism of the suicides and madmen of Andreyev and Artzibachev. Pragmatism, which so effectively moves humanity to action, is at bottom a relativist and skeptical school of thought. Hans Vaihinger, the author of *The Philosophy of "As If,"* has properly been classified as a pragmatist. For this German philosopher, there are no true absolutes;

but there are relative absolutes that govern human life as if they were absolute. "Moral principles, just like esthetic ones, legal criteria, just like the concepts upon which science operates, the very fundamentals of logic, all have no objective existence; they are our own fictitious constructs which only serve as regulatory precepts for our actions, which are conducted as if they were true." The Italian philosopher Guiseppe Rensi thus defines the philosophy of Vaihinger in his *Features of Skeptical Philosophy*, which, as I see in a bibliographical note in Ortega y Gasset's journal, has begun to attract attention in Spain, and therefore in Spanish America.

This philosophy, then, does not invite us to renounce action. It solely claims to deny the Absolute. But I recognize in human history the same value and efficacy for the temporal truth of each epoch as for an absolute and eternal truth. This philosophy proclaims and confirms the necessity of myth and the usefulness of faith. Although he entertains the thought that all truths and all fictions are finally equal, Einstein, a relativist, comports himself in his life as an optimist of the ideal.

V

The desire to overcome skeptical philosophy fires the new generation. In the contemporary chaos, the materials of a new mysticism are being elaborated. The world in birth will not place its hope where it was placed by fallen religions. "The strong persist and struggle," says Vasconcelos, "to hasten somewhat the work of heaven." The new generation wishes to be potent.

Modern Philosophy and Marxism[*]

In 1919, the poet Paul Valery sketched the following genealogical line in biblical language: "And Kant begot Hegel, who begot Marx, who begot. . . ." Although the Russian revolution was already in course, it was still too soon not to prudently content oneself with these ellipses in discussing the descendants

---

[*] Published in *Defense of Marxism* (1928).

of Marx. But in 1925, C. Achelin replaced them with the name of Lenin. And it is likely that Paul Valery himself would not find this too bold a manner of completing his thought.

Historical materialism recognizes three streams at its source: classical German philosophy, English political economy, and French socialism. This is precisely Lenin's concept. In conformity with it, Kant and Hegel precede and bring forth, first, Marx and, later, Lenin—we add him ourselves—in the same way that capitalism precedes and brings forth socialism. This obvious lineage of historical materialism is certainly not contrary to the attention that such conspicuous representatives of idealist philosophy as the Italians Croce and Gentile have dedicated to the philosophical background of Marx's thought. The transcendental dialectic of Kant prefigures the Marxist dialectic in the history of modern thought.

But this lineage does not signify the subjection of Marxism to Hegel or his philosophy, which, according to the famous phrase, Marx turned on its feet against the intent of its author, who left it on its head. In the first place, Marx never proposed the elaboration of a philosophical system of historical interpretation destined to serve as an instrument for carrying out his political and revolutionary ideas. His work is, in part, philosophical, because this type of speculation is not reducible to a system (in the proper sense of the word) in which, as Benedetto Croce warns—someone for whom any thought with a philosophical character is a philosophy—one at times only encounters outward appearances. Marx's materialist conception is born, dialectically, as the antithesis of Hegel's idealist conception. And this very relationship does not seem very clear even to critics as sagacious as Croce. "The connection between these two conceptions," says Croce, "seems to me more psychological than anything else, since Hegelianism was the pre-culture of the young Marx, and it is natural that everyone connect new to old ideas as evolution, as correction, as antithesis."

The efforts of those, such as Henri de Man, who summarily condemn Marxism as a simple product of nineteenth-century rationalism could therefore not be more hasty or capricious. Historical materialism is precisely not metaphysical or philosophical materialism, nor is it a Philosophy of History superseded by scientific progress. Marx had no reason to create anything more than a method of historical interpretation of modern society. Refuting Professor Stamler, Croce claims that "the presupposition of socialism is not a Philosophy of History, but a historical conception determined by the present conditions of society and the manner in which they have appeared." Marxist criticism studies capitalist society concretely. As long as capitalism has not been definitively overcome, Marx's canon remains valid. Socialism or, rather, the struggle to transform the social order from capitalism to collectivism keeps this critique alive, continues it, confirms it, corrects it. Any attempt to categorize it as a simple scientific theory is in vain, since it historically unfolds as the gospel and method of a mass movement. Because, as Croce also says, "historical materialism arose from the need to take account of a particular social configuration, not for the purpose of an investigation of the factors of historical existence; and it was developed in the minds of political leaders and revolutionaries, not those of cold and measured academic scholars."

Marx lives in the struggle for socialism unleashed throughout the world by the innumerable multitudes animated by his theories. The fate of the scientific or philosophical theories that he utilized, surpassed, and transcended as elements of his theoretical work do not in any way compromise the validity and relevance of his ideas. They are radically extraneous to the mutable fortunes of the scientific and philosophical ideas that accompany or immediately precede them.

Henri de Man formulated his criticism in the following manner:

Marxism is a child of the nineteenth century. Its origins go back to the epoch in which the reign of intellectual knowledge, which was begun by humanism and the Reformation, reached its apogee in the rationalist method. This method took its watchwords from the precise natural sciences, to which it owed the progress of productive technique and communications; it consists of transporting the principle of mechanical causality, which manifests itself in technology, to the interpretation of psychic actions. It sees rational thought, which modern psychology recognizes only in its function as regulator and inhibitor of the psyche, as the ruler of all human desire and all social development.

He adds that "Marx made a psychological synthesis of the philosophical thought of his era" (agreeing that it was "so singularly new and vigorous in the sociological realm itself that it is unjust to doubt its brilliant originality"), and that "what is expressed in Marx's theories is not the movement of ideas, which have only arisen from the depths of working-class life and social practice since his death; it is the causal materialism of Darwin and the teleological idealism of Hegel."

These are not very different from the unappealable sentences against Marxist socialism pronounced, on the one hand, by futurism and, on the other, by Thomism. Marinetti ties Marx, Darwin, Spencer, and Comte into a single bundle to more rapidly and implacably execute them, without taking account of the distance that might separate their equally nineteenth-century, and therefore exterminable, ideas. And the neo-Thomists, from the opposite extreme—the remonstrance of the medieval against modernity—find in socialism the logical conclusion of the Reformation and all Protestant, liberal, and individualist heresies. Thus de Man lacks even the merit of originality in his perfectly reactionary attempt to catalog Marxism among the most particular mental processes of the "stupid" nineteenth century.

It is unnecessary to defend that century against the contrived and superficial diatribes of its detractors to refute the author of *Beyond Marxism*. Nor is it necessary to show that Darwin, like Spenser and Comte, in any case, corresponds in different ways to the capitalist method of thought, like Hegel, from whom descends (as does the revolutionary rationalism of Marx and Engels) the conservative rationalism of historians who apply the formula "Everything that is rational is real" as a justification for despotism and plutocracy. Marx could not base his political plans or his historical theories on De Vries's biology, or Freud's psychology, or Einstein's physics, just as Kant had to content himself with Newtonian physics and the sciences of his era in elaborating his philosophy. Marxism—or rather, its intellectuals—in its later development, has continually assimilated the most substantive and relevant of post-Hegelian or post-rationalist philosophical and historical speculation. Georges Sorel, so influential in the spiritual formation of Lenin, illuminated the revolutionary socialist movement—with a talent that Henri de Man certainly must know, although his book omits any reference to the author of *Reflections on Violence*—in the light of Bergsonian philosophy, continuing Marx, who fifty years earlier had done this in the light of the philosophy of Hegel, Fichte, and Feuerbach. Revolutionary literature, despite the wishes of de Man, does not abound in erudite discourses on psychology, metaphysics, esthetics, etc., since it must attend to the concrete objectives of agitation and criticism. But outside the official party press, in journals like *Clarté* and *La Lutte des Classes* in Paris, *Unter den Banner des Marxismus* in Berlin, etc., one will find expressions of philosophical thought much more serious than his attempts at revisionism.

Vitalism, activism, pragmatism, relativism: none of these philosophical currents, insofar as they can bring something to the revolution, have remained marginal to the Marxist intellectual movement. William James is no stranger to Sorel's theory of socialist myth, which, on the other hand, was so markedly influenced by Wilfredo Pareto. And the Russian revolution, in Lenin, Trotsky, and others, has created a type of individual who thinks and acts, which should give certain shabby philosophers, full of all the rationalist prejudices and superstitions of which they imagine themselves purged and immune, something to consider.

Marx was the first of this type of man of action and thought. But this ideologue-actor appears with a clearer profile in the leaders of the Russian revolution. Lenin, Trotsky, Bukharin, and Lunarcharsky philosophize in theory and practice. Along with his works on the strategy of class struggle, Lenin left his *Materialism and Emperiocriticism*. In the midst of his comings and goings during the Civil War and the party discussion, Trotsky found time for his meditations on *Literature and Revolution*. And wasn't Rosa Luxemburg always both fighter and artist? Who among the professors that Henri de Man so admires live with more fullness and intensity of thought and action? The time will come, despite the conceited academics who now hoard their positions as the official representatives of culture, when the amazing woman who wrote such marvelous letters from prison to Luisa Kautsky will inspire the same devotion and find the same recognition as a Theresa de Avila. Her spirit, active and contemplative at the same time, more philosophic and modern than the pedantic crowd that ignores her, infused the tragic poetry of her life with a heroism, beauty, agony, and joy taught in no school of knowledge.

Instead of accusing Marxism of backwardness or indifference in respect to modern philosophy, it would be more appropriate to accuse the latter of a deliberate and fearful incomprehension of the class struggle and socialism. A liberal philosopher like Benedetto Croce—a real philosopher and a true liberal—had already raised this issue in unassailably just terms, before that other philosopher Giovanni Gentile, also an idealist and liberal and the continuator and interpreter of Hegelian thought, accepted a position in the brigades of fascism, in the promiscuous company of the most dogmatic neo-Thomists and the most flaming anti-intellectuals (Marinetti and his gang).

The bankruptcy of positivism and scientism as a philosophy in no way compromises the position of Marxism. Marx's theory and politics are invariably grounded in science, not scientism. And as Benda observes, all political programs now wish to base themselves on science, even the most reactionary and anti-historical. Doesn't Brunetiere, who proclaims the bankruptcy of science, hope to wed Catholicism and positivism? And doesn't Maurras also claim to be a child of scientific thought? If some belief must rise to the rank of a genuine religion, the religion of the future, as Waldo Frank thinks, will rest upon science.

Marxist Determinism[*]

Another common approach of intellectuals who entertain themselves by denigrating the Marxist oeuvre is to self-interestedly exaggerate the determinism of Marx and his school, with the aim of declaring them from this viewpoint a product of the mechanistic mentality of the nineteenth century, which is incompatible with the heroic, voluntaristic conception of life to which the

---

* Published in *Defense of Marxism* (1928).

modern world is inclined since the war. These reproaches do not accord with a critique of the rationalist and utopian superstitions and the mystical foundation of the socialist movement. But Henri de Man could not eschew an argument that so easily creates such commotion among twentieth-century intellectuals, who are seduced by the reactionary snobbism against the "stupid nineteenth century." The Belgian revisionist observes a certain prudence in this regard. He declares:

> One must point out that Marx does not merit the reproach that is frequently directed against him, that of being a fatalist, in the sense that he denies the influence of human will in historical development; actually, he considers this will to be predetermined.

He adds that "Marx's disciples are right when they defend their teacher from the reproach of having preached this type of fatalism." But none of this keeps him from accusing them of "a belief in another sort of fatalism, that of categorical, inevitable ends," since " . . . according to the Marxist conception, there is a social will, subject to laws, which is fulfilled by means of the class struggle and is the inevitable result of an economic evolution that creates opposed interests."

Neo-revisionism basically adopts the idealist critique that reaffirms the action of the will and spirit, although with discreet emendations. But this critique only pertains to social democratic orthodoxy, which, as we have already established, is not and was not Marxist but, rather, Lasallean—a fact proven by the vigor with which the slogan "Back to Lasalle" is disseminated inside German social democracy. For this critique to be valid, it would have to begin by proving that Marxism is social democracy, an effort that Henri de Man avoids attempting. On the contrary, he recognizes the Third International as the heir to the International Working Men's Association, in whose congresses breathed a mysticism quite close to that of the Christianity of the catacombs. And he corroborates this explicit judgment in his book:

> The vulgar Marxists of communism are the real usufructs of the Marxist heritage. Not in the sense that they understand Marx better in reference to his era, but because they more effectively use it for the tasks of their own era, to realize their objectives. The image of Marx that Kautsky offers us appears more like the original than the one Lenin popularized among his disciples. But Kautsky has expounded politics in which Marx has never prevailed, while the words that Lenin took from Marx as holy writ after his death are his very politics, and they continue creating new realities.

In his *The Agony of Christianity*, Unamuno praises a phrase attributed to Lenin that he once pronounced in contradicting someone who observed that his efforts went against reality: "So much the worse for reality!" Marxism, where it has shown itself to be revolutionary—that is, where it has been Marxist—has never obeyed a passive and rigid determinism. The reformists opposed the revolution during the post-war revolutionary wave with the most rudimentary economic determinist arguments—arguments that were basically identified with the conservative bourgeoisie and that gave notice of the absolutely bourgeois and non-socialist character of such determinism. To the majority of its critics, the Russian revolution appears rather as a rationalist, romantic, anti-historical effort of utopian fanatics. All caliber of reformists primarily rebuked the revolutionaries' tendency to force history, censuring the tactics of the Third International's parties as "Blanquist" and "putschist."

Marx could only conceive or propose realistic politics, and he therefore carried to extremes his demonstration that the very processes of the capitalist economy lead to socialism to the degree they are fully and energetically realized. But he always understood the spiritual and intellectual capacity of the proletariat to create a new order through the class struggle to be its necessary condition. Before Marx, the modern world had already reached the moment when no political and social doctrine could appear in contradiction to history and science. The decline of religion has its quite visible origin in its increasing alienation from historical and scientific experience. And it would be absurd to ask a political idea like socialism, so eminently modern in all its aspects, to be indifferent to this order of consideration. As Benda observes in his book *The Treason of the Intellectuals*, all contemporary political movements, starting with the most reactionary, are characterized by their efforts to attribute to themselves a strict correspondence with the course of history. For the reactionaries of *Action française*, who are literally more positivist than any revolutionary, the whole period inaugurated by the liberal revolution is monstrously romantic and anti-historical. The limits and function of Marxist determinism have been fixed for some time. Critics alien to any party criteria, such as Adriano Tilgher, subscribe to the following interpretation:

> Socialist tactics, to lead to success, must take into account the historical situation in which they must operate, and where this is still too immature for the installation of socialism, they must certainly avoid having their hand forced. But, on the other hand, they must not quietistically defer to the course of events, but rather, inserting themselves in this advance, always tend even more to orient them in a socialist sense so as to make them ripe for the final transformation. Marxist tactics are thus as dynamic and dialectical as Marxist theory itself. The socialist will does not agitate in a vacuum, does not disregard the pre-existing situation, does not delude himself that he can change things with calls to humanity's better emotions, but cleaves solidly to historical reality, without resigning himself passively to it. Rather, it reacts against them always more energetically in the sense of economically and spiritually reinforcing the working

class, accentuating its consciousness of its conflict with the bourgeoisie, until, having reached the end of its rope and the bourgeoisie having reached the end of the power of the capitalist regime and become an obstacle for the productive forces, they can be usefully overthrown and replaced by a socialist regime, to everyone's advantage (*La Crisi Mondiale e Saggi critice di Marxismo e Socialismo*).

The voluntarist character of socialism is really no less evident than its determinist foundation, even if it is less understood by critics. To give it its true value, though, it is nevertheless enough to follow the development of the proletarian movement from the actions of Marx and Engels in London at the origin of the First International to the present, dominated by the first experience of a socialist state: the USSR. Every word, every act of Marxists in this process has a resonance of faith, of will, of heroic and creative conviction, whose impulse it would be absurd to seek in a mediocre and passive determinist sensibility.

The Heroic and Creative Meaning of Socialism*

All those, like Henri de Man, who preach and proclaim an ethical socialism based on humanitarian principles, instead of contributing in some way to the moral elevation of the working class, unconsciously and paradoxically work against its advancement as a creative and heroic force, that is, against its civilizing role. By way of "moral" socialism and such anti-materialist chatter, one can only manage to relapse into the most sterile and lachrymose humanitarian romanticism, the most decadent, "pariah-like" apologetics, and the most sentimental and useless plagiarism of evangelical epigrams about the "poor in spirit." And this is tantamount to returning socialism to its romantic, utopian period, when its demands were mostly nurtured by the sentiments and ramblings of an aristocracy that, after having entertained itself in an idyllic, eighteenth-century way by dressing as shepherds and shepherdesses and being converted to the Encyclopedia and liberalism, strangely

---

* Published in *Defense of Marxism* (1928).

dreamed of nobly leading a revolution of the shirtless helots. Obeying a tendency to sublimate one's emotions, this type of socialist—whose services no one thinks of denying, and among whom some extraordinary and admirable spirits rise to great heights—pulled from the gutter the sentimental clichés and demagogic images of the era of sansculottes so as to inaugurate a paradisiacally Rousseauean age throughout the world. But, as we have known for some time, this was absolutely not the road to socialist revolution. Marx discovered and taught that one had to begin by understanding the necessity and, especially, the value of the capitalist stage. Socialism, after Marx, appeared as the conception of a new class, as a theory and movement that had nothing in common with the romanticism of those who repudiated the work of capitalism as an abomination. The working class has succeeded the bourgeoisie in the work of civilization. And it assumed this mission, conscious of its responsibility and capacity—gained in revolutionary activity and the capitalist factory—when the bourgeoisie, having fulfilled its destiny, ceased being a force for progress and culture.

For this reason, Marx's work has a certain tone of admiration for the work of capitalism, and *Capital*, as it lays the bases for socialist science, is the best history of the epoch of capitalism (something that seemingly does not escape Henri de Man's view, but that does in its deeper sense).

Ethical, pseudo-Christian, humanitarian socialism, which anachronistically tries to oppose itself to Marxist socialism, might be the more or less lyric and innocuous exercise of a tired and decadent bourgeoisie, but not the theory of a class that has reached its adulthood, overcoming the greatest objectives of the capitalist class. Marxism is completely foreign and contrary to these mediocre, altruistic, and philanthropic speculations. We Marxists do not believe that the job of creating a new social order, superior to the capitalist order, falls to an amorphous mass of oppressed pariahs led by evangelical preachers of goodness. The revolutionary energy of socialism is not nurtured by compassion or envy. In the class struggle, where all the sublime and heroic elements of its ascent reside, the working class must elevate itself to a "producers' morality," quite distant and distinct from the "slave morality" that its gratuitous professors of morals, horrified by its materialism, officiously attempt to provide. A new civilization cannot arise from a sad and humiliated world of miserable helots with no greater merits or faculties than their servility and misery. The working class only enters history politically, as a social class, at the moment it discovers its mission to build a superior social order with elements gathered by human effort, whether moral or amoral, just or unjust. And it has not gained this ability miraculously. It has won it by situating itself solidly on the terrain of the economy, of production. Its class morale depends on the energy and heroism with which it operates on this terrain, and the extent to which it understands and masters the bourgeois economy.

De Man touches upon this truth at times, but he generally avoids adopting it. He thus writes, for example, "The essential part of socialism is the struggle for it. According to the formula of a representative of the German Socialist Youth, the purpose of our existence is not paradisiacal, but heroic." But this is not exactly the conception that inspires the thought of the Belgian revisionist, who, a few pages before, confesses, "I feel closer to reformist than extremist practice, and I value a new sewer in a working-class neighborhood or a flower garden in front of a worker's house more than a new theory of class struggle." In the first part of his book, de Man criticizes the tendency to idealize the working class, just as the peasant, the primitive, simple man, was idealized in the age of Rousseau. And this indicates that his thinking and practice are almost solely based on the humanitarian socialism of intellectuals.

It is undoubtedly true that this humanitarian socialism has been propagated more than a bit among the working masses. The Internationale, the hymn of the revolution, addresses itself in its first verse to the "wretched of the earth," a phrase clearly reminiscent of the gospels. The spirit of its motivation becomes clear if we recall that the author of these words is a popular French poet of a purely bohemian and romantic stripe. The work of another Frenchman, the great Henri Barbusse, is impregnated with this same sentiment: the idealization of the mass—the timeless, eternal mass, the caryatidic mass—upon which the glory of heroes and the burden of culture weighs oppressively. But this mass is not the modern proletariat, and its generic demands are not revolutionary and socialist.

The particular merit of Marx consists in having discovered the working class in this sense. As Adriano Tilgher writes:

> Marx stands before history as the discoverer, one could almost say the *inventor*, of the working class. In effect, he not only has given the proletarian movement the consciousness of its nature, legitimacy, and historical necessity, of its internal laws and the ultimate goal toward which it is moving, and has thus imbued the working class with the consciousness which it had previously lacked; he has created, one could say, the very idea, and besides the idea, the reality of the working class as the class essentially antithetical to the bourgeoisie, and the true and sole bearer of the revolutionary spirit in modern industrial society.

Materialist Idealism*

A friend and comrade whose intelligence I greatly appreciate writes to me that, in his opinion, the merit of Henri de Man's work is as an effort to spiritualize Marxism. In his dual role as intellectual and academic, my friend is right to have been scandalized at more than one gathering by the simplistic and elemental materialism of its orthodox catechists. I am aware of many such cases, and I myself had this experience in the early stages of my investigations into the revolutionary phenomenon. But even without advancing practically with this investigation, it is enough to consider the nature of the ingredients with which such a judgment contents itself to see its uselessness. My friend would find it absurd to claim to understand and appraise Catholicism through the sermons of a parish priest. He would demand a serious and profound treatment of scholasticism and mysticism in such a critique. And any honest investigator would join him in such a demand. How, then, can he agree with a first-year philosophy student who has just picked up a distaste and disdain for Marxism from a phrase of his professor about the need to spiritualize this theory, too gross for the academic palate as it is understood and propagated by its vulgarizers at a meeting?

Above all, what kind of spiritualization do we want? If capitalist civilization, in a decline similar to that of Roman civilization in so many ways, renounces its own philosophic thought and abdicates its own scientific certitude in search of drug-like Oriental occultism and Asian metaphysics, then the best sign of the health and power of socialism as the source of a new civilization is undoubtedly its resistance to all these spiritualist ecstasies. In comparison with the return of the decadent and menaced bourgeoisie to mythologies that did not trouble it in its youth, the most solid affirmation of the creative power of the proletariat would be its peremptory rejection of and comical contempt for the afflictions and nightmares of a menopausal spiritualism.

Against the sentimental—and non-religious—raptures, the extra-worldly nostalgias, of a class that senses its mission to be concluded, a new ruling class disposes of no more valid defense than its confirmation of the materialist principles of its revolutionary philosophy. What would distinguish socialist thinking that began by sharing all the clandestine tastes of the most senile and rotten capitalist thought? No, nothing is more nonsensical than to suppose

---

* Published in *Defense of Marxism* (1928).

that the incipient tendency of a professor or banker to revere Krishnamurti, or at least to show himself able to understand his message, is a sign of superiority. None of his clients asks the same banker, no one in his audience asks the same professor, that they show themselves similarly capable of understanding Lenin's message.

What person who follows the development of modern thought with critical lucidity can fail to note that the return to spiritualist ideas, the escape to Asian paradises, has clearly decadent causes and origins? Marxism, as philosophical reflection, discovers the work of capitalist thought at the point where it abandons its forward march and begins its retreat, hesitating before its extreme consequences, a hesitation that precisely corresponds on the economic and political plane to a crisis of the liberal bourgeois system. The mission of Marxism is to continue this work. Revisionists like Henri de Man, who, according to the phrase of Vandervelde, de-bone Marxism for fear of appearing backward in relation to philosophical attitudes of a clearly reactionary impulse, intend nothing else than an apostatized rectification in which socialism would attenuate its materialist premises to the point of making them acceptable to spiritualists and theologians for the frivolous purpose of adapting itself to current fashion.

The first false position in this reflection is that of supposing that a materialist conception of the universe is not suitable for producing great spiritual values. The theological—and not philosophical—prejudices that cling to minds that imagine themselves free of vanquished dogmatisms lead them to associate materialist philosophy with an unrefined existence. Innumerable historical examples contradict this arbitrary idea. The biographies of Marx, Sorel, Lenin, and a thousand other protagonists of socialism find nothing to envy as to moral beauty and the full affirmation of the power of the spirit in the biographies of those heroes and ascetics who had earlier worked in accord with a spiritual or religious conception, in the classical sense of these words. The USSR combats bourgeoisie ideology with the most extreme weapons of materialism. The work of the USSR nevertheless tests the current limits of rationalism and spirituality in its declarations and objectives, if the object of rationalism and spiritualism is to improve and ennoble life. Do those who aspire to a spiritualization of Marxism believe that the creative spirit is less present and active in the actions of those who struggle for a new world order than among those New York moneylenders and industrialists who, marking the moment of capitalist exhaustion, disown potent Nietzschean ethics—the sublimated morality of capitalism—to flirt with fakirs and occultists? Just as Christian metaphysics have not kept the West from great material accomplishments, Marxist materialism, as I have already claimed at other occasions, encompasses all of our era's possibilities for moral, spiritual, and philosophical ascent.

Piero Gobetti, a disciple and heir of Crocean idealism, has considered the most active and pure part of this problem in admirably proper terms. Gobetti writes:

> Christianity reached the world of truth inside us, the intimacy of our spirit, and pointed out to humanity a duty, a mission, a redemption. But having abandoned Christian dogma, we have found richer, more conscious, more actionable spiritual values. Our problem is moral and political. Our philosophy sanctifies the value of practice. Everything is reduced to a criterion of human responsibility; if the earthly struggle is the only reality, everyone has value insofar as they work, and it is all of us that make our own history. This is progress because ever richer new experiences unfold. It is not a matter of reaching a goal or denying oneself through an ascetic renunciation; it is a matter of always more intensely and consciously being oneself, of overcoming the chains of our weakness in a perpetual superhuman effort. The new criterion of truth is work that is adequate to each person's responsibility. We are in the era of struggle (the struggle of man against man, of class against class, of state against state), because only through struggle are capabilities tempered and does everyone, intransigently defending their position, collaborate in the vital process that has transcended the death of Greek asceticism and objectivism.

A Latin mind could not find a more classically precise formula than this: "Our philosophy sanctifies the value of practice."

The classes that have succeeded in dominating society have always disguised their material interests with a mythology that credits the idealism of its conduct. Since socialism, consistent with its philosophical premises, renounces this anachronistic garb, all spiritualistic superstitions rebel against it, in a conclave of international Pharisaism to whose holy decisions timid intellectuals and ingenuous academics feel obliged to appear considerate.

But because bourgeois philosophical thought has lost that security and stoicism with which it wished to be characterized in its affirmative and revolutionary era, should socialism imitate its withdrawal to the Thomist cloister or its pilgrimage to the pagoda of the living Buddha, following the Parisian itinerary of Jean Cocteau or the tourism of Paul Morand? Who are more idealistic in the higher, abstract sense of the word, the idealists of the bourgeois order or the materialists of the socialist revolution? And if the word *idealism* is discredited and compromised by its service to systems that signify all the old class interests and privileges, what historical need has socialism of resorting to its protection? Idealist philosophy is historically the philosophy of liberal society and the bourgeois order. And we already know the results that it has theoretically and practically given since the bourgeoisie has become conservative. For every Benedetto Croce who loyally develops this philosophy and denounces the inflamed conspiracy of academia against socialism, which is unrecognized as an idea that arises from the development of liberalism, how many Giovanni Gentiles serve a party whose ideologues are sectarian supporters of a spiritual restoration of the Middle Ages who repudiate modernity in toto? During the era when the formula "All that is real is rational" sufficed against egalitarian rationalism and utopianism, the historicist and evolutionist bourgeoisie dogmatically and forcibly disposed of almost all "idealists." Now that the myths of History and Evolution no longer serve to resist socialism, they become anti-historicist, reconcile with all religions and superstitions, favor the return to transcendence and theology, adopt the principles of the reactionaries whom they furiously fought when they were revolutionary and liberal, and once again discover the solicitous suppliers of all sermons useful for the rejuvenation of the oldest myths in the ranks and leading circles of a "one size fits all" idealist philosophy (neoKantian, neopragmatist, etc.), whether dandies and gallants like Count Keyserling or pamphleteers and provincials à la Leon Bloy, like Domenico Giulliotti.

It is possible that academics who are vaguely sympathizers of Marx and Lenin, but more particularly of Jaurés and Macdonald, feel the lack of a feverishly spiritual socialist theory or literature with abundant citations from Keyserling, Scheller, Stammler, and even Steiner and Krishnamurti. It is logical that Henri de Man's revisionism, and others of lesser distinction, would find disciples and admirers among such elements, who are often ignorant of any serious knowledge of Marxism. Few among them will bother to investigate if the ideas of *Beyond Marxism* are at least original, or if, as Vandervelde himself certifies, they add nothing to the older revisionist critique.

Both Henri de Man and Max Eastman draw their best arguments from the critique of the materialist conception of history formulated some years ago in the following terms by Professor Brandenberg:

> It wishes to base all the *variations* of the collective life of humanity in the changes that take place in the realm of productive forces, but it cannot explain why the latter must constantly change, and why this change must necessarily occur in the direction of socialism.

Bukharin responds to this criticism in an appendix to *Historical Materialism*. But it is easier and more convenient to content oneself with reading Henri de Man than to investigate his sources and inform oneself of the arguments of Bukharin and Professor Brandenberg, which are circulated less widely by news distributors.

On the other hand, the following proposition is peculiar and exclusive to Henri de Man's attempt to spiritualize socialism:

> Living values are superior to material ones, and among living values, the highest ones are spiritual. Eudemonistically, this could be expressed as follows: Under equal conditions, the most desirable satisfactions are those

which one feels in one's conscience when reflecting what is most enduring in the reality of the self and the medium that surrounds it.

This arbitrary categorization of values has no other purpose than to satisfy
those pseudo-socialists who wish to be furnished a formula equivalent to
that of the neo-Thomists: "the primacy of the spirit." Henri de Man could
never satisfactorily explain how living values differ from material ones. And
to distinguish material from spiritual values would require a reliance on the
most archaic dualism.

In the previously cited appendix to his book on historical materialism,
Bukharin passes judgment on a tendency in which one could place de Man:

> According to Marx, the relations of production are the material base of
> society. Nevertheless, among numerous Marxist (or, rather, neo-Marxist)
> groups, there is an irresistible tendency to spiritualize this material base.
> The progress of the psychological school and method in bourgeois sociol-
> ogy could not fail to contaminate Marxist and semi-Marxist milieus. This
> phenomenon went hand in hand with the growing influence of idealist
> academic philosophy. The Austrian school (Böhm-Bawerk, L. Word, and
> all the rest) began to remake Marx's construction, introducing the "ideal"
> psychological base into the material base. The initiative in this task fell to
> Austro-Marxism, theoretically in decline. They began to treat the material
> base in the spirit of the Pickwick Club. The economy, the mode of
> production, became a category inferior to that of psychological reactions.
> The solid cement of the material disappeared from the social edifice.

Let Keyserling and Spengler, those sirens of decadence, remain on the
margins of Marxist thought. More harmful and disturbing to socialism at its
current stage is the fear of not seeming intellectual and spiritual enough to
academic critics.

As Sorel wrote in the introduction to his *Reflections on Violence*:

> Men who have received an elementary education are generally imbued
> with a certain reverence for print as such, and they readily attribute genius
> to the people who attract the attention of the literary world to any great
> extent; they imagine that they must have a great deal to learn from authors
> whose names are so often mentioned with praise in the newspapers; they
> listen with singular respect to the commentaries that these literary prize-
> winners present to them. It is not easy to fight against these prejudices,
> but it is very useful work; we regard this task as being absolutely of the
> first importance, and we can carry it to a profitable conclusion without
> ever attempting to direct the working-class movement. The proletariat
> must be preserved from the experience of the Germans who conquered
> the Roman Empire; the latter were ashamed of being barbarians, and put
> themselves to school with the rhetoricians of the Latin decadence; they
> had no reason to congratulate themselves for having wished to be civilized

(Georges Sorel, *Reflections on Violence*, translated by T. E. Hulme and J. Roth [Glencoe, Illinois: Free Press, 1950], pp. 61–62).

This warning, from the man of thought and learning who took for socialism the best parts of Bergson's teachings, has never been as relevant than during this temporary period of capitalist stabilization.

PART VI
Literature, Art, and Culture

Nearly half of Mariátegui's written work takes up questions of artistic and cultural production, reflecting not only his own interests and literary predilections, but also his views on the importance of the mutual influence between ideological developments and the social and political realm. The following essays, therefore, offer only the slightest taste of his cultural criticism, which would require a separate anthology and a more expert introduction. Included are a few articles that discuss general questions about literature and art in capitalist society, as well as analyses of some movements and individuals with close ties to the revolutionary movement in Europe. For Mariátegui's perspective on the development of Peruvian literature, see "Literature on Trial," the last and most impassioned of the *Seven Interpretive Essays on Peruvian Reality*. The final essay here, on Chaplin, attests to the power of a new medium; as Mariátegui wrote in his introduction to *The Contemporary Scene*, "The best method to explain and translate our era is, perhaps, one that is a bit journalistic and a bit cinematic."

The Artist and the Epoch*

I

The contemporary artist frequently complains that this society or civilization does not do him justice. This complaint is not arbitrary. The conquest of happiness and fame is really quite hard these days. The bourgeoisie wants of its artists an art that courts and flatters its mediocre taste. In any case, it wants an art consecrated by its connoisseurs and appraisers. In the bourgeois market, the work of art does not have an intrinsic value, but a fiduciary one. The purest artists are almost never the most valued. The success of a painter depends, more or less, on the same conditions as the success of a business. His paintings need one or more dealers who administer them skillfully and wisely. Fame is manufactured on the basis of publicity. It has an unsurpassed value for the financial stock of the poor artist. Sometimes, the artist does not even demand to make a fortune. He is modestly content to be allowed to do his work. He only aspires to fulfill his personality. But this just ambition seems to be thwarted, too. The artist must sacrifice his personality, his temperament, his style, if he does not want to heroically die of hunger.

The artist takes vengeance for this unjust deal by generically defaming the bourgeoisie. In opposing his squalor, or because of a limited imagination, the artist invariably represents the bourgeois as coarse, lewd, and piggish. The artist seeks the rabid spur for his satires and ironies in this creature's real or imagined blubber.

The painter, the sculptor, the writer are not the most active or apparent of the capitalist order's discontents. But they are intrinsically the harshest and most inflamed. The worker senses that his labor is exploited. The artist feels his genius oppressed, his creations coerced, his right to glory and happiness stifled. The injustice he suffers seems tripled, quadrupled, multiplied many times over. His protest is in proportion to his generally disproportionate vanity, to his almost always exorbitant pride.

II

But in many cases this protest is a reactionary one in its conclusions or consequences. Disgusted with the bourgeois order, the artist declares himself,

---

* *Mundial,* October 14, 1925.

in these cases, skeptical or distrustful of proletarian efforts to create a new order. He prefers to adopt the romantic sentiments of those who repudiate the present in the name of their nostalgia for the past. He disempowers the bourgeoisie to rejoin the aristocracy. He disowns the myths of democracy to accept the myths of feudalism. He thinks that the artist of the Middle Ages, the Renaissance, etc., found a more intelligent, more understanding, more generous ruling class in those times. He compares the pope, the cardinal, or the prince to the nouveau riche. The nouveau riche naturally fares quite poorly in this comparison. The artist therefore reaches the conclusion that the era of the aristocracy and the church were better than that of democracy and the bourgeoisie.

III

Were the artists of feudal society really freer and happier than the artists of capitalist society? Let us examine the arguments of this theory's supporters.

First of all, the elite of aristocratic society had more artistic education and more esthetic aptitude than the elite of bourgeois society. Its function, habits, and tastes were more open to art. It pleased the popes and princes to surround themselves with painters, sculptors, and writers. Elegant discourses on arts and letters were heard in their social gatherings. Artistic creation constituted a fundamental human purpose according to the theory and practice of the era. A Renaissance lord did not comport himself before a painting of Raphael as a modern bourgeois does before an Archipenko statue or a work of Franz Marc. The aristocratic elite was composed of refined admirers and lovers of arts and letters. The bourgeois elite is made up of bankers, industrialists, and technicians. Their practical activities exclude all esthetic activity from these people's daily lives.

Second, criticism was neither a profession nor an occupation in that era as it is in ours. The ruling class itself exercised it worthily and eruditely. The feudal lord who hired Titian knew quite well himself what a Titian was worth. There were no intermediaries, no brokers between art and its purchasers or patrons.

Third and most important, the press did not exist. The basis of an artist's fame, whether great or modest, was exclusively his own work. It did not rest, as now, on a ream of newsprint. The rotary presses did not judge the merits of a painting, a statue, or a poem.

IV

The press stands particularly accused. The majority of artists feel themselves opposed and oppressed by its power. Teophile Gauthier, a romantic, wrote many years ago that "the periodicals are a sort of broker interposed between the artist and the public. The reading of periodicals obstructs the existence of real scholars and real artists." All the romantics of our era subscribe to this judgment without reservation or mitigation.

The dictatorship of the press weighs excessively on the fate of modern artists. Periodicals can raise a mediocre artist to the first rank and relegate the best to last. The journalist-critic understands his influence and uses it arbitrarily. He consecrates all the mundane successes. He flatters all the official reputations. He always has in mind the taste of his important clientele.

But the press is only one of the instruments of the celebrity industry. The press is merely responsible for carrying out what this industry's biggest interests decree. The managers of art and literature have all the means for producing fame in their hands. In an era in which fame is a question of publicity, of propaganda, one cannot claim that it is nevertheless granted equitably and impartially.

Advertising and publicity are generally omnipotent in our era. An artist's fate consequently often depends merely on having a good promoter. The merchants of books and those of paintings and statues decide the destiny of most artists. They launch an artist in much the same way as any product or business. And this system that on the one hand bestows fame and well-being on a Beltrán Masses, on the other hand condemns a Modigliani to misery and suicide. The Montmartre and Montparnasse quarters of Paris know many such stories.

V

Capitalist civilization has been defined as the civilization of Power. It is therefore natural that it is not organized spiritually and materially for esthetic activity, but for practical activity. The representative men of this civilization are its Hugo Stinneses and its Pierpont Morgans.

But the modern artist should not oppose these aspects of the present reality with a romantic nostalgia for past reality. The correct position on this matter is that of Oscar Wilde, who, in his essay *The Soul of Man under Socialism*, sees the liberation of art in the liberation of labor. The image of an aristocracy magnificent and provident with artists is a mirage, an illusion. It is absolutely untrue that aristocratic society was a society of gentle patrons. It is enough to remember the tormented life of so many noble artistic figures of that era. Neither is it true that the merit of the great artists was much better recognized and rewarded then than now. Vulgar artists also prospered exorbitantly at that time (for example, the most mediocre Cavalier d'Arpino enjoyed honors and favors that the era refused or doled out to Caravaggio). Art today depends on money, but yesterday it depended on a caste. Today's artist is a courtesan of the bourgeoisie, but yesterday's was a courtesan of the aristocracy. And, in any case, one servitude is as valid as another.

Art, Revolution, and Decadence*

We should hasten the elimination of an ambiguity that disorients some young artists. To correct certain hasty definitions, it should be established that not all new art is revolutionary, nor really new. Two spirits coexist in the modern world, that of revolution and that of decadence. Only the presence of the former gives a poem or painting value as new art.

We cannot accept as new any art that merely brings us a new technique. This would mean amusing ourselves with the one of the most fallacious modern illusions. No esthetic can lower artistic work to a question of technique. "A new technique should also correspond to a new spirit. If not, the only things that change are the trappings, the decorations. And an artistic revolution does not content itself with formal conquests."

Distinguishing between these two contemporaneous categories of artists is not easy. Just as they coexist in the same world, decadence and revolution coexist in the same individuals. The artist's consciousness is the agonistic ring of struggle between these two spirits. The understanding of this struggle almost always escapes the artists themselves. But, in the end, one of the two spirits prevails. The other is left strangled in the arena.

The decline of capitalist civilization is reflected in the atomization, the dissolution, of its art. In this crisis, art has above all lost its essential unity. Every one of its principles, every one of its elements, has demanded its autonomy. Secession is its most characteristic result. Schools multiply infinitely, because only centrifugal forces are at work.

But this anarchy, in which the spirit of bourgeois art is dying, irreparably segmented and divided, is the prelude and preparation of a new order. It is the passage from dusk to dawn. The elements of the art of the future are being elaborated separately in this crisis. Cubism, dadaism, expressionism,

---

* *Amauta*, November 1926.

etc., as they announce a crisis, also announce a reconstruction. Each movement in isolation bears no method, but all contribute an element, a value, a principle to its elaboration.

The revolutionary aspect of these contemporary schools or tendencies is not their creation of a new technique. Neither is it the destruction of the old technique. It is the repudiation, the removal, the taunting of bourgeois universals. Consciously or not, art always feeds, at the least, on the universals of its era. The contemporary artist, in most cases, bears an emptiness in his soul. The literature of decadence is a literature without universals. But one can only take a few steps in this manner. Humanity cannot advance without a faith, because to lack faith is to lack a goal. To proceed without a faith is to skate in place. The artists that consider themselves the most peevishly skeptical and nihilistic are generally those most desperately in need of a myth.

The Russian futurists have affiliated with communism; the Italian futurists have affiliated with fascism. What better historical demonstration that artists cannot escape the pull of politics? Massimo Bontempelli says that in 1920 he felt himself nearly a communist, and in 1923, the year of the March on Rome, felt himself nearly a fascist. Now he seems fully fascist. Many have mocked Bontempelli for this confession. I defend it; I find it sincere. The empty soul of poor Bontempelli had to adopt and accept the myth that Mussolini laid at his altar (the Italian vanguardists are convinced that fascism is the revolution).

Vicente Huidobro claims that art is independent of politics. The reasoning and motivation of this assertion are so ancient and decrepit that I cannot imagine even an ultraist poet holding to it, if one considers the extent to which ultraist poets discourse upon politics, economics, and religion. Since politics for Huidobro is exclusively that of the Palais Bourbon, we can grant his art all the autonomy he desires. But the truth is that, as Unamuno says, for those of us who raise it to the category of a religion, politics is the very plot of History. In a classical era, or at the height of any order, politics can be simply an administration and a parliament. In romantic eras, or in those of crisis, politics occupies the foreground of life.

Louis Aragón, André Breton, and their comrades of *La Révolution Surréaliste*—the greatest spirits of the French vanguard—proclaim this with their actions on their march toward communism. Drieu La Rochelle, who was so near this spiritual state when writing *Mesure de la France* and *Plainte contre inconnu*, has been unable to follow them. But, as he also has been unable to escape from politics, he has shown himself to be vaguely fascist and clearly reactionary.

In the Hispanic world, Ortega y Gasset is partially responsible for this error about the new art. His view is such—since he did not distinguish between schools or tendencies, at least in modern art, he did not distinguish revolutionary elements from decadent elements. The author of *The Dehumanization of Art* did not give us a definition of the new art. But he took characteristics that typically correspond to a decline as those of a revolution. Among other things, this led him to claim that "the new inspiration is always, unfailingly, cosmic." His picture of the symptoms is generally correct, but his diagnosis is incomplete and wrong.

Method is not enough. Technique is not enough. Paul Morand, despite his imagery and modernity, is a product of decadence. One breathes an atmosphere of dissolution in his writing. Jean Cocteau, after having flirted for a time with dadaism, now leaves us with his *Call to Order*.

We should now illuminate the issue until the last ambiguity vanishes. It is a difficult job. It takes much effort to understand many points. Images of decadence are often present in vanguard art until it proposes truly revolutionary goals, overcoming the subjectivism that weakens it at times. Hidalgo, situating Lenin in a poem of many dimensions, says that "Salome breasts" and "boyish hair" are the first steps toward the socialization of women. And this should not be surprising. There are poets who think the jazz band is a herald of the revolution.

Fortunately there are still artists like Bernard Shaw, who are able to understand that "art has never been great when it has not supplied an iconography for a living religion, and it has only been fully contemptible when imitating this iconography after the religion has become a superstition." This latter path seems to be that which various new artists have taken in French and other literatures. The future will laugh at the simple stupidity with which some critics of their era called them "new" and even "revolutionary."

Freudianism in Contemporary Literature*

Freudianism in literature is neither prior nor subsequent to Freud: it is simply contemporaneous. Ortega y Gasset considers Freudianism to definitely be one of the distinctive ideas of the twentieth century (it might be more

---

* *Variedades*, August 14, 1926.

precise to say insight rather than idea). And, in fact, Freudianism is incontestably a nineteenth-century idea. The seed of Freud's theory was in the world's consciousness before the official advent of psychoanalysis. Theoretical, conceptual, active Freudianism spread rapidly because it coincided with a potential, latent, passive Freudianism. Freud was simply the agent, the instrument, of a revelation that awaited someone to express it rationally and scientifically, but whose presentiment already existed in our civilization. This naturally does not diminish the merit of Freud's discovery. On the contrary, it magnifies it. The function of genius seems to be precisely that of formulating the thought, translating the intuition of an era.

The Freudian attitude of modern literature seemed evident far before Freud's studies were popularized among men of letters. At a time when Freud's theses were barely known among a public of psychiatrists, Pirandello and Proust—to cite only two of the loftiest names—displayed quite distinctive elements of Freudianism in their work.

Freud's presence in the work of Pirandello does not appear as a result of his knowledge of the theory of the learned Viennese genius, but of what Pirandello has written in his profession as dramatist. But Pirandello, before being a dramatist, is a novelist and, more specifically, a storyteller. And in many of his older stories, which are now gathered in a twenty-four-volume collection, one finds the most strictly Freudian psychological processes. Pirandello has always carried out Freudian psychology in his writing. It is not as mere anti-rationalist sport that his work constitutes a potent satire, a furious attack on the old conception of the human personality or psyche. Even in *The Late Mattía Pascal*, published twenty years ago, one sees an incipient Freudian tendency. Mattía Pascal, the Pirandellian protagonist, who appears to everyone to have died because of the false identification of a body that seemed just like his and who wishes to take advantage of this mistake to actually escape a world that was stifling and trapping him, could not kill himself. Adriano Meis, the new man who wishes to be, has no reality. He is unable to free himself from Mattía Pascal, who obstinately continues to live. The childhood and youth of the escapee pulls on his conscience more strongly than his own free will. And Mattía Pascal returns, revives. To feel himself real again, the misfortunate Pirandellian character must give up his existence as a fictional creature born through the artifice of accident.

In Pirandello's latest works, this Freudianism becomes conscious and deliberate. *Each in His Own Way*, for example, is proof of his reading and adoption of Freud. One of its characters, Doro Pallegari, during a distinguished gathering, defends a woman whose name is mentioned in good society only along with a rebuke. This conduct is scandalously explained the following day as Doro Pallegari arrives at his home. When questioned, Doro responds that he had done it as a reaction to the exaggerations of his friend

Francesco Savio. He is not convinced of what he said in defense of Delia Morello. Quite the opposite. One of those present, Diego Cinci, then maintains the thesis that his true feelings are those which caused the explosion the previous evening. I would like to quote this passage:

DIEGO: You're now agreeing with Francesco Savio! But do you know why? It's to hide a feeling which you've had inside you without your knowing that it was there.

DORO: Nothing of the kind! You make me laugh!

DIEGO: It's true! It's true!

DORO: You make me laugh, I say!

DIEGO: In the excitement of the argument last evening that feeling suddenly came to the top in your mind. It caught you off guard . . . and you said things you didn't realize you were saying. . . . Of course you didn't! Of course you didn't! And you imagine you never even thought those things! And yet you did think them . . . you did think them!

DORO: What do you mean? When?

DIEGO: Secretly . . . unknown even to yourself! Oh, my dear Doro, just as we sometimes have illegitimate children, so we sometimes have illegitimate thoughts!

DORO: Speak for yourself, eh!

DIEGO: Yes, I'll speak also for myself! . . . We all yearn to marry, and for our whole life long, some one particular soul . . . the soul which brings us in dowry the faculties and qualities most likely to help us attain the goals to which we aspire. But later on, outside the honest, conjugal household of our consciousness, we have . . . well . . . one affair after another, numberless little sins with all those other souls which we have rejected and buried in the depths of our being, and from which actions and thoughts are born— actions and thoughts which we refuse to recognize, but which, when we are forced to it, we adopt or legitimize . . . with the appropriate adaptations, reserves, and cautions. Now, in this case, one of your own poor, fatherless thoughts has come home to you. You deny paternity . . . but look it over carefully! It's yours! You were really in love with Delia Morello . . . head-over-heels in love, as you said! (*Naked Masks*, translated by Arthur Livingston [New York: Dutton, 1952], pp. 296–297)

There is no similar reasoning or theorizing in the rest of the comedy. But, on the other hand, the action and development are themselves patently Freudian. Pirandello has adopted Freud more enthusiastically than Italian psychologists and psychiatrists, among whom a positivist mentality still prevails that, moreover, is quite in accord with the Italian and Latin temperament (in this regard, I will refer to a work of two thick volumes I have read recently, *La psicanalisi*, by Professor Enrico Morselli [Turin: Fratelli Bocca, 1926], to peripherally note that this eminent Italian psychiatrist favorably cites the works of the Peruvian professor Dr. Honorio Delgado, whom he points to as one of the best interpreters of Freud's theory).

The case of Proust is even more curious. The relationship between Proust's work and Freud's theory has been carefully studied in France—another country in which Freudianism has found more favor in literature than science—by the late lamented director of the NRF (Nouvelle Revue Française), Jacques Riviére, who, with unimpeachable authority, asserts that Proust was acquainted with Freud only by name, and that he never read a line of his writings. Proust and Freud coincide in their distrust of the ego, in which Riviére finds them opposed to Bergson, whose psychology is founded, in his judgment, on a confidence in the ego. According to Riviére, Proust "has instinctively applied the method established by Freud." On the other hand, "Proust is the first novelist who has dared to take the sexual factor into account in the exposition of his characters." Riviére's testimony establishes, in short, that Freud and Proust, one as an artist, the other as a psychiatrist, have simultaneously and synchronously employed the same psychological method without knowing each other, without communicating.

Currently, Freudianism seems to have spread among the literati to such an extent that Jean Cocteau, who himself does not escape the influence of psychoanalysis, proposes the following prayer to young writers: "My Lord, keep me from believing the century's evil, protect me from Freud, stop me from writing the expected book!" François Mauriac, whom the French Academy just awarded a prize for his novel *The Desert of Love*, states with a certain pride that the generation of novelists to which he belongs writes under the sign of Proust and Freud, adding in that regard: "When I wrote *A Kiss for the Leper* and *The River of Fire*, I had never read a line of Freud and knew almost nothing of Proust. Moreover, I never deliberately wanted my heroes to be as they are."

This Freudian current grows daily larger in all literatures. The Latin spirit seems the least apt to understand and accept psychoanalytic theories, for which its Italian and French objectors blame its Nordic and Teutonic background, if not its Jewish origins. We have, nevertheless, already seen how two of the most representative writers of France and Italy are characterized by their Freudian method, and how the new generation of French novelists show themselves perceptibly influenced by psychoanalysis. The propagation— and, in some cases, the exaggeration—of Freudianism in other literatures should therefore not surprise us. Judging by what I know—my other studies and readings do not allow me too many literary investigations—I would point to Waldo Frank, author of the novel *Rahab*, of which I published a quick impression, as the North American writer who penetrates most deeply into the subconscious of his characters. Waldo Frank, a Jew, infuses them with a sexuality one might call religious, along with a messianic mysticism.

And so as not to fix on the most illustrious and notorious cases, I will make the last stop on my tour on the far bank of the new Russian literature, almost unknown in Spanish at this point, and the case of Boris Pilnyak. The sexual factor has a primary role in this author's characters. And the following pansexualist thesis belongs to one of them—comrade Xenia Ordynina:

> Karl Marx must have made a mistake. He only considered physical hunger. He didn't take into account the other factor: love, love as red and powerful as blood. Sex, family, race: humanity hasn't been wrong in worshiping sex. Yes, there's physical hunger and sexual hunger. But this isn't quite right; better yet, physical hunger and sexual religion, the religion of blood. Sometimes I feel, even with real, physical pain, that the whole world—civilization, humanity, everything; chairs, sofas, dressers, chests—are permeated with sexuality—no, permeated isn't right . . .—and the people, too; the nation, the state, this handkerchief, this bread, this belt. I'm not the only one who thinks so. Sometimes my head spins and I feel the revolution is saturated with sexuality.

Freud, in an incisive study on the resistances to psychoanalysis, examines their origin and character in the scientific and philosophical milieus. Among the adversaries of psychoanalysis, he points to the philosopher and the doctor. Preoccupied by his polemic, Freud forgets to dedicate some words of recognition in his essay to poets and writers. While, according to Freud, the resistance to psychoanalysis is not of an intellectual order but has an emotional origin, it is possible that, because of their subconscious inspiration and irrational process, art and poetry had to understand his theory better than science.

Reality and Fiction[*]

Fantasy is regaining its privileges and position in Western literature. Oscar Wilde is thus an authority on contemporary esthetics. His current expertise depends neither on his work nor his life, but on his conception of reality and art. We live in an epoch propitious for his paradoxes. Wilde claimed that the London fog was invented by painting. It isn't true, he said, that art

---

* *Perricholi*, March 25, 1926.

copies nature; it is nature that copies art. In our times, Massimo Bontempelli has taken this theory to the extreme. According to Bontempelli's bizarre thesis, brought on during a summer meditation in a mountain village, the earth was almost solely mineral in its earliest days. There was only man and stone. Humanity was nourished by mineral nutrients. But its imagination discovered the other two realms of nature. The trees and animals were imagined by artists. These floras and faunas began to really exist in nature after having existed ideally in art. Having furnished the planet, man's imagination created new things. Machines appeared. The civilization of the machine was born. The earth was electrified and mechanized. But after mechanization had reached its fullest extent, the process was repeated in reverse. Mineral, vegetable, machine, etc., were reabsorbed by nature. The Earth gradually petrified, mineralized, and returned to its original state. This evolution has occurred many times. Today, the world is once more in its machine and mechanical period. Bontempelli is one of the most fashionable writers in contemporary Italy. Some years ago, when Verism dominated Italian literature, his book would have had a different fate. Bontempelli, who originally was more or less a classicist, would not have written it. Today, he is a Pirandellian; then, he would have been a D'Annuzianist.

A D'Annuzianist? But do we not also find more invention than realism in D'Annunzio? In D'Annunzio's work, fantasy is more external than internal. D'Annunzio adorned his novels fantastically, byzantinely, but their frame-work is not much different from naturalistic novels. D'Annunzio attempted to be aristocratic, but he did not dare to be implausible. Pirandello, on the other hand, in a novel as bare of ornamentation and simple in form as *The Late Mattía Pascal*, presented a case study which the critics immediately censured as odd and implausible, but which life faithfully reproduced years later.

Realism in literature distances us from reality. The realist experiment has merely served to show that we can only encounter reality along the path of fantasy. And this has produced surrealism, which is not only a French liter-ary school or movement, but a tendency, a method of world literature. The Italian Pirandello is a surrealist; the North American Waldo Frank is a sur-realist; the Romanian Panait Istrati is a surrealist; the Russian Boris Pilniak is a surrealist. It doesn't matter that they work outside of and far from the surrealist brigade that Aragón, Bretón, Eluard, and Soupalt head in Paris.

But fiction is not free. More than uncovering the fantastic, it seems des-tined to unveil the real. Fantasy serves us little when it does not approach reality. Philosophers avail themselves of artificial concepts to reach the truth. Writers use fiction for the same purpose. Fantasy only has value when it creates something real. This is its limitation. This is its drama.

The death of the old realism has in no way prejudiced our understanding of reality. On the contrary, it has facilitated it. It has liberated us from dogmas and prejudices that have restricted it. There is sometimes more truth, more humanity in the implausible than the plausible. An implausible farce of Pirandello penetrates the depths of the human soul more profoundly than a plausible comedy of **Monsieur** Capus. And *The Magnificent Cuckold*, by the brilliant Fernand Crommelynck, is certainly worth more than the whole mediocre French theater of adultery and divorce, to which *L'Adversaire* and *Na Falena* belong.

Today, the prejudice toward the plausible seems to have greatly obstructed art. Artists of the most moderate sensibility have shown themselves to be violently opposed to it.

Pirandello writes:

> Life, for all the shameless absurdities, both big and small, with which it is beautifully filled, has the inestimable privilege of being able to do without that verisimilitude which art is obliged to obey. Life's absurdities need to seem lifelike because they are true, unlike art, which needs to be lifelike to seem true.

Freed of this tie, artists can engage in the conquest of new horizons. Works are now written that would be impossible without this freedom—Joseph Delteil's *Joan of Arc*, for example. In this novel, Delteil shows us the maiden of Domremy talking ingenuously and naturally with St. Catherine and St. Margaret, as if with two country girls. The miracle is narrated with the same simplicity, the same candor as a children's fable. The implausible parts of this novel do not pretend to be believable. And it is by accepting the miracle—that is, the fabulous—that we more closely approach the truth of the Maiden. Delteil's book offers us a more truthful and living image of Joan of Arc than the book of Anatole France.

Modern literature draws some of its best energy from this new concept of the real. What makes it anarchic is not fantasy itself. It is that aggravation of individualism and subjectivism that constitutes one of the symptoms of the crisis of Western civilization. One need not seek the root of this evil in its excess of fictions, but in the lack of a great fiction that could be its myth and guiding star.

The Clarté Group*

The sorrows and horrors of the great war have produced an explosion of revolutionary and pacifist ideas. Only the few and the mediocre have sung its praises. Its literature is poor, vulgar, and obscure. Its great monuments number but one. The best pages that have been written about the war are not those that exalt it, but those that vilify it. The best writers, the most profound artists, have almost unanimously felt a critical need to denounce and damn it as a monstrous crime, a terrible sin of Western humanity. The heroes of the trenches have found no illustrious minstrels. The spokesmen of their glory have been journalists and functionaries lacking any grand poetic sensibility. Isn't Poincaré—a lawyer, a bureaucrat—the greatest troubadour of the French victory? The war to end all wars, contrary to what the skeptics say, has not meant a setback for pacifism. Its effects and influence have been especially favorable to pacifist theories. This bitter test has not diminished pacifism; it has magnified it. And instead of causing despair, it has created rage (the war, moreover, was won by a preacher of peace—Wilson. Victory has fallen to those people thought to be defeated, since this was the war to end wars). It can be claimed that a period of decline has begun for war and martial heroism, at least in the history of ideas and art. Ethically and esthetically, war has lost much ground in recent years. Humanity has stopped thinking of it as beautiful. Martial heroism does not interest artists as it did before. Contemporary artists prefer an opposed and antithetical theme: military suffering and horror. *Under Fire* will probably remain the most honest chronicle of the contest and Henri Barbusse the best chronicler of its trenches and battles.

The modern mind, in short, has acquired a pacifist attitude. But this pacifism does not have the same consequences among all its adherents. Many intellectuals believe that world peace can be ensured through the realization of Wilson's program. They await messianic results from the League of Nations. Other intellectuals think that the old social order, within which an armed peace and nationalist diplomacy are inevitable, is powerless and inadequate for the realization of the pacifist ideal. The seeds of war are lodged in the very organism of capitalist society. To defeat them it is therefore necessary to destroy this regime whose historical mission, moreover, has already been exhausted. The central nucleus of this tendency is the Clarté group, which Henri Barbusse heads, or better, represents.

* Published in *La escena contemporánea* (1925).

Clarté at first attracted not only revolutionary intellectuals to its ranks, but also some intellectuals standing on liberal and democratic ideas. But the latter could not follow the line of march of the former.

Barbusse and his friends solidarized themselves more and more with the revolutionary proletariat. They therefore took part in its political activities. They led the International of Thought toward the path of the Communist International. This was the inevitable trajectory of *Clarté*. One cannot surrender oneself to the revolution only in part. The revolution is a political task. It is a concrete action. No one can truly and effectively serve it at a distance from the masses who make it. Revolutionary work cannot be solitary, individualist, detached. Truly revolutionary intellectuals have no choice but to accept their role in collective action. Barbusse today is a member, a soldier, of the French Communist Party. A short time ago, he presided over a congress of war veterans in Berlin. And from the platform of this congress, he told the French soldiers in the Ruhr that they should never shoot at the German workers, even if their officers order them. These words led to a trial and could have earned him a prison term. But, for him, pronouncing them was a political duty.

Intellectuals are generally averse to discipline, programs, and systems. Their psychology is individualistic and their thought heterodox. Their sense of individuality is particularly excessive and overwhelming. The intellectual's individuality almost always feels itself above the usual rules. Finally, a disdain for politics is common among intellectuals. Politics seems to them an activity for bureaucrats and shysters. They forget that this is perhaps the case in placid historical periods, but not in revolutionary, stormy, pregnant periods when a new social state and new political forms are in gestation. In these periods, politics is no longer the job of a routinist political caste. In these periods, politics transcends these vulgar levels and invades and dominates all arenas of human life. A revolution represents a great and vast human concern. Only the prejudices and threatened privileges of an egoistic minority can oppose the triumph of this higher interest. No liberated spirit, no sensitive mind, can be indifferent to such a conflict. Currently, for example, a thinking person for whom the social question does not exist is inconceivable. The insensitivity and deafness of intellectuals to the problems of their time abound, but this insensitivity and deafness are abnormal. They must be classified as pathological exceptions. Barbusse writes:

> To do politics is to pass from dreams to reality, from the abstract to the concrete. Politics is the real work of social thought; politics is life. To allow a loosening of the cohesion between theory and practice, to abandon its consummators to their own efforts, even if it means conceding them an amiable neutrality, is to desert the cause of humanity.

Behind an apparent esthetic repugnance for politics sometimes lurks a vulgar conservative sensibility. The writer and the artist do not like to openly and explicitly declare themselves reactionaries. There is always a certain intellectual shame in solidarizing oneself with the old and the decrepit. But intellectuals are actually no less docile or prone to conservative prejudices and interests than common people. It is not only that power disposes of academies, honors, and riches sufficient to ensure a large clientele of writers and artists. Most of all, it happens that one does not come to the revolution by a coldly conceptual route. The revolution is an emotion more than an idea. It is a passion more than a concept. To understand it, one needs an instinctive spiritual attitude, a special psychological capability. The intellectual, just like any fool, is subject to the influence of his environment, his education, and his interests. His intelligence does not operate freely. He has a natural inclination to adapt himself to the most convenient ideas, not the most just. In a word, the backwardness of an intellectual grows from the same motives and sources as the backwardness of a shopkeeper. The language is different, but the mechanism of the attitude is identical.

Clarté no longer exists as an outline or beginning of an International of Thought. The International of the revolution is singular and unique. Barbusse has recognized this, giving his support to communism. In France, *Clarté* remains a nucleus of vanguard intellectuals committed to the work of preparing a proletarian culture. Its proselytism will be successful to the degree that a new generation matures, a new generation that is not content to sympathize with revolutionary demands in theory, but knows how to accept, cherish, and support them without mental reservations. The Clarté group, Barbusse has said, has no official links with communism, but maintains that international communism is the living incarnation of a well-conceived social vision. *Clarté* is now but a face, a sector of the revolutionary party. It signifies an effort by the intelligentsia to commit itself to the revolution, and an effort by the revolution to win over the intelligentsia. Revolutionary ideas must dislodge conservative ideas not only from the institutions, but also from the mind and the spirit of humanity. The revolution undertakes the conquest of thought at the same time as the conquest of power.

A Balance Sheet of Surrealism*

None of the vanguard literary and artistic movements of Western Europe have had either the historical significance or content of surrealism, despite what simple appearance might suggest. Other movements have been limited to affirming certain esthetic postulates and experimenting with certain artistic principles.

Italian "futurism" has undoubtedly been an exception to the rule. Marinetti and his followers claimed to represent a new Italy not only artistically, but also politically and emotionally. But "futurism," which, considered at a distance, might entertain us more with its histrionic megalomania than any other of its aspects, had already joined the forces of "order" and the academy some time before; fascism assimilated it effortlessly, which proves the fundamental innocuousness of the futurists rather than the digestive power of the blackshirt regime. Futurism has also had the virtue of persistence to some degree. But, in this regard, it has been a matter of longevity rather than continuity or development. At each reappearance, the old pre-war futurism was recognizable. The wig, the makeup, the tricks could not keep us from noting the broken voice and mechanical gestures. Marinetti, considering the impossibility of gaining a continued, dialectical presence for futurism in Italian literature and history, saved it from oblivion with ruinous *rentrées*. In the end, futurism was corrupted primarily by its taste for the spectacular, its abuse of the histrionic—so Italian, certainly, and this is an excuse that an honest critic might concede it—which condemned it to a life on the proscenium, to an artificial, false, declamatory role. That one cannot speak of futurism without using the vocabulary of the theater confirms this dominant aspect of its character.

Surrealism has another sort of endurance. It is truly a *movement*, an *experience*. It is no longer, for example, where it was left two years ago by those who were then observing it with the hope that it would disintegrate or be pacified. Those who imagine they know and understand surrealism through a formula or definition of one of its stages are totally uninformed. Since its appearance, surrealism has distinguished itself from other artistic and literary tendencies or programs. It did not appear fully armed and perfected from

---

* *Variedades*, February 19 and March 5, 1930.

the head of its inventors. It has developed. Dada is the name of its infancy. If we follow its development attentively, we can note an adolescent crisis. Reaching adulthood, it has sensed its political responsibilities, its civic duty, and has joined a party and adopted a doctrine.

And on this plane, it has comported itself quite differently than futurism. Instead of letting loose a surrealist political program, it accepts and subscribes to a concrete, current revolutionary program: the Marxist program of proletarian revolution. It recognizes the unique validity of the Marxist program on the social, political, and economic terrain. It does not occur to them to submit politics to the rules and taste of art. In the same way that it is impossible to oppose the facts of science in the domain of physics, it would be childish and absurd to attempt any original speculation in the realm of politics and economics based on the facts of art. The surrealists only exercise their right to absurdity, to absolute subjectivism, in art. They carry themselves prudently in all other realms, and this is one of the things that differentiates them from the shameful variety of their predecessors, both revolutionary and romantic, in the history of literature.

But the surrealists reject nothing as much as voluntarily confining themselves to pure artistic speculation. The autonomy of art, yes, but not the confinement of art. Nothing is more foreign to them than the formula of art for art's sake. The artist who, at a given moment, does not fulfill his duty to throw one of Mr. Tardieu's *flics* (policemen) into the Seine, or to interrupt a speech of Briand with an interjection, is a poor devil. Surrealism denies one the right to seek shelter in esthetics so as not to feel the repugnance and malevolence of Mr. Chiappe's profession or the oral anesthetics of the pacifism of the United States of Europe. Some dissidence and defections have had their origins precisely in this conception of the unity between the man and the artist. Explaining the estrangement of Robert Denos, who for a time made copious contributions to *La Révolution Surréaliste*, André Breton says that "he believed himself able to devote himself with impunity to one of the most dangerous activities that exist, journalism, and in its exercise avoid responding to a small number of brutal intimations that surrealism has faced in its forward march: Marxism or anti-Marxism, for example."

It would be quite difficult, perhaps impossible, for those in our tropical America who imagine that surrealism is libertinism to accept this statement: that it is a difficult, laborious discipline. I could temper and moderate this with a more scrupulous definition—that it is the difficult, laborious search for a discipline. But I absolutely insist on the rare quality—unattainable and forbidden to snobbism, to artifice—of the surrealists' experience and work.

La Révolution Surréaliste has reached its twelfth issue and its fifth year. Issue #12 opens with a balance sheet of one part of its operation, which André Breton titles "The Second Manifesto of Surrealism."

Before commenting on this manifesto, I would like to call attention in a few paragraphs to the scope and value of surrealism, a movement I have followed to a degree that has been reflected more than once in my articles, and not just episodically. This attention, nourished in sympathy and hope, guarantees the fidelity of my writing when I polemicize with surrealist texts and intentions. As to issue #12, I will add that its text and tone confirm the character of the surrealist experiment and the journal that displays and interprets it. An issue of *La Révolution Surréaliste* almost always represents a test of conscience, a new inquiry, a perilous effort. Each issue announces a new regroupment of forces. The very administration of the journal, in its functional or personal sense, has often changed, so André Breton has assumed the post to give it the stamp of continuity. A journal of this type cannot be published with a precise regularity. All its assertions should be faithful to the tormented, dangerous, challenging line of its explorations and experiments.

In the second surrealist manifesto, André Breton stages a trial of those writers and artists who had participated in the movement and then disowned it more or less openly. In this respect, the manifesto is a sort of indictment, and has not been long in provoking a violent reaction against the author and the members of his team. But there is as little personal in the matter as possible. The trial of these apostasies and desertions in this polemical piece especially tends to insist upon the difficult and courageous spiritual and artistic discipline to which the surrealist experiment leads. Breton writes:

> It is noteworthy, moreover, that when they are left to their own devices, and to nothing else, the people who one day made it necessary for us to do without them have straightway lost their footing, have been immediately forced to resort to the most miserable expedients in order to reintegrate themselves with the defenders of *law and order*, all proud partisans of leveling via the head. This is because unflagging fidelity to the commitments of surrealism presupposes a disinterestedness, a contempt for risk, a refusal to compromise, of which very few men, in the long run, prove to be capable. Were there to remain not a single one, from among all those who were the first to measure by its standards their chance for significance and their desire for truth, yet would surrealism continue to live (*Manifestoes of Surrealism*, translated by Richard Seavers and Helen R. Lane [Ann Arbor: University of Michigan Press, 1972], p. 129).

The notorious, older dissidents of the movement are scarcely mentioned by Breton in this manifesto, which does, though, rigorously examine the conduct of those who have recently separated from surrealism. Breton carries to an extreme his personal attack against Pierre Naville, who so distinguished himself, along with Marcel Fourrier, in the liquidation of *Clarté* and its substitution by *La Lutte des Classes*. Naville is presented as the arriviste son of a millionaire banker desperately seeking notoriety, guided on his voyage by the devil of ambition from his time as editor of the surrealist journal through *La Lutte des Classes*, *La Verité*, and the Trotskyist Opposition. It seems to me that there is something much more serious in Naville. And I do not exclude the possibility that Breton will change his attitude about him later on—if Naville corresponds to my own hopes—with the same nobility with which he recognized, after a long quarrel, the persistence of Tristan Tzara in his bold efforts and rigorous work.

The same fairness, the same scrupulousness is shown in appreciations such as those which are given us in this balance sheet of surrealism, stating that "more than anything else, surrealism attempted to provoke, from the intellectual and moral point of view, a *crisis of conscience*, of the most general and serious kind, and that the extent to which this was or was not accomplished alone can determine its historical success or failure" (ibid., p. 123).

Breton says:

> From the intellectual point of view, it was then, and still is today, a question of testing by any and all means, and of demonstrating at any price, the meretricious nature of the old antimonies hypocritically intended to prevent any unusual ferment on the part of man, were it only by giving him a vague idea of the means at his disposal, by challenging him to escape to some meaningful degree from the universal fetters.

We cannot approve of the sentences that follow—precisely for the reasons that come with this definition, this specifying of surrealism as an experiment:

> Everything tends to make us believe that there exists a certain point of the mind at which life and death, the real and the imagined, past and future, the communicable and the incommunicable, high and low, cease to be perceived as contradictions. Now, search as one may one will never find any other motivating force in the activities of the surrealists than the hope of finding and fixing this point.

The spirit and program of surrealism are not expressed in these or other high-minded phrases of shocking and extremist intent. Perhaps the best passage of the manifesto is another in which André Breton, with a historical understanding of romanticism a thousand times clearer than that reached by scholars of romanticism and classicism in their often quite banal inquiries, affirms the romantic connections of the surrealist revolution:

> But, at a time in history when the officials in France are getting ready to celebrate grotesquely the hundreth anniversary of romanticism with public ceremonies, we say, and insist on saying, that this romanticism which we are today willing to consider as the tail, *but then only as an amazing prehensile tail*, by its very essence remains unmitigated in its negation of these officials and these ceremonies, and we say that to be a hundred is

for it to be still in the flower of its youth, that what has been wrongly called its heroic period can no longer honestly be considered as anything but the first cry of a newborn child which is only beginning to make its desires known through us and which, if one is willing to admit that what was thought "classically" before it came into being, was tantamount to good, undeniably wishes *naught but evil.*

But the manifesto is not lacking in sentences with a dadaist flavor—"I ask for the profound, the veritable occultation of surrealism," "no concessions to the world," etc.—which gives an infantile tone to these passages that is no longer possible to excuse, considering the point this movement has reached historically as experiment and inquiry.

Maxim Gorky and Russia*

Maxim Gorky is the novelist of the vagabonds, the pariahs, the miserable. He is the novelist of the lower depths, the profligate life, and hunger. Gorky's work is a special, spontaneous one, representative of this century of the masses, the Fourth Estate, and the social revolution. Many contemporary artists draw their themes and characters from the plebeian strata, the lower classes. The bourgeois soul and passions are somewhat passé. They are overexplored. In the proletarian soul and passions, on the other hand, there are new shadings and unexpected lines of development.

The plebeian of Gorky's novels and dramas is not the Western plebeian. But he is authentically the Russian plebeian. And Gorky is not only a narrator of the Russian romance, but also one of its protagonists. He did not make the Russian revolution, but he has lived it. He has been one of its critics, chroniclers, and actors.

Gorky has never been a Bolshevik. Intellectuals and artists habitually lack the necessary faith to enroll themselves as factional, disciplined, and sectarian members of a party. They tend toward a personal, particular, and arbitrary attitude toward life. Gorky, meandering, disquiet, and heterodox, has not rigidly followed any program or political faith. In the early days of the revolution, he published a revolutionary socialist daily, *Novy Zhinh.* This daily received the Soviet regime with disconfidence and enmity. It accused

* Published in *La escena contemporánea* (1925).

the Bolsheviks of being adventurers and utopians. Gorky wrote that the Bolsheviks were carrying out an experiment useful to humanity, but deadly for Russia. But the source of his resistance was more recondite, intimate, and spiritual. It was a state of mind, a basic counterrevolutionary spirit common to the majority of intellectuals. The revolution scrutinized and treated them as potential enemies. And they became upset that the revolution, so boisterous, so impetuous, so explosive, discourteously disturbed their dreams, research, and discourse. Some persisted in this state of mind. Others were infected and inflamed by revolutionary faith. Gorky, for example, did not take long in moving closer to the revolution. The Soviets charged him with the organization and directorship of an institution of intellectuals. This institution, chosen to safeguard Russian culture from the revolutionary tide, sheltered, nourished, and provisioned Russia's men of science and culture with the rudiments of research and labor. Gorky, given over to the protection of Russia's scholars and artists, thereby became one of the essential collaborators of Lunacharsky, the commissar of public education.

Days of drought and famine came to the Volga region. A failed harvest unexpectedly and totally impoverished various provinces already weakened and emaciated by long years of war and blockade. Many millions of people were left without bread for the winter. Gorky felt his duty was to move and arouse humanity about this immense tragedy. He sought the collaboration of Anatole France, Gerard Hauptmann, Bernard Shaw, and other great artists. And he left Russia, now more distant and alien than ever, to tell Europe of it. But he was no longer the vigorous vagabond, the robust nomad, of earlier times. His old case of tuberculosis attacked him along the way and forced him to stop in Germany and take shelter in a sanatorium. A great European, the explorer and sage Nansen, crisscrossed Europe demanding help for the famished provinces. Nansen spoke in London, in Paris, in Rome. With the guarantee of his indubitable and apolitical position, he stated that this was not communism's responsibility, but a scourge, a cataclysm, a calamity. Russia, blockaded and isolated, could not rescue all its starving. There was no time to lose. The winter was approaching. Not to aid the hungry immediately was to condemn them to death. Many generous souls responded to this call. The working masses gave their pennies. But the moment was not propitious for charity and philanthropy. The atmosphere in the West was too charged with rancor and anger against Russia. The major European newspapers gave Nansen's campaign an uninterested response. The European states, insensitively poisoned by emotion, were not dismayed by Russia's affliction. Help was not given in proportion to its magnitude. Some millions were saved, but other millions perished. Gorky, despondent over this tragedy, cursed Europe's cruelty and prophesied the end of European civilization. The world, he said, had just witnessed a weakening of the moral sensibility of Europe. This weakening is a symptom of the decline and degeneration of the Western world. European civilization had not only been notable for its technical and material wealth, but also for its moral assets. Both had given it authority and prestige in the East. Once in decline, nothing can defend European civilization from the assaults of barbarism.

Gorky hears a subconscious, internal voice announcing the ruin of Europe. This same voice tells him the peasant is an implacable and fatal enemy of the Russian revolution. The revolution is the work of the urban working class and of socialist ideology, also essentially urban. The peasants have supported the revolution because it has given them land. But other sections of its program are not equally intelligible to agrarian minds and interests. Gorky despairs that the egoist and impure peasant psychology cannot assimilate itself to the ideology of the urban worker. The city is the center, the home, of civilization and its creations. The city is civilization itself. The psychology of the city person is more altruistic and disinterested that the psychology of the country person. This can be observed not only among the peasant masses, but also among the peasant aristocracy. The temperament of the agrarian *latifundista* is much less elastic, active, and comprehensive than that of the industrial *latifundista*. The rural magnates are always on the extreme right; the magnates of finance and industry prefer a centrist position and tend to come to agreements and compromises with the revolution. The city adapts humanity to collectivism, the country savagely stimulates their individualism. And, for this reason, the final battle between individualism and socialism could perhaps break out between the city and the country.

Various European statesmen implicitly share this preoccupation of Gorky. Caillaux, for example, looks with disquiet and apprehension at the tendency of the peasants of Central Europe to free themselves from urban industrialism. Rural petty industry is on the rise in Hungary. The peasant is again spinning his own wool and forging his own tools. He is attempting to resurrect a medieval, primitive economy. Gorky's intuition and vision coincide with the proof, the verification, of the man of science.

I spoke of this and other things with Gorky in December of 1922 in the Neue Sanatorium of Saarow Ost. His quarters were closed to all extraneous and unexpected visitors. But Maria Feodorowna, Gorky's wife, opened their doors to me. Gorky speaks only Russian. Maria Feodorowna speaks German, French, English, and Italian.

At that time, Gorky was writing the third volume of his autobiography and beginning a book about Russians.

"Russians?"

"Yes. People I saw in Russia; people I have known; not famous people, but interesting ones."

I questioned Gorky about his relationship with Bolshevism. Some newspapers claimed that Gorky was distancing himself from its leaders. Gorky denied the story. He intended to return to Russia soon. His relations with the Soviets were good, normal.

There is something of the old vagabond, the old pilgrim, in Gorky: his sharp eyes, his rustic hands, his body a bit doubled over, his Tatar whiskers. Gorky is not physically a metropolitan; he is rather a rural and peasant type. But he does not have a patriarchal and Asian soul like Tolstoy. Tolstoy preached a peasant and Christian communism. Gorky admires, loves, and respects Western machinery, technology, and science, all those things that offended Tolstoy's mysticism. This Slav, this vagabond, is secretly and subconsciously a devotee, a supporter, a lover of the West and its civilization.

And under the lindens of Saarow Ost, where neither the rumors of communist revolution nor the shouts of fascist reaction arrive, his sickly and hallucinating eyes saw with anguish the coming twilight and death of a marvelous civilization.

Outline of an Interpretation of Chaplin*

In any interpretation of our era, the topic of Chaplin seems to me no less important than the topic of Lloyd George or MacDonald (if we look for an equivalent only in Great Britain). Many have considered the assertion of Henri Poulaille, that *The Gold Rush* is the greatest modern novel, to be excessive. But—always situating Chaplin in his country—I feel, in any case, that the human resonance of *The Gold Rush* largely surpasses that of H. G. Wells's *The Outline of History* and the plays of Bernard Shaw. This is a fact that Wells and Shaw would certainly be the first to recognize (Shaw exaggerating it extremely and bizarrely, and Wells attributing it somewhat melancholically to deficiencies in secondary education).

For its subjects, Chaplin's imagination chooses matters of no less importance than the issue of Methuselah or the legal rights of Joan of Arc: gold;

---

* *Variedades*, October 6 and 13, 1928.

the circus. And he realizes his ideas with greater artistic efficacy. The regulatory intellectualism of the guardians of the esthetic order would be scandalized by such a proposition. In their cerebral formulas, Chaplin's success is explained like that of Alexandre Dumas or Eugene Sue. But, without resorting to Bontempelli's arguments on the mystery novel or subscribing to his re-evaluation of Dumas, this simplistic judgment can be quickly disproved by recalling that Chaplin's art is enjoyed with the same relish by the learned and the illiterate, by the intelligentsia and by boxers. When one speaks of the universality of Chaplin, one is not appealing to the test of popularity. Chaplin wins everyone's vote: the majority and the minority. His fame is at the same time rigorously aristocratic and democratic. Chaplin is a real member of the elite, if we remember that *elite* is a derivative of *elect*.

The search for and conquest of gold, the gold rush, was the romantic chapter, the bohemian phase of the capitalist epic. The capitalist era begins when Europe renounces finding a theory of gold, to instead seek real gold, physical gold. For this reason especially, the discovery of America is so intimately and fundamentally linked to its history (Canada and California are the great way stations of this itinerary). Undoubtedly, the capitalist revolution was principally a technological revolution: its first great triumph is the machine; its greatest invention is finance capital. But capitalism has never been able to free itself from gold, despite the tendency of the productive forces to reduce it to a symbol. Gold has never ceased insinuating its way into its body and soul. Bourgeois literature, nevertheless, has almost completely neglected this theme. In the nineteenth century, only Wagner sensed and expressed it in his grandiose and allegorical manner. The novel about gold does appear in our day: *Gold* by Blaise Cendars and Crommelnyk's *Tripes d'or* are two different but related specimens of this literature. *The Gold Rush* legitimately belongs to it, also. In this case, Chaplin's thought and the images through which it is revealed arise from a great modern sensibility. The creation of a great satire about gold is imminent. We now have its foretaste. Chaplin's work grasps something that moves deep in the world's subconscious.

Chaplin incarnates the bohemian in the cinema. Whatever his costume, we always imagine Chaplin in the vagrant role of the Little Tramp. To attain the deepest and most naked humanity, the purest and most mysterious drama, Chaplin absolutely requires the poverty and hunger, the bohemianism, the romanticism, and the insolvency of the Little Tramp. It is difficult to define the bohemian precisely. Navarro Monzó—for whom Francis of Assisi, Diogenes, and Jesus himself are the sublimation of this spiritual type—says that the bohemian is the antithesis of the bourgeois. The Little Tramp is anti-bourgeois par excellence. He is always ready for adventure, for change, for departure. No one imagines him with a savings account. He is a little Don Quixote, God's minstrel, humorist, and beggar.

It is therefore logical that Chaplin could only interest himself in that bohemian and romantic capitalist enterprise: the search for gold. The Little Tramp could leave for Alaska, enrolled in that greedy and miserable phalanx that takes off to discover gold in the rugged and snowy mountains. He could not stay and make it with capitalist cunning in commerce, industry, or the stock market. This was the only way to imagine the Little Tramp getting rich. The ending of *The Gold Rush*—which some find vulgar, because they would prefer the Little Tramp to return to his disheveled bohemia—is absolutely just and accurate, not even minimally observing the reason of Yankee methodology.

The whole work is insuperably constructed. The sentimental, erotic element intervenes with mathematical precision, with rigorous artistic and biological necessity. Jim McKay finds the Little Tramp, his old comrade in poverty and vagrancy, at the exact moment that the Little Tramp, in romantic tension, can decide with the maximum energy to accompany him in search of a gigantic lost mine. Chaplin, as author, knows that erotic arousal is a propitious state for creation and discovery. Like Don Quixote, the Tramp must fall in love before undertaking his daring voyage. In love, vehemently and bizarrely in love, it is impossible for the Tramp not to find the mine. No power, no accident can stop him. It wouldn't matter if the mine didn't exist. It doesn't matter that Jim McKay, his mind dulled by a blow that erases his memory and makes him lose his way, has deluded him. The Little Tramp will find the fabulous mine. His pathos gives him super powers. The avalanche, the storm, cannot defeat him. On the edge of a precipice, he will have abundant energy to fight off death and take an acrobatic leap over it. He must return from this trip a millionaire. And, considering the contradictions of his life, who would be his logical comrade in this victorious adventure? Who but Jim McKay, this ferocious, brutal, imperious gold miner who, mad from hunger in the mountains, one day wants to kill the Tramp and eat him? McKay has the full, complete, and perfect constitution for a gold miner. The ravenous, insane ferocity that Chaplin attributes to him is not overblown. McKay could not be the consummate hero of this story if Chaplin had not conceived him as prepared in extremity to eat a comrade. The first duty of a gold miner is to live. His logic is Darwinian and pitilessly individualistic.

In this work, then, Chaplin has not only brilliantly seized upon an artistic idea of his time, but has expressed it in strictly scientific psychological terms. *The Gold Rush* confirms Freud. As myth, it descends from the Wagnerian tetrology. Artistically and spiritually, it transcends the theater of Pirandello and the novels of Proust and Joyce.

The circus is the bohemian spectacle, the bohemian art par excellence. On the one hand, this is its first and most profound relationship with Chaplin.

On the other, the circus and the cinema have a visible bond in the context of their technical and essential autonomy. Despite their distinct manner and style, the circus, like the cinema, is the movement of images. Notwithstanding the effort to make cinema speak, pantomime is at the source of its art, which is silent par excellence. Chaplin comes precisely out of pantomime or, rather, from the circus. Cinema has killed the theater as bourgeois theater. It has been unable to do a thing against the circus. The spirit of the circus, all the living bohemian, romantic, nomadic sense of the circus, has freed Chaplin, the film artist. Bontempelli has uncomplimentarily dismissed the old, literary, wordy bourgeois theater. The old circus, though, is alive, active, and unchanged. While the theater needs to reform itself, remake itself by returning to the medieval "mystery," the plastic spectacle, or the agonistic or Circean technique, or approximate the cinema with the synthetic action of the movable stage, the circus needs only to continue; it finds all the elements necessary for its development and continuation within its own tradition.

Chaplin's latest film is subconsciously a sentimental return to the circus, to pantomime. It spiritually has much Hollywood-style subterfuge. It is significant that this has not upset, but rather favored its finished cinematographic realization. I have encountered objections to The Circus as an artistic work in a seasoned vanguardist journal. I think exactly the opposite. If the cinematographic is what is artistic in the cinema above all else, Chaplin has hit the target as never before in The Circus. The Circus is purely and absolutely cinematic. Chaplin in this work has succeeded in expressing himself solely in images. The titles are reduced to a minimum. And they could be totally eliminated without having the comedy expressed any less to the spectator.

According to a fact always insisted upon in his biography, Chaplin comes from a family of clowns, circus artists. In any event, he himself was a clown in his youth. What power could have taken him from this art, so consonant with his bohemian soul? To me, the attraction of the cinema, of Hollywood, seems neither the only nor most decisive reason. I prefer historical, economic, and political explanations, and even in this case I think it possible to attempt one that is perhaps more serious than humorous.

The English clown represents the highest degree of evolution of the genre. It is the farthest possible from those quite vicious, excessive, strident Mediterranean ones that we are used to finding in traveling, nomadic circuses. He is an elegant, measured, mathematical mime who exercises his art with a perfectly Anglican dignity. Great Britain has come to produce this human type as it does the racing or hunting thoroughbred—in conformity with a rigorous and Darwinian principle of selection. The laugh and visage of the clown is an essential, classic mark of British life, a cog in the magnificent machine of Empire. The clown's art is a ritual, his comicality absolutely serious. Metaphysical and religious Bernard Shaw, in his country, is nothing more than a clown who writes. The clown is not a type, but rather an institution, as respectable as the House of Lords. The clown's art signifies the domestication of the wild and nomadic buffoonery of the bohemian in accord with the taste and needs of a refined capitalist society. Great Britain has done with the clown's laugh what it has done with the Arabian horse: trained it through capitalist art and zootechny as a Puritan recreation for the Manchester and London bourgeoisie. The clown notably illustrates the evolution of the species.

No clown emerging in the era of a persistent and regular British ascendancy, not even the great genius Chaplin, could have deserted his art. The discipline of the tradition, the mechanics of its undisturbed and unshaken customs, would have been enough to automatically bridle any impulse to escape. In a normal period of British evolution, the spirit of rigid, corporate England was enough to maintain fidelity to the profession, to the trade. But Chaplin entered history at a moment when the axis of capitalism was silently shifting from Great Britain to North America. The disequilibrium of the British machine, recorded precociously by his ultrasensitive spirit, acted on his centrifugal and secessionistic impulses. His genius felt the attraction of the new capitalist metropolis. The pound sterling humbled by the dollar, the crisis of the coal industry, the stopping of Manchester's looms, the agitation for autonomy in the colonies, Eugene Chen's communication on Hankow: all these symptoms of the weakening of British power were anticipated by Chaplin—an alert receptor of the most secret messages of the era—when the Little Tramp, the film artist, was born from the rupture of the internal equilibrium of the clown. Without a series of breaks in the high-tension lines of British history, the gravitational attraction of the United States, in the midst of rapid capitalist development, would have been unable to draw Chaplin from the destiny he would have normally fulfilled as a clown. How different Chaplin's destiny would have been in the Victorian age, even if the cinema and Hollywood had already lit their searchlights!

But the United States has not spiritually assimilated Chaplin. Chaplin's tragedy and humor receive their intensity from the innermost conflict between the artist and North America. The prosperity, the energy, the élan of North America hold and excite the artist, but its bourgeois puerility, its arriviste prosaity, are repugnant to the bohemian, who is romantic at heart. North America, in turn, does not like Chaplin. As is well known, Hollywood's bosses consider him subversive, antagonistic. North America feels that there is something in Chaplin that escapes them. Among the neo-Quakers of Yankee finance and industry, Chaplin will always be accused of Bolshevism.

One of the greatest and purest modern artistic phenomena feeds from this contradiction, this contrast. The cinema allows Chaplin to assist humanity in its struggle against sorrow with a breadth and a simultaneity that no artist has ever reached. The image of this tragically comic bohemian is a daily rite of happiness across five continents. With Chaplin, art reaches the height of its hedonistic and liberating function. With his pained smile and costume, Chaplin alleviates the world's sadness and contributes more to the miserable happiness of humanity than any of its statesmen, philosophers, industrialists, or artists.

Glossary of Spanish and Quechua Terms

Amauta—wise man or teacher (Quechua); Mariátegui himself came to be known as the Amauta

Aprismo—the ideology of the APRA (American Popular Revolutionary Alliance), a Peruvian nationalist movement founded by Haya de la Torre

Argentinidad—"Argentineness"; the sense of being part of the Argentine nation (cf. *Peruanidad*)

ayllu—Incan term referring to a group of people linked by ties of consanguinity; an indigenous community

cacique—Native American chief; later, a boss

cholo—a person of indigenous American and European ancestry

Civilismo—the ideology of the Civilista party, the major bourgeois political movement of the late nineteenth and early twentieth centuries in Peru

criollo—relating to Americans of mainly European ancestry

enganche—literally, a hook; a method of forcibly recruiting labor gangs

encomendero—a Spanish recipient of a grant of land and/or a group of indigenous people as slaves or serfs

gamonal—rural boss; large landowner

hacendado—the owner of a hacienda

indigenismo (indigenista)—the ideology of supporters of the rights of the indigenous peoples of Latin America

Kaswa—Incan dance

kelkere—notary, clerk (Quechua)

latifundista—owner of a large estate

mita—group labor required by the Spanish of indigenous communities and peasants

peón—agricultural worker; day laborer

Peruanidad—"Peruvianness"; the sense of being part of the Peruvian nation

Porfirismo—the ideology of the regime of Porfirio Díaz, the president of Mexico (1877–1880, 1884–1911)

raza (la)—literally "the race"; the people of Latin America

195

Suggestions for Further Reading

José Carlos Mariátegui's classic study of Peru, *Seven Interpretive Essays on Peruvian Reality*, was published by the University of Texas Press in 1971, translated by Marjory Urquidi and introduced by Jorge Basadre.

There are four book-length studies of Mariátegui available in English:

John M. Baines, *Revolution in Peru: Mariátegui and the Myth* (University, Alabama: University of Alabama, 1972).

Marc Becker, *Mariátegui and Latin American Marxist Theory* (Athens, Ohio: Ohio University Monographs in International Studies, Latin American Series no. 20, 1993).

Jesus Chavarría, *José Carlos Mariátegui and the Rise of Modern Peru, 1890–1930* (Albuquerque: University of New Mexico Press, 1979).

Harry E. Vanden, *National Marxism in Latin America: José Carlos Mariátegui's Thought and Politics* (Boulder, Colorado: Lynne Rienner, 1986).

The best of these is by Chavarría, a Mexican-American activist and academic, who gives a sensitive reading of Mariátegui's revolutionary nationalism in the context of Peruvian political and intellectual history; the book also contains an excellent bibliographical essay. Becker's book is a well-documented study of Mariátegui's influence among Latin American Marxists, especially in Cuba, Nicaragua, and Central America.

Mariátegui's writings have been published in an inexpensive, popular edition by Empresa Editora Amauta of Lima, under the direction of his children. Their twenty-volume *Obras completas* includes nearly all of his post-1919 work, along with a number of biographical essays and an index of *Amauta* and *Labor*. A separate collection of important political and personal letters of Mariátegui has been published under the title *Correspondencia, 1915–1930*. Editora Amauta also produces a yearly *Anuario Mariateguiano* that includes interesting essays, documents, and bibliographic materials. Their most recent publication is *Mariátegui total*, a two-volume edition of his collected works—including his pre-Marxist writings, which they had previously collected under the title *Escritos juveniles: La edad de piedra* (Youthful Writings: The Stone Age).

The number of Spanish-language anthologies keeps growing. They include:

Ensayos escogidos (Lima: Editorial Universo, 1971), introduced by Augusto Salazar Bondy, 248 pages.

Invitación a la vida heroica (Lima: Instituto de Apoyo Agrario, 1989), edited by Alberto Flores Galindo and Ricardo Portocarrero Grados, 450 pages.

Obra política (Mexico City: Ed. Era, 1979), edited and introduced by Rúben Jiménez Ricárdez, 327 pages.

197

Textos Básicos (Lima: Fondo de Cultura Económica, 1991), edited and introduced by Aníbal Quijano, 404 pages.

Two of the best and most complete studies of Mariátegui's thought are:

Aníbal Quijano, *Introducción a Mariátegui* (Mexico City: Ed. Era, 1982).

Robert Paris, *La Formación Ideológica de José Carlos Mariátegui* (Mexico City: Siglo XXI, 1981).

A collection of essays reflecting the divergent interpretations of Mariátegui is *Mariátegui y los orígenes del Marxismo latinoamericano* (Mexico City: Ed. Pasado y Presente, 1978), edited and introduced by José Aricó.

Index